COMMON WORSHIP
ALL-AGE TALKS

COMMON WORSHIP
ALL-AGE TALKS

SUSAN SAYERS

Kevin
Mayhew

First published in 2000 by KEVIN MAYHEW LTD
Buxhall, Stowmarket, Suffolk IP14 3BW

Common Worship All-age Talks is taken from *Living Stones,* Years A, B and C, first published in 1997, 1998 and 1999.

The publishers wish to express their gratitude to Phoenix House, a Division of the Orion Publishing Group, for permission to use the extract from *The Solitaire Mystery* by Jostein Gaarder, translated by Sarah Jane Hails, copyright © 1996.

0 1 2 3 4 5 6 7 8 9

ISBN 1 84003 562 5
Catalogue Number 1500360

Cover Design by Jonathan Stroulger
Edited by Katherine Laidler
Typesetting by Louise Selfe

FOREWORD

All-age talks are not the same thing as talks for children, with the adults present. They are aimed rather at the whole worshipping community, when children, young people and adults from 18 to 98 are in church together.

Naturally that poses some problems. What on earth have all these different age groups got in common? How can we possibly preach the gospel in a meaningful way to such a broad age and culture range? How will anyone benefit? Won't we end up by devaluing the gospel and teaching no one?

All these fears are valid and it is essential that they are asked. I ask them regularly myself.

However, I wonder if, when we ask such questions, we have in our minds a school image of what we are about on Sundays, rather than a family or household image. In educational terms there is much to be said for splitting the age groups and organising the curriculum accordingly, whereas in a family or household it is expected that all the different age groups are living together, along with the affection and irritations, the shared jokes, worries, celebrations and memories. Through such living together, we are given the practice for learning to love. It seems appropriate, then, for there to be at least some occasions each month when the household of faith gathers and explores the gospel together.

People will be at different stages as well as ages; there may be adults who are hovering on the brink of faith or rejection of it, and children who enjoy God's love and talk to him every day. There may be middle-aged adolescents and adolescents with profound maturity. Our joy as the people of God is knowing that we are all accepted and loved wherever we are at the moment, and that we are all in the process of learning to love, however many years have passed since our birth and whatever our choice in clothes.

The profound truths of the gospel need to come across in how we speak as well as in what we say. The all-age talk gives the church a wonderful opportunity to enjoy unpacking the gospel together, sometimes playfully, sometimes in a very moving or challenging way. In Christ we are all brothers and sisters. Whatever family we have or don't have biologically, as Christians we are family members, and the all-age talk takes that truth and celebrates it.

The talks in this book are from the *Living Stones* parish programme, published separately for the convenience of those given responsibility for this part of the worship on any particular Sunday. Accordingly, the appropriate lectionary readings are given, together with the thought for the day. In preparing to give a talk, prayerful reading of these passages is vital. The suggested talks can then be used either as written, or as a springboard to set you off expressing your own insights, in the light of the needs of your congregation.

Practise the talk aloud, and ensure that any signs or posters are clearly written and well produced. Be fair in who you choose as volunteers, and include different age groups; it doesn't always have to be the children. Prepare well in advance, so that there is time to contact any 'experts' whose help may be needed, and adapt the talks in any way you want to. They are provided as a help, not a straightjacket.

The whole point of speaking during worship like this is to help people get to know God better; to excite them into deepening their faith, their understanding of God's love, and their response to God. I pray that God will speak through you to get in touch with each of those in your congregation, and that their hearts and minds will be open to receive his love.

SUSAN SAYERS

CONTENTS

YEAR B

YEAR C

YEAR A

FIRST SUNDAY OF ADVENT

Isaiah 2:1-5
Psalm 122
Romans 13:11-14
Matthew 24:36-44

We are to wake up and make sure we stay ready for the second coming.

All-age talk

Begin by explaining that today is Advent Sunday, the first Sunday of the year as far as the Church is concerned. Advent means 'coming', and over the next four weeks we will be getting ourselves ready for the coming of Jesus which we celebrate on Christmas Day.

Today's readings tell us to keep ourselves ready and alert for God's coming, which happens all the time and will happen in a very dramatic way at the end of time when Jesus returns in all his glory. The children will be helping to show us all how to make sure we don't miss out by being unprepared for this.

Invite all the children and young people to walk quickly around the centre aisle, changing direction every time you clap your hands or blow a whistle. Two claps or whistle blows means stand still and listen to a new instruction. Give them a few goes at changing direction, and then make the standing-still and listening signal. Explain that one clap will now mean change direction, two will mean walk backwards, and three will mean stand still and listen. Try this out for a short while and then, when they are standing still and listening, thank them for their demonstration and ask them to sit down where they are.

Explain that if we are to keep ourselves ready and alert while we get on with our lives, it will mean listening out all the time for the good and loving direction that God whispers to us to follow, just as the children were doing so well. As they walked about their lives, they were listening out, so that whenever there was a need to change direction, they were ready to do it straightaway. If they hadn't listened so carefully, they wouldn't have been able to do it nearly so well.

Tell the children that this time when they hear the signal it will mean 'Go back to your seat'. As you start them moving about the aisle again, remind everyone to keep listening to God's loving direction as they walk about through life, so they are always ready. Make the last signal, and thank the children for their help as they go back to their seats.

All-age ideas

- At the beginning of the service tell everyone that at some point the first candle of the Advent ring will be lit. It won't be announced, so everyone is to watch out for it. When anyone sees it happening, they raise their hand, until everyone has noticed. (Arrange beforehand for the candle to be lit at an appropriate time, and as soon as everyone has raised their hand the usual short prayer can be said.)

- Read the Isaiah passage chorally, using the voices of men, women and children. Work through the reading together, trying out different voice combinations, and finish with verse 5 spoken all together.

- As an introduction to the Gospel reading, have small groups of people miming various everyday activities in different parts of the church during the Gradual hymn, and have the Bible, or book of the readings, held high just before the Gospel is read. Some of those miming notice straightaway and turn to face the reader, walking towards them and standing attentively. Gradually the others follow.

SECOND SUNDAY OF ADVENT

Isaiah 11:1-10
Psalm 72:1-7, 18-19
Romans 15:4-13
Matthew 3:1-12

Get the road ready for the Lord!

All-age talk

In the aisle lay down some 'holes' (cut from black paper) and some blocks (chairs with cardboard boxes or trays leaning against them).

Talk about John the Baptist coming out of the desert and urging everyone to 'Get the road ready!' Some people may have seen a new road being built, with some parts being banked up and others tunnelled through, in order to cut out the steep hills. Most people will at some time have been stuck in traffic jams while roads are being mended, or widened.

John the Baptist was imagining us getting a nice new road ready so that God can travel straight into our lives without finding any holes to fall down, or blocks in the way. He was saying to the people, 'You need to get yourselves ready like a good straight road.'

Ask a couple of volunteers to inspect the 'road' in the aisle, finding all sorts of blocks and holes along it that need putting right. This is a bit like our lives, and the lives of the people John was talking to about two thousand years ago. There are 'holes' of selfishness and meanness, and gaping holes in our loving. They need to be filled in with loving kindness and thoughtfulness. Perhaps there are gaps in our honesty, because we don't always tell the truth, or live the truth. These holes need filling up with truthfulness and integrity. There are perhaps holes of superiority, because we sneer at people who aren't like us, or as clever or handsome or rich as us.

Then there are those roadblocks which block God from getting through to us: blocks such as 'I

16

don't need God', 'I'm fine as I am, thanks', 'I don't want to change', and 'It's not my fault I'm bad tempered so you'll have to put up with it'. (The blocks can have these labels written on them clearly.)

When today we hear John the Baptist rushing out of the desert and shouting, 'Get the road ready for our God!', it's a good idea to listen to him, look at our own life-road, see where the holes and blocks are, and ask God to help us put them right straightaway, so that God can come to us easily without any hold-ups.

All-age ideas

- For the time of Penitence and Confession, give everyone a piece of paper and a pencil so they can draw their road and ask God to help them make it ready. Other people will only see the holes and blocks; what these stand for will be known only by the person drawing them.

- Read the Isaiah passage chorally. This helps to bring out both the meaning and the poetry.

- Act out the Gospel with someone dressed up as John the Baptist. This person can then light this week's Advent candle.

THIRD SUNDAY OF ADVENT

Isaiah 35:1-10
Psalm 146:5-10 or
  Canticle: Magnificat
James 5:7-10
Matthew 11:2-11

Great expectations. Jesus fulfils the great statements of prophecy.

All-age talk

Beforehand wrap some objects as presents. Some should be obvious, such as a tennis racket, a balloon and a bottle of wine. Others should be harder to guess from the shape, such as a boxed toy and a book.

Display the wrapped presents, and talk about the way Christmas is getting nearer and we're all getting our presents ready. Perhaps some of us are really hoping for a particular present, even though we know it's the thought that counts and we'll be happy with whatever we get because it means someone has thought of us.

Draw attention to the wrapped presents you have brought in, and pick up the first group of obvious presents, asking people to guess what is inside. Then go on to the second group, discovering that some things are harder to guess – we might look at the parcel and expect something completely different to be inside.

John the Baptist knew that God was coming to his people, and he had done a good job of getting them ready. But exactly how this would happen was like a wrapped present – still hidden from view because it hadn't happened yet. Perhaps John was expecting Jesus to be more of a mighty warrior, judging everyone and destroying those who didn't make the grade.

What *did* Jesus do? We heard about it in the first reading from the prophet Isaiah: he was going around healing the sick, making the deaf hear again, the blind see again and the lame walk again. He was letting the weak and downtrodden know that God was on their side and loved them.

Once Jesus pointed out that he was doing these things, John could see that it really did fit in with the 'shape' he had been expecting, even though it wasn't quite the same, rather like our wrapped-up bottle of red wine which we had perhaps been expecting to be white wine, or sherry. Or like the boxed game that you might have expected to be 'Guess Who' and it turned out to be 'Mr Pop'.

As we wrap our presents, let's remember that God's ways are often hidden and unexpected – he is a God who sometimes takes us by surprise. But the surprises will always be true to his good and loving nature.

All-age ideas

- On banners or posters have the words of Isaiah 35:10 celebrated and decorated, so that the very building proclaims them.

- The Isaiah reading contains wonderful poetry. Think how best to bring this out; you could try choral reading, or a combination of reading and music to give the words 'soaking in' time.

FOURTH SUNDAY OF ADVENT

Isaiah 7:10-16
Psalm 80:1-7, 17-19
Romans 1:1-7
Matthew 1:18-25

Through the willing participation of Mary and Joseph, God is poised to come among his people as their Saviour.

All-age talk

Ask for two volunteers. Stand one on a chair and have the other lie down on the floor. Talk with the volunteers about what they can see from their particular viewpoint. Although nothing else in the church has changed, the descriptions will be different because of where the volunteers are.

You could also suggest that everyone looks at something central, first through one eye and then the other. They can then all notice the change of view even when looking out from the same head!

What our readings today are reminding us is that we need to get into the habit of looking at everything from God's point of view. What we then see may sometimes come as a surprise to us, because we are so used to looking from our own point of view. Take Joseph, for instance. He was in for a surprise. He thought he had worked out the kindest way of dealing with the embarrassing problem of Mary expecting a baby before they were married. He had it all worked out. He'd divorce Mary without a big fuss, so that she needn't be noticed too much.

But through the dream God helped him look at things from another point of view. Joseph saw that Mary's baby was all part of God's plan, and, rather than divorcing her, he had an important job to do – to look after Mary and this very special baby. Joseph must have been a very brave man, as well as a good and kind one. He knew people would think he was stupid; perhaps they would stop being friends with him; his life would never be nice and straightforward again. But he did that brave, good thing because he had seen the situation from God's point of view and was happy to go along with that.

It was the same with Mary. If she had only seen the angel's message from her own point of view she might have refused to go along with God's plan, which was bound to turn her own hopes and dreams upside down. But she saw it from God's point of view – that the people of our earth needed a Saviour; God needed to be born as a human baby so he could rescue humans as an insider. And a baby needed a mum. So she agreed and that made Christmas possible.

All-age ideas

- During the first reading, at the reference to the sign of a virgin being with child, have the Mothers' Union banner carried slowly around the church.

- Use nativity play costumes and dress people up as Joseph and Mary, who can then mime the actions as the Gospel is read.

CHRISTMAS DAY

Isaiah 52:7-10
Psalm 98
Hebrews 1:1-4 (5-12)
John 1:1-14

The Word of God is made flesh.
In the birth of Jesus we see God
expressed in human terms.

All-age talk

Begin by getting different people to say, 'Happy Christmas, everyone!' in whatever way they like. A group of friends might like to shout it together; someone might like to stand at the front; others will choose to say it quietly to their neighbour.

Point out how all the 'Happy Christmas!' messages are much appreciated, and they all show the wonderful way we're all different. You don't have to be a particular sort of person to be a Christian. The only sort of person you have to be is yourself! God loves you that way.

Today we've been expressing ourselves when we spoke our Christmas messages, and Christmas is about God expressing himself: Jesus being born as a human baby is God saying to all of us, 'I love you!'

All-age ideas

• Gather the collection in a model manger (made from a box and filled with straw) and use different age groups to do the collecting.

• Ask everyone to bring bells and ring them at the Gloria.

• Gather the children round the crib during the intercessions, and round the altar at the eucharistic prayer.

FIRST SUNDAY OF CHRISTMAS

Isaiah 63:7-9
Psalm 148
Hebrews 2:10-18
Matthew 2:13-23

Jesus, the expression of God's love, lives as a vulnerable boy in the real and dangerous world we all inhabit.

All-age talk

If you have a member of the congregation whose job involves rescue (for example in the fire, ambulance, lifeboat or mountain rescue services), ask if they would be willing to take part in a brief interview before the talk. Talk with them about the kind of dangers they themselves have to accept in order to rescue people, and the way they get alongside the people who need rescuing in order to help them. If you are not having a live interview, talk briefly about these rescuers.

Explain how Jesus is a rescuer, who comes in person to save us and help us. Stand someone on a paper island in the middle of a flood. God doesn't stand a long way off and shout to us. (Stand a long way off and shout to them to get into a boat and sail away.) That's no good, because the person feeling drowned by sadness or guilt or evil can't do what you are shouting even if they wanted to. We can't rescue ourselves; only God can set us free by accepting us, loving us and forgiving us. So instead of being a long way off and telling us what to do, God came in person to rescue us. (Pretend to row over to the person and then rescue them.) That's what happened at Christmas – God came to live among us in the person of Jesus, and he is still with us now. We are all his brothers and sisters.

All-age ideas

• Have the first reading read by a parent who is carrying a young child. Or have a parent walking up to the front of the church, and at the last verse, they lift the child up in their arms.

- During the Gospel, have the holy family moving from one place to another, settling down, and then setting off again.

- Have a collection of money or gifts for homeless families or refugees, with some pictures and figures to help people understand the problems experienced.

Second Sunday of Christmas

Ecclesiasticus* 24:1-12
(* also called Sirach)
Canticle: Wisdom of
    Solomon 10:15-21
Ephesians 1:3-14
John 1:(1-9) 10-18

The grace and truth revealed in Jesus show God's freely-given love; through Jesus, God pours out his blessings on us and gives us real freedom.

All-age talk

Bring something with you to offer as a small gift – a chocolate bar, a sticker, a few flowers or a piece of fruit, perhaps.

Over Christmas we have all been busy giving one another presents. Explain that you have brought something with you to give away today, so that we can understand a bit more about God's Christmas present to us. In Jesus we see God giving himself to set us free from sin and evil because he loves us so much.

Show everyone what your gift is, and ask them to put their hands up if they would like to be considered for it. Choose someone using some random method, such as their name being first in the alphabet, or their birthday coming up this week. When God gives us his present no one has to get left out. Everyone who asks, gets.

Stand a short distance away from the person chosen, and hold out the gift. Can they receive the gift without moving? No, they can't. If we are going to receive a gift we have to change our position a bit. (The person can demonstrate this and receive the gift.) It's the same with us all receiving God's gift – we are bound to change if we receive Jesus into our daily living.

Just as Joseph and Mary's lives changed when Jesus was born into their family, so our lives will change. As we reach out to receive Jesus, we shall find we are able to reach out to one another in a more loving, positive way; we shall find we are more

25

concerned about justice and mercy being written into our social system; we shall find we are wanting to be more truthful to others and ourselves.

So be prepared – if you don't want to change into a happier, more loving person, freed from guilt and able to be truly yourself, then don't take God up on his offer!

All-age ideas

- At the same time as the collection plate is passed around, have a basket of coloured shapes with the reference to John 3:16 written on them. These are given to everyone, so that they are given a message which they can then decide to receive.

- Just before the Gospel is read, have a single candle carried by a young child ahead of the Bible, or book of readings, into the centre of the congregation.

THE EPIPHANY

Isaiah 60:1-6
Psalm 72:(1-9) 10-15
Ephesians 3:1-12
Matthew 2:1-12

Jesus, the hope of the nations, is shown to the world.

All-age talk

Beforehand arrange for a knitter to bring a completed garment to church, together with a ball of wool and needles. Also prepare a large paper cut-out of a similar garment, which is folded up so that the first bit that would be made is the only piece showing. Alternatively use the actual garment, folded up at that point.

Begin by showing everyone the wonderful garment that the knitter has made and asking how long it took to make and who it is for. What did it look like at first, when they started making it? The knitter can show the ball of wool and needles, and do a couple of stitches. Hold up the needles with these stitches and point out that it doesn't look much like a jumper/scarf yet! But the knitter went on working at it, knowing that one day it would be ready.

God knew that one day everything would be ready for Jesus to come into the world, but he, too, took a long time making things ready. He started by calling one person, Abraham. (Show the folded garment, but don't refer to it – it is there to be visual reinforcement of what you are saying.) Over the years God went on to prepare all Abraham's family. (More of the garment is revealed.) Until over more years that family became one nation. (Reveal some more of the garment.) But God's plan still wasn't finished. He went on to include not one nation but all the nations and everyone in them. (Shake the whole garment out and display it.) Today is called the Epiphany because the word 'epiphany' means 'showing' or 'revealing' or 'manifesting', and when those wise men arrived at Bethlehem with

27

their presents, God was showing or revealing himself not just to Abraham or his family, not just to the whole nation of Israel, but to all the rest of us in the world as well.

Whatever country you come from, whatever you look like and whatever language you speak, God is saying to us today that he is there for you and no one is left out. You don't have to have the right ancestors to know God. You don't have to pass any exams to know God.

We sometimes get so interested in the presents the wise men were bringing to Jesus that we forget what brought them there in the first place. It was God who called these wise men from other nations to be there when Jesus was still a baby, so he could welcome them as well. They were there representing all the nations, so when God welcomed them he was welcoming each of us.

All-age ideas

- Today's Gospel can be acted out, preferably with costumes, as these may well be available from a nativity play. I am not suggesting a full-blown production with hours of rehearsal. All that is needed is a sensitive narrator, and the characters to mime what the narrator says.

- The wise men can take the collection and offer the gifts today. This emphasises their role as representatives of all the nations coming to be welcomed and offer their gifts. A globe can be offered at the same time.

- Have a bowl of burning incense, gold and myrrh arranged among flowers as a display either as people come in or near where they will come to receive communion.

THE BAPTISM OF CHRIST: FIRST SUNDAY OF EPIPHANY

Isaiah 42:1-9
Psalm 29
Acts 10:34-43
Matthew 3:13-17

As Jesus is baptised, the Spirit of God rests visibly on him, marking him out as the One who will save his people.

All-age talk

Ask various children if they know what job they would like to do when they grow up. Ask various adults what they wanted to be when they were children, and whether they did it or not. Ask some of the children if they have seen pictures of their mums and dads when they were babies and toddlers. Do they look anything like that now? Ask some of the mums and dads if they can imagine what their children will be like in twenty years' time.

A week or two ago we were thinking about when Jesus was a baby. Now, suddenly, we're looking at what he was like when he grew up. Here he is at about thirty years old. He's a carpenter, so he's probably quite strongly built. He's heard that his cousin, John (do they remember John?), is washing people in the River Jordan as a sign that God has forgiven their sins. We wash to get our bodies clean. John baptised people to show they were getting their souls clean. They were all getting ready for the Messiah, or Christ.

And now here comes Jesus, wading into the river, and wanting John to baptise him as well! (We know that Jesus is the Christ they were waiting for, but the people didn't know that yet.) John realises who Jesus is, and is shocked that he wants to be baptised. 'It ought to be the other way round!' says John. '*You* ought to be baptising *me*!'

Jesus insists. 'No, it's right for you to baptise me. God's work of putting things right all through the centuries is coming together now in this Baptism.'

So John agrees to baptise Jesus. He pushes Jesus down under the water in the river, and when Jesus comes up out of the water, something amazing happens.

It's as if the heavens are opened up, and Jesus sees the Spirit of God coming to him and resting on him. Matthew tells us it looked something like a dove flying down to him. Jesus hears God his Father speaking to him deep into his being. God is saying that Jesus is indeed his well-loved Son, chosen and marked out for a special life that will save the world.

So that tiny baby, born in the stable, visited by shepherds and wise men, looked after by Joseph and Mary all through his childhood, is now at the start of his important work on earth. His job is to show the world God's love.

All-age ideas

- Decorate the font today, and have the renewal of baptismal promises displayed beside it. Suggest that people go and visit it after the service or during the week, thinking over their own Baptism as being the start of their Christian ministry.

- During the time of confession, have the sound of water being poured out during the absolution.

- Have some floating candles in a shallow tray of water incorporated in an arrangement that people will see as they come up to receive communion.

SECOND SUNDAY OF EPIPHANY

Isaiah 49:1-7
Psalm 40:1-11
1 Corinthians 1:1-9
John 1:29-42

Jesus is recognised and pointed out by John to be God's chosen one.

All-age talk

Start by hiding some treasure while a volunteer 'seeker' covers their eyes. Everyone else needs to know where it is hidden. Now set the treasure-seeker off to search, with everyone else guiding them by calling out whether they are colder or hotter. With all this help it shouldn't take too long for the seeker to find.

Lots of people are truth-seekers. They want to find out the truth about life and about God and about the reason we are here. These are the deep questions that humans have always asked, and it is important that we ask them. Questions are good things; never stop asking them, just because you're grown up. Grown-ups need to learn from the children here – children are very good at asking important questions!

When we are seeking for the truth about God, it helps if there are people who have already found him, who are happy to tell us when we're getting nearer or drifting further away. John the Baptist is one of those who is calling out to us, 'Warmer! You're getting warmer . . . you're boiling hot!' That's what he was doing to his disciples when Jesus came by. 'Look!' he said. 'That's the one I was telling you about – this is the one you've been waiting for! This is the Son of God!' And the two disciples took John's advice and started following Jesus.

One of those disciples was Peter's brother, Andrew. Peter was probably a truth-seeker as well, and his brother Andrew helped guide him to the truth. He told Peter they had found the Messiah, took hold of his brother and led him to Jesus. (Get two brothers to walk this through as you say it.)

Think about whether you ever help other people

31

find the truth about God. Think about whether other people help you, and how they do it. And if you don't think you've been doing much helping, today's readings are giving you some ideas as to how to start:

- telling people what you have noticed and found out about God;

- mentioning that he's worth spending time with;

- suggesting that they come with you to find out more;

- and introducing them to God by the way you live.

All-age ideas

- Have the Gospel acted out while it is being narrated. Use the whole church so there is a real sense of walking about in the real world.

- Have a display of different Bible reading schemes for people to browse through and order after the service.

THIRD SUNDAY OF EPIPHANY

Isaiah 9:1-4
Psalm 27:1, 4-9
1 Corinthians 1:10-18
Matthew 4:12-23

The prophecies of Isaiah are fulfilled in a new and lasting way in Jesus of Nazareth.

All-age talk

Out of strong card (or a wooden broom handle) make a demonstration yoke to show, on a brave volunteer, how conquerors used to subdue their captives. When you release the volunteer captive, talk to them about how good it feels to be free of the yoke.

Explain how in our first reading today we heard from a man called Isaiah. He was a prophet – someone who clearly speaks out God's words to the people. At the time, the people he was speaking to were being threatened by another country. It looked as if Assyria might well come and yoke the people up as captives, and take them far away from their own homes and their temple and their country, to live in exile in the country of their conquerors.

Isaiah showed the people that if they went on turning away from him by treating the poor unfairly, and spoiling themselves while others starved, then God would not save them from this attack. They were already 'yoked' up as slaves to their greed and selfishness, and their worries about the Assyrians.

Through Isaiah the prophet, God spoke to his people. He told them that he loved them, and that he longed for them to sort their lives out and trust him again. God would then be able to look after them and keep them and their holy city of Jerusalem safe. It would be like their yokes being broken in pieces, so they would be completely free.

Show the demonstration yoke again on another volunteer. Do any of us wear invisible yokes and need to be set free? We may be wearing yokes of selfishness, or resentment; we may be always wishing for things we can't have. We may still feel guilty about something we did. We may need healing of some emotional damage which is holding us back from living freely.

33

Jesus came so that we could be set free from all these yokes. He's an expert 'yoke shatterer'! He's the kind of light that makes all the darkness in our lives and minds and hearts disappear. If we let him in to walk around our own lives, as well as the lake of Galilee, he will set us free from all those yokes that hold us captive. And then we'll be able to walk through life with a new spring in our step, full of hope.

All-age ideas

• Gather as mixed a group as possible to work on this mime about Jesus setting captives free. First have the line of captives, wearing card yokes and roped together, walking dejectedly up the aisle, sometimes flinching as if from a captor's whip. At the front of the church stands the Christ figure with arms outstretched, both in welcome to the captives and also in the shape of a cross. As the others approach they stretch out their hands towards the human cross, and begin to line themselves up against its shape. As they do this the Christ figure unties their yoke and sets them free. Eventually the captives are helping each other until all are free. Then all stretch out their arms (this time because they want to, and not because the yoke makes them) towards one another and the whole congregation. This could lead into the sharing of Christ's peace.

• Have a light arrangement, rather than a flower arrangement, using lots of different containers and candles, perhaps in conjunction with a mirror.

• Use this prayer of penitence:
   All Father, forgive us, for we have sinned.
   A Into the darkness of our selfishness
   All shine with the light of love.
   B Into the darkness of our thoughtlessness
   All shine with the light of love.
   A Into the darkness of our unkindness
   All shine with the light of love.
   B Into the darkness of our greed
   All shine with the light of love.
   Father, forgive us, for we have sinned.

FOURTH SUNDAY OF EPIPHANY

1 Kings 17:8-16
Psalm 36:5-10
1 Corinthians 1:18-31
John 2:1-11

Jesus shows us in action the loving provision of the God who made us.

All-age talk

Ask a volunteer to stand at the front, holding a large piece of card in front of them so that no one can see their face. Point out that we can't be certain whether the person is looking happy, sad or angry, because we can't see for ourselves. Ask the volunteer to make one of those expressions behind the card. We can talk to them and listen to them, but we can't see them. It was a little like that for the people of Israel. Sometimes the prophets would speak out God's word to them, and they prayed to God, but it wasn't until Jesus came that people could see what God was like.

(Take the card from the volunteer's face.) We can now see clearly whether the person is happy, sad or angry, and we can see how s/he behaves, and what s/he thinks is important. When Jesus came to live as a human being on our earth, walking about in the actual place of Galilee and in the actual time of Roman-occupied Palestine, people could see exactly what God thought was important, and how much he loved them.

They saw that God really is interested in our everyday worries such as having enough food, or enough time or energy to get our work done. (In the story we heard today, Jesus was interested in the problem of a wine shortage at a wedding.)

They saw that God goes on loving us right to the very limit and still carries on loving! (Jesus went on loving and forgiving right through being put to death on a cross.)

They saw that God likes to work with us in solving some of our problems, and, if we are happy to work with him, amazing things can happen. (The servants

35

went ahead and filled the water pots with water, as Jesus had told them, and started pouring it out *before* they had seen it was now wine.)

There will be lots of times this week when we can choose to do 'exactly what Jesus tells us' and, if we agree, God will be able to use us in providing lovingly for someone's needs. Perhaps we will be giving our complete attention to someone when they talk to us, or providing financial help or emotional support. Perhaps our smile will cheer someone up, or our help will give someone a well-needed rest. Perhaps by letting someone play we will be making them feel less lonely and happier. Perhaps the spare curtains we remember to take into the charity shop will be exactly what someone is hoping to find as they struggle to furnish a home with very little money.

Let's make sure that this week we listen out for the ways God asks for our help, and then do what he whispers in our hearts, so that the people in this town can actually see God's love in action.

All-age ideas

- After the talk, provide a time for everyone to listen attentively to anything God may suggest is a need they might be able to help with, either at home, at school or work, or in the local neighbourhood or the wider world environment. Have some music played during this time – for example, *Show me the way of the cross once again* (Matt Redman) or *I, the Lord of sea and sky* (Dan Schutte).

- Have the words 'Do exactly as he tells you' cut out large and separately from black paper and fix them to the wall.

- Have twin flower arrangements, one incorporating a little jug of oil, a bowl of flour and a small flat loaf, and the other incorporating a carafe of wine, a glass or two, and some wedding ribbon. Place Bible references beside them.

PROPER 1

Sunday between 3 and 9 February inclusive (if earlier than the Second Sunday before Lent)

Isaiah 58:1-9a (9b-12)
Psalm 112:1-9 (10)
1 Corinthians 2:1-12
   (13-16)
Matthew 5:13-20

We are commissioned to live so that we shine like lights which direct others on to God, the source of Light.

All-age talk

You will need a large saucepan, a pack of spaghetti, a jar of Italian sauce and a large carton of salt, a jug, a teacup and a tablespoon. You will also need a table lamp and a bright spotlight.

Produce the first set of items, setting them out and talking about cooking pasta. Invite a good cook from the congregation to supervise! Explain that the best cookery books say that pasta can't be seasoned after it's cooked, so we need to add the salt to the cooking water. Pick up the salt, and wonder aloud how much salt to use. A jugful? Get the cook to explain what would happen if you put in that much salt. A teacupful? Still too much! A tablespoonful? Still too much. If we use that much all we will taste will be the salt, and the whole idea of salt is that it isn't really noticed but brings out the flavour of the other ingredients.

That's what we are called to do as Christians: not to take over and dominate or possess people, or want to control them, but in humility to make ourselves available and useful in helping to give other people the freedom and the confidence to be themselves. That may mean more listening and less speaking; it may mean being less concerned about being thought important and more concerned about other people's needs being recognised. It is the way of quiet, loving service.

Now flash the spotlight around so that it goes in people's eyes (but don't overdo this!). Explain that Jesus also calls us to be light. That doesn't mean trying to blind people with our natural brilliance, or trying subtly to impress others, so that we're more like disco lights, designed for a flashy effect. The kind of light we are called to be is a much more practical sort, rather like a table lamp, perhaps, which simply helps people to see better, so they don't bump into things and hurt themselves, and so they can get on with living more effectively.

Salt and light are just simple things, but they are things which can make a great difference. As Christians we are called to be like that – just our ordinary selves, but through our faith in God, able to make a difference.

All-age ideas

- Have a salt mill and a table lamp included in one of the flower arrangements today.

- Read the Isaiah passage chorally, with a group of men, women and children.

- Include actions with this penitential meditation:
  We have used our words selfishly.
  (touch lips)
  We are sorry. Lord, have mercy.
  We have used our hands selfishly.
  (look at open hands)
  We are sorry. Christ, have mercy.
  We have used our minds to think selfishly.
  (touch heads)
  We are sorry. Lord, have mercy.

PROPER 2

Sunday between 10 and 16 February inclusive (if earlier than the Second Sunday before Lent)

Deuteronomy 30:15-20
or Ecclesiasticus
    15:15-20
Psalm 119:1-8
1 Corinthians 3:1-9
Matthew 5:21-37

To live God's way is to choose the way of life.

All-age talk

Begin by drawing attention to the direction everyone is facing in church. Obviously this will vary according to your architecture and the age of the building. The architecture reflects a focus and a general direction which the planners thought of most importance. Perhaps if you were all about to start planning from scratch, you might arrange things slightly differently!

Once you have established the general seating focus, move to another part of the church, such as the baptistry. If people are going to continue facing you, they will all have to turn round. That is because at the moment the important thing going on is you speaking, and that takes over in importance from the general focus of the building.

Now move somewhere else so that everyone has to turn round again. Today we heard Jesus teaching about the Law, which is summed up in the ten commandments. Have these displayed on card, or on an OHP, or walk to the part of the church where they are written on the wall. They are good rules to live by and our whole law system is still based on them. But with all rules there is a problem. Jesus wanted his followers (and that includes us) to remember that the really important thing is to stay focused on God in everything we do.

Perhaps you haven't ever killed someone. But the spirit of the law means more than that, just as our focus is more than just sitting facing the front. It also means making sure we haven't got unkind or destructive thoughts about people, that we're not making people feel stupid or useless, that we aren't putting other people down or running them down behind their backs, because those things are in the destructive spirit of hate, which is the opposite of God's law of love. As you mention each of these, move around the building so people have to move their 'attitudes' to see you.

What we need to do is keep our eyes fixed on Jesus, and whatever we are doing we can think to ourselves, 'Does this thing I'm doing or saying or thinking make Jesus happy? Is it a loving thing to do or think or say?'

And if it is, carry on. If it isn't, stop and change direction.

All-age ideas

- Have two people standing in different places in the church, calling out the following contrasting attitudes alternately:

I want!
  What do you need?
Me first!
  Let's share!
Why should I?
  I'll help!
I believe in freedom so I can do whatever I like!
  If we think of one another we can all be free!
You've got to look after number one. Never mind anyone else.
  Love God – and love your neighbour as yourself.
This is the way of death.
  This is the way of life.

- Fix to the floor four footprints with the letters L, I, F and E on them, so that people can read them as they come in.

PROPER 3

Sunday between 17 and 23 February inclusive (if earlier than the Second Sunday before Lent)

Leviticus 19:1-2, 9-18
Psalm 119:33-40
1 Corinthians 3:10-11, 16-23
Matthew 5:38-48

We are called to be holy; to be perfect in our generous loving, because that is what God our Father is like.

All-age talk

Bring along a rubber stamp and ink pad, making sure it isn't permanent ink. Begin by putting the stamp on a number of volunteers. Talk about the way we sometimes get stamped at theme parks or discos to show that we have a right to be there because we have paid our entrance fee.

When we are baptised we have the sign of Jesus Christ marked on our foreheads. (What is that sign? It's the cross.) It's as if we've got God's stamp on us. (You could get everyone to trace a cross on their foreheads with their thumb to feel it freshly.) We are marked out as his children, whether we are one-day-old children, twenty-three-year-old children or ninety-seven-year-old children, and we have been freely given the right to belong in God's kingdom, which is a kingdom full of love and peace and joy, patience and kindness, goodness, gentleness and self-control.

As well as us belonging in God's kingdom, God's kingdom now belongs in us! As we've got God's stamp on us we will be wanting to behave like him, and he will help us to do that. Our behaviour will then be a visible sign to other people that we really do belong to God as his children. When they see us being honest and kind and patient and joyful, loving and working for peace and justice, they will be able to say, 'That must be a child of God – look how generous he is, even when he isn't going to gain anything by it!' And, 'That must be a child of God – look how loving she is with those difficult people!'

The whole point is this: we don't work to behave nicely so that God will love us. We don't need to do

41

that, and we can't ever earn his love anyway. God simply loves us! He thinks we're really special, and he always wants the best for us.

When we love him back, and let him work in us, we will find we are beginning to behave more like our God. The closer we get to God, the more generous loving we will find ourselves doing. Instead of looking out for what we can get all the time, we'll find we're looking out eagerly for ways we can give instead! Instead of making sure we are doing whatever *we* want, we'll find we are looking to check if other people are OK. And that is actually a much happier and more fulfilling way to live.

All-age ideas

- Print out in large letters: 'Love your friends, hate your enemies!' with a line crossing through the second part and the alteration written in: 'Love your enemies too!'

- Just before the exchange of the greeting of peace, have the choir or music group playing all kinds of different songs at once, so it sounds terrible. The worship leader gets their attention, points out that they're all pleasing themselves, and it would work much better if they decide to work together instead, listening to one another. The group voice their approval of this idea, and play or sing something beautiful. The peace can then be introduced as a sign of God's peace which binds us into a loving community.

- Express God's extravagant generosity by having some lavish flower arrangements with garlands and cascades.

SECOND SUNDAY BEFORE LENT

Genesis 1:1-2:3
Psalm 136 or 136:1-9,
   23-26
Romans 8:18-25
Matthew 6:25-34

God is creative and good; seeking his rule, as our priority, will mean that everything else falls into place.

All-age talk

Beforehand prepare some large speech bubbles from thin card, with the typical worries of those in the congregation written clearly on them. Here are some suggestions:

• My hair's going grey/thin on top!

• What can I wear?

• Weetabix or cocopops or toast?

• Suppose they don't like me?

• Brut or Denim – and how much of it?

• I'm the wrong shape!

Ask some volunteers to hold these worries up high. They're the kind of things we all waste our time and energy worrying about. Jesus was sad to see people worrying their lives away, and he wanted them to be free of this constant worrying. Point out that the volunteers will start to get aching arms if they have to go on holding the worries up for too long.

In our Gospel reading today Matthew tells us that Jesus says to us, 'Put all those worries down – they're heavy to carry and are making your arms ache.' Let the volunteers put the worries down, and talk about what a relief it is to have our worries sorted out.

Jesus wants us to know that although life is bound to be full of difficult and uncomfortable times as well as easy and happy times, we don't need to worry about it as well as live through it! That makes it twice as bad for us. The way to be free of worry is not to be massively rich or refuse to grow up, or bury your head in the sand and pretend not

43

to see the problems. The way to be free of worrying yourself sick is to trust that your Parent God loves you, likes you, and is well able to help you cope with everything you'll face in your life.

Jesus suggests we live one day at a time, instead of worrying about things that might never happen, or which are bound to happen, and God will bring us safely through it all to heaven, where we will be safe with God for ever.

All-age ideas

• To celebrate the way God looks after us as a loving parent, have a display of photographs showing young children being fed, washed, cared for and played with; young children simply being absorbed and happy in what they're doing. Mount them all on the wall or on a display board and have various scriptures written out among the pictures. Here are some possible texts to use: Matthew 6:9, Genesis 1:27, Genesis 1:31, 1 Corinthians 3:16.

SUNDAY BEFORE LENT

Exodus 24:12-18
Psalm 2 or Psalm 99
2 Peter 1:16-21
Matthew 17:1-9

In Jesus the full glory of God is revealed and encountered.

All-age talk

Bring along a family photograph album with snaps of holidays or celebrations in it, and if possible a camera which takes instant pictures. Also have two cards to hold up, one with a large plus sign on and the other a large minus sign.

If you have an instant camera, begin by taking a picture of some people or the day's flower arrangement. Show the album and talk about the way we all like to snap away to capture the moments when we are on holiday or at a special celebration, or when our children and grandchildren are growing up. We want to hang on to the moment and cherish it for years to come, because we know the moment itself won't last. The children will soon grow up, and we may never have the chance to visit the Eiffel Tower or Southend illuminations ever again!

The 'plus' side of taking pictures like this (encourage everyone's suggestions) may be that we will remember better if we look back at the picture – it may help us see the importance of the occasion, it helps us pass on the family tradition to the next generation, and it lets us enjoy more at our leisure later than we were able to take in at the time.

The 'minus' side may be that we're so busy taking pictures at the time that we aren't able to concentrate properly on the actual moment.

In the Gospel we heard about something amazing which happened on a mountain in Galilee. Three of Jesus' friends – Peter, James and John – saw Jesus shining with God's glory as he prayed. It was one of those times when Peter wanted to reach for the camera (except that cameras hadn't been invented then) so they could hold on to the wonderful moment for ever. Perhaps they had never before felt God quite so close to them! They even heard God's voice. He wasn't saying, 'I hope you're watching carefully and I'm sorry cameras haven't been invented yet or you could have got a pretty dramatic picture here today!' He was helping them understand the real, actual experience they were in, assuring them that Jesus really was God's Son, and wanting them to listen to Jesus in a way they had never listened before.

God doesn't just want Peter, James and John to know – he wants St Peter's church and St James's and St John's and all the other churches to know. He wants all the people in all the world to know who Jesus is, and he wants us all to pay attention to what Jesus says, and really listen to him with our hearts and minds as well as our ears.

All-age ideas

- Arrange one flower display on a mirror, or combined with a shallow tray of water, with lots of candles near it, so that the whole arrangement shines and reflects.

- If you have an OHP draw the word 'Life' in bubble writing with a black outline on one acetate and have this displayed during the intercessions or the time of confession. On another acetate decorate all around the word outline using several different colours and swirls. Either during the response to each section of the intercessions, or during the absolution, lay this second acetate on top of the first, showing visually the way God can transform life with shining richness and love.

- Use music with the Gospel reading, beginning the music quietly at verse 2.

FIRST SUNDAY OF LENT

Genesis 2:15-17; 3:1-7
Psalm 32
Romans 5:12-19
Matthew 4:1-11

*Jesus knows all about temptation;
and he can deal with our sin.*

All-age talk

Talk about some of the rules we are given, such as 'Wear your seatbelt', 'Don't lean out of the window of a moving train', 'Don't play on the railway line' or 'Don't keep poisons in old lemonade bottles'. Gather ideas about why they are good, sensible rules which are worth keeping. Point out that they are good rules whether we actually know the reasons or not.

Now ask for some volunteers to stand around as trees in the garden of the story from Genesis. Give the volunteers real or paper fruits to hold. God's rule for Adam and Eve was 'Don't eat fruit from this tree'. Hang this rule round the tree in the centre of the garden. Now God has very good reasons for making this rule, based on his love for Adam and Eve and his concern for them. And since God is God, that rule is the most important thing for Adam and Eve to remember. However tasty the fruit looks, whatever they may be told it will do to help them, they are always to keep hold of God's rule (what was it?), and stick to keeping that. Anything that cuts across God's rule must be wrong.

Ask two people who think they will be able to keep to God's rule without disobeying it. These two are going to be Adam and Eve. Show them how tasty the fruit looks and try to persuade them to try it. Tell them that it will do wonderful things for them, and make them wise like God. When they (hopefully) manage to resist the temptation to do what God's rule told them not to, praise them, and then point out that they managed it this time, but we are always being tempted to be disobedient to God's rule of love, and when it next happens we

47

need to stick close to God, and remember his rule: 'Love God and love one another'.

Adam and Eve in the story stand for all of us who are human. And humans tend not to be very good at resisting temptation. God loves us and understands what it is like to be humans being tempted. We know that because Jesus was tempted during his life on earth. He will give us the strength we need to resist those pressures of temptation, but that doesn't mean it's going to be easy. Resisting temptation is *very hard*, and that's why Jesus told us to pray about it every day of our life: 'Lead us not into temptation but deliver us from evil.' Let's use the strength God offers; we need all the help we can get!

All-age ideas

- The Genesis reading can be accompanied by a group of people miming the action.

- Have different voices to read the Gospel, either using the *Dramatised Bible* or simply going through the text together and deciding how the meaning and drama can best be brought out.

- Give everyone a cut-out paper shape of a bitten apple, and during the time of confession ask them to hold it and look at it as they bring to mind the times they have gone along with temptations instead of holding on to God's rule of love. After the confession the shapes can be collected and placed at the foot of the cross as the words of forgiveness are proclaimed.

Second Sunday of Lent

Genesis 12:1-4a
Psalm 121
Romans 4:1-5, 13-17
John 3:1-17

Anyone who believes in Jesus can know his power to save and set us free.

All-age talk

You will need a hand-held hairdryer (and possibly an extension lead).

Begin by talking about the wind, and how we can tell it is windy, even though the wind itself is invisible. Collect examples of the signs from the congregation. Draw together the signs with the principle that wind makes things move.

Now ask some volunteers to scatter some cut-out paper people on the ground, fixing some firmly to the ground with Blu-Tack or paperweights. In the Gospel today we overheard a conversation between Jesus and a man called Nicodemus. We know Nicodemus was a Pharisee, and knew lots of clever things. But Jesus puzzled him. He could see that the miracles Jesus was doing made it look as if Jesus really was God's promised Messiah who they were all waiting for. The problem was, Jesus didn't seem to be sticking rigidly to the rules Nicodemus and the other Pharisees felt he ought to be. He seemed far too broad-minded. He was spending time with sinners.

The good thing about Nicodemus was that he didn't keep his worries to himself, or pretend they weren't there, or reject Jesus because he was making him think about things in a new way. He went to find Jesus one night and talked to him about it all. And that's what we need to do with all our doubts and puzzles and questions.

Jesus gave him some funny answers, and one of the answers was about the wind. He said that living in the Spirit is rather like being blown by the wind. God wants to move us along and he can do that so long as we don't fix ourselves down. Watch how the wind from the hairdryer can move these people. (Switch on the hairdryer and blow the people along.)

Look at these people who were stuck down to

49

the floor. The wind blew but they haven't moved anywhere. And sometimes we are like that. We might sing on Sundays about wanting to live in God's Spirit, but when that means being ready to move or change in our life or our attitudes or ideas, we start fixing ourselves to the floor where we feel safer, and can enjoy moving a little to the breath of God, but not enough to be actually moved along.

This Lent let's work at being brave enough to come to Jesus with the deep worries and puzzles of life, knowing that God is quite able to cope with them and won't suddenly disappear or be offended. And let's work at being brave enough to stand out in the wind of God's Spirit, without fixing ourselves to the spot, but willing for him to move us as a parish and as individuals wherever he wants to move us.

All-age ideas

- During one of the hymns wave streamers and flags. If you have warm air heating you could position streamers nearby, so that the wind blows them.

- This song can be accompanied with actions which help the understanding of the words:

  For God so loved the world (*point up, then trace a large circle with both hands moving outwards from the top centre*)

  he gave his only Son (*mime a giving action with both hands*)

  that whoever believes in him (*point with eye contact to different people and yourself, then up*)

  shall not die (*crouch with hand over head*)

  but have eternal life. (*stand with arms raised*)

  L is for the love that he has for me. (*first finger of right hand on palm of left hand, then hug yourself*)

  I am the reason he died on the tree. (*point to second finger of left hand, then make cross shape with arms*)

  F is for forgiveness and now I am free. (*first two fingers of right hand crossing first two fingers of left hand, then clench fists and cross them as if in handcuffs, and break hands apart as if being freed*)

  E is to enjoy being in his company. (*point to first finger of left hand, then turn around, dancing*)

THIRD SUNDAY OF LENT

Exodus 17:1-7
Psalm 95
Romans 5:1-11
John 4:5-42

God both knows us completely and loves us completely; meeting us where we are, he provides us with living water, to satisfy all our needs.

All-age talk

You will need some paper cups, one with holes poked in it, a washing-up bowl or bucket and a jug of water.

Remind everyone of the way the people in the desert were very thirsty, and Moses asked God how their thirst could be quenched. He also told God how grumpy everyone was getting – they were so grumpy that Moses began to think they might take their anger out on him physically! God answered by providing water tumbling out of a rock, fresh and pure and delicious. There's nothing more wonderful when you're thirsty than the refreshing sound and taste of water. Now pour some water out and enjoy the sound of it. Invite some thirsty person to drink some from the proper cup. The people wanted to be back in the past, but God wanted to lead them on into the future.

We heard about two more water supplies today. Did anyone notice what they were? One was a well, where a woman had come to collect water, and where Jesus was sitting, feeling thirsty. Perhaps his own thirst reminded him of the people getting grumpy with Moses in the desert, and the way God had given them the flowing, living water they needed.

The other water supply is a bit unusual. Jesus told the woman about some water which would quench her thirst completely, and become a spring of water inside her, welling up to give her life that lasts for ever. At first the woman thought this

51

sounded too good to be true! What Jesus was doing was explaining the way God fills our lives, and leads us into the future, satisfying us all the way along, and refreshing us when we are sad and longing for good and right and fair and helpful things to happen in our world. The more we go to God to be filled with his living water of life and love, the more we shall find that we too are becoming sources of love and comfort and fairness and truthfulness for other people.

Let's see what happens when we pour some water into this cup with holes in it. (Station some people around with proper cups.) Pretend this hol(e)y cup is a Christian drinking the living water of life and love from the living, loving God. Can you see how the Christian then pours out that love to other people he or she meets? There's no problem that God will suddenly dry up, because God is living, flowing, for ever. And the other people may well want to become hol(e)y themselves, drinking that eternal supply which they can see is changing us for the better.

So if your life feels rather dry or thirsty or stuck in the past, go to Jesus; keep going to Jesus; and let him fill you up with the living spiritual water that really satisfies. And don't keep it all to yourself – pass it on!

All-age ideas

- Make streamers for the children from green and blue crepe paper, and have them sweeping and twirling like water during one of the hymns.

- Have the Gospel read as a conversation between a man and a woman.

FOURTH SUNDAY OF LENT: MOTHERING SUNDAY

Exodus 2:1-10 or
  1 Samuel 1:20-28
Psalm 34:11-20 or
  Psalm 127:1-4
2 Corinthians 1:3-7 or
  Colossians 3:12-17
Luke 2:33-35 or
  John 19:25-27

Thanking God for our earthly opportunities for mothering and being mothered, we also remember the mothering parenthood of God.

All-age talk

Begin by interviewing a couple of mothers, one young and one older, using such questions as: What do you like best about being a mum? What do you find hardest? How has being a mum helped you grow as a person? What advice would you give to a young Christian couple about to become parents?

Talk about the way we all need to look after each other in this unselfish, loving way which we think of as mothering, and how that is the way our loving God treats us. He doesn't smother us or stop us exploring our world and trying everything out, but he encourages us and guides us so we know where to walk safely. If we fall over and hurt ourselves in life, he's there to comfort us and make us better, and if we go off and get ourselves lost in bad or stupid behaviour, he comes to search for us until he finds us, calling our name again and again until we hear him and shout out, asking to be rescued.

When we are little, our parents have to dress us, because we can't do our buttons up or tie our laces on our own. A good way to remember that we are all called to look after one another in a loving, caring way, is to think about it as dressing ourselves in clothes of kindness, forgiveness and patience, compassion, humility and gentleness. As you say this, dress a volunteer or a rag doll in various garments. Finally, to bind everything together, we need love (a belt is tied around the other clothes).

53

So tomorrow, and every morning when you get dressed, think of yourself also putting on the clothes of kindness, forgiveness and patience, compassion, humility and gentleness, and tie everything together with love. That way we'll be learning to look after one another the way our God looks after us.

All-age ideas

- Stage the interview with a younger and an older mum, either just before the all-stage talk or between the readings.

- Have a family or parent and child leading the intercessions.

- Have a group of different aged people reading one of today's Bible readings, working on it beforehand to use the variety of voices effectively, sometimes alone and sometimes together.

- If posies of flowers are being distributed today, first light a special candle of thanksgiving to remember all those mothers who have died and commend them to God's safekeeping.

- Have a collection of food or toiletries for those families who are at present having to live in refuge or asylum housing, or who are homeless.

- Have a scribble wall (a length of lining paper and some crayons) for people to draw or describe qualities they are thankful for in their own mothers or in God's parenting, as they pray their thanks during a time of quietness and reflective music.

FIFTH SUNDAY OF LENT

Ezekiel 37:1-14
Psalm 130
Romans 8:6-11
John 11:1-45

Jesus is the resurrection and the life. He can transform death and despair, in any form, into life and hope.

All-age talk

You will need an inflatable ball or a balloon, and, if possible, a dummy used for teaching mouth-to-mouth resuscitation. Otherwise, bring along a large baby doll.

Begin by asking everyone to breathe in deeply, hold their breath while you count to twenty and then let their breath out. They will all have noticed how much we need that air. By the end of just twenty seconds we're getting desperate! Most of the time we breathe in and out without even thinking about it. Although it's such a vitally important thing to do, we're designed so that the breathing mostly goes on automatically so we can do lots of other things at the same time. Yet without that breathing we wouldn't be able to do any of those other things because we would be dead. That's how important breath is – it's a matter of life and death.

Ask a volunteer to demonstrate what we have to do if we come across someone whose breathing has stopped. Point out that what is happening when we are doing mouth-to-mouth resuscitation is that we actually do the breathing for the other person. With our living breath we can save someone's life.

Today in the Gospel we have heard an amazing story of Jesus actually bringing someone back to life. It was his friend Lazarus, and when Jesus' voice, as the Lord of life, broke into the place of death, Lazarus heard his name being called and walked out into life again towards that voice.

Jesus calls each of us by name. He calls into the place we are, even if that place is full of darkness and sadness, or if the noise of unimportant things we like wasting our time on nearly drowns his voice, or if we're running as fast as we can away from God's way of living. Wherever we are, Jesus keeps calling because he wants to bring us out into new life. He knows his breath in us will transform our time in this life, and beyond that into the time after our physical death. As Jesus breathes his life into us it will make such a difference to us that we'll wish we'd gone for it ages ago!

Ask someone to blow up the ball or balloon, and as they do so point out what a difference it is making to have that breath inside. Once they are filled with our breath they have a whole new dimension – they're much more useful and they're much more their true selves. It's the same with us. When we let God breathe his life into us every minute of every day, we become much more our true selves, our life has a whole new dimension, and we are of more use to God in caring for the world he loves.

All-age ideas

- Have the Gospel read by a group, with people taking the different parts, so that the different conversations in the story are brought out.

- With a group of musicians work out some sound effects to accompany the Ezekiel reading, perhaps using blocks of wood and shakers, a rain stick or coconut shells.

- Ask some of the creative people in the congregation to make a poster or banner about God's power to renew us, using the 'dry bones into living people' image.

PALM SUNDAY

Liturgy of the Palms:
Matthew 21:1-11
Psalm 118:1-2, 19-29

Liturgy of the Passion:
Isaiah 50:4-9a
Psalm 31:9-16
Philippians 2:5-11
Matthew 26:14-27:66
   or Matthew 27:11-54

Jesus rides into Jerusalem cheered by the crowds. Days later crowds will be clamouring for his death.

All-age talk

Have the London Underground map printed out on the weekly sheet, or have some larger versions available to show everyone.

Look at the plan and talk about the way it is simple sign language to help us make sense of a huge complicated network of rails and tunnels criss-crossing under the streets. The whole thing is so enormous to understand that we need this simple map.

But when we travel on the underground it only works because, as well as the simple map in our hand or on the station wall, the real massive tracks are laid in all those dark tunnels, and the electrical power is surging through all the thick cables, and the tilers have been busy fixing tiles on the station walls, and the computers are busy checking where each train is so that they don't bump into one another, and those moving stairs, the escalators, are well oiled and running smoothly. Although all this doesn't show up on our plan of coloured lines and blobs, we only have to look at it and we know that all the real stuff is right there.

In a way the cross shape is like one of those plans. Draw people's attention to the crosses they can see around them in church. It is only a simple shape, and we can all make it ourselves by placing one index finger across the other. (Do that now.) When people say 'fingers crossed' what do they do? (Ask some people to show this.) Today it usually means hoping we'll be lucky, but a long time ago it was people making the sign of the cross as they prayed about something they were worried about. (We could go back to using the sign that way!)

Now if the shape of the cross is like the underground train plan, what is all the real, deep stuff that the cross reminds us of? Ask everyone to find or make a cross and look at it, as you tell them about the deeper meaning: God loves the world so much that he was willing to give up everything, and come and live with us in person as Jesus. That loving led him to a cross where he gave up his life for us, taking all the selfishness and sin on himself, and stretching out his arms in welcome and forgiveness, because he so longs for us to be free.

All-age ideas

- Have a very large, plain cross made of paper fixed on the floor in the central aisle. During the time of confession, some people can come and write on it the sin and evil of our world and our society.

- During the intercessions, candles can be placed along the cross.

- The reading of the Passion can be sung by the choir, or dramatised using different voices, with the whole congregation joining in the crowd's words. These can be displayed at the appropriate time either on sheets of paper or on an OHP.

- A drama group could prepare a short mime to bring out the meaning of the crucifixion. Rather than having set movements to follow, give them some familiar religious keywords to pray about, unpack and express, such as *Saviour, Redemption* or *Justification*.

EASTER DAY

Acts 10:34-43 or
  Jeremiah 31:1-6
Psalm 118:1-2, 14-24
Colossians 3:1-4 or
  Acts 10:34-43
John 20:1-18 or
  Matthew 28:1-10

It is true. Jesus is alive for all time. The Lord of life cannot be held by death. God's victory over sin and death means that new life for us is a reality.

All-age talk

Bring along a few fresh eggs in a carton, and a chocolate egg.

Begin by reminding everyone that we are here for an exciting celebration. Draw attention to all the flowers, and the cleaning that has been going on, and any banners or other special Easter decorations and symbols. What is it we're celebrating? That Jesus had died on the cross and is now alive – alive for ever!

Introduce the chocolate egg. For some reason we've been seeing a lot of these at Easter. No doubt some people gave some away. No doubt some ate one before breakfast! What have they got to do with Jesus? Why do we all like to give one another eggs at Easter time?

One reason is that people were giving one another eggs around the time of Easter long before they had heard about Jesus. This is springtime, and eggs are all part of the spring, with its promise of new life.

New life! That's interesting – we've been hearing about the new life that Jesus gives us. When people came to our country and told us about Jesus, they thought the egg was a very good way of explaining the Gospel, so they kept it.

How does an egg help us to understand the Easter story? Show everyone the carton of ordinary eggs, and hold one up on its own. What is it? (An egg.) What comes out of a fertilised egg like this? (A chicken.) Yes, it's a new life – in this case a chicken. An egg is the way new creatures come into being. And Easter is about Jesus being alive in

59

a new way and making it possible for all of us to be given new life.

What does the inside of an egg look like? (It's got yellow yolk and some thick runny stuff which is white when it's cooked.) What are some favourite ways of eating an egg? (Gather suggestions.) So what is inside the shell turns into something quite different. Jesus' life now, as from the first Easter Day, is different. For a start, he's never going to die again; his new life isn't a life that runs out. Even though Jesus has now been alive again for about two thousand years, he is outside time, so he hasn't got old. And he isn't tied to space like us, so he can come and go without having to catch a bus or open doors. He doesn't have to be seen to be real.

Now break one of the eggs. When we enjoy eating an egg the shell needs to be broken; otherwise we wouldn't be able to get at the white and the yolk. When a chick is ready to live in the big wide world it has to crack the eggshell before it can climb out. What does that tell us? Sometimes we want to hang on to things just as they are. We don't always want to change, even if change in our lives is for the best.

Will we let our shells be broken ready for the new life Jesus wants us to have? God is calling us out of our shells into a whole new, different way of living. It is the loving way of living, trusting in God with our heart and soul and mind and strength, and loving one another. That may mean that some of our habits and fears may, like shells, have to be broken before we can live freely in the loving way. The good news of Easter is that Jesus has already broken through death and sin, so if we hold on to him, he can bring us through the shell breaking and out into the light and space of day – a daylight which lasts for ever.

All-age ideas

- If part of the children's worship on Good Friday has involved art and craft work, such as banners or posters or Easter gardens, these can be used to decorate the church today.

- Make a celebration arch of flowers at the entrance of the church, either by attaching oasis in chicken wire around the doorway, or actually constructing an archway using three ladders, lashed together and fastened securely. Weave plenty of greenery in and out of the ladder rungs to hide the main structure, and then decorate with flowers and ribbons.

- Encourage everyone to bring bells to ring in a burst of praise with the organ or music group just before singing the Gloria.

- If you have a small congregation, consider supplying an ordinary fresh egg for each person to use at the time of confession. Give out the eggs from baskets lined with straw. At the time of confession ask everyone to hold their egg very carefully, and remember that this is the way our loving God holds us – carefully in the palm of his hand. Think of the times we have failed to respond to his love, and reject his offer of new life in him. Think of the times we fail to treat other people with care, ignoring their brokenness; think of the times we treat one another carelessly or harshly and without consideration. Think of one area in our life where we need to be broken and made new. Then, during the words of absolution, hold the egg as a symbol of our hope which we celebrate today.

- Rather than a traditional Easter garden, consider a cross made of wire and deadwood, which has flowers in oasis fixed into it.

Second Sunday of Easter

Acts 2:14a, 22-32
Psalm 16
1 Peter 1:3-9
John 20:19-31

Through the risen Jesus we have a living hope which will never spoil or fade.

All-age talk

Ask for one volunteer who is brave and one who is more scared and timid. Tell the timid one that you are asking them to fall backwards. You promise them they won't come to any harm (but you don't say you will catch them). Suggest that they watch the brave volunteer to try it first, so they can see what happens. Now ask the brave volunteer to fall backwards, and make sure you catch them, or arrange to have someone strong to catch them.

Now ask if the timid person is able to try it, now that they have seen that it is safe. If they are, let them try it, making certain they are safely caught!

Sometimes it is very hard to know whether we can trust something or not unless we have seen it in action. Perhaps we have bought a tape recorder, or a jigsaw puzzle at a boot sale or a jumble sale, and it looks fine, and we are assured that it's in good working order. But when we get home we find the tape recorder chews up our favourite tape, and the jigsaw puzzle has two or three pieces missing.

It's all very disappointing to be let down like that. And the longer we live, and the more we are let down by things or by people, the more disappointed we get, and the more determined we are not to trust anyone or anything in case we are let down again. Thomas was a bit like that. He had probably been badly let down by people during his life. Like lots of us, it made him scared to trust good news. We and Thomas would love good news to be true, but we'd rather not trust it at all than trust it and risk being let down.

Now Jesus himself knows that he is alive, and will stay alive for ever. He knows it would be quite safe for us to believe this, because he knows it's true! He hopes very much that we will be able to believe, because he knows it will make such a wonderful difference to our lives – we'll be able to live in a new kind of freedom, and become more and more our real selves.

So what does he do about it? In our Gospel reading today we heard how Jesus came into the room, joining his friends as they were praying, so that they knew he was there. And Jesus still does that, nearly two thousand years later. He is here now, with us, his friends. Whenever we gather in Jesus' name, he joins us. When we live on the lookout for him, we'll find we start noticing him more and more. We won't see him with our eyes, but we'll feel his love and peace, and suddenly know he is there.

All-age ideas

- Try this short sketch to alert people to the way we don't see what we aren't expecting, or what doesn't seem relevant.

  Phil and Robert are waiting with their coats on at a bus stop. Both have briefcases. Robert is reading his newspaper. Phil is checking his watch.

  Phil   Excuse me, but has the 7:42 gone yet? The 25A?

  Robert   The 25A? I wouldn't know. I'm waiting for the 26. That's the bus I catch.

  Phil   Well, how long have you been waiting?

  Robert   Oh, since 7:40. But it isn't due till 7:50, and it's always late.

  Phil   Is the 7:42 ever late? (*Checks watch.*)

  Robert   I wouldn't know. I wait for the 26, you see.

  Phil   Well, have any other buses come since you've been waiting?

  Robert   Oh yes, there's been a few others, I think.

Phil	What numbers were they?
Robert	I wouldn't know. I wait for the 26 you see. That's the bus I catch.
Phil	Oh. Thanks. *(Folds arms in resignation and looks the other way.)*
Phil	Hey there's a bus coming . . . It's the 25A! So I haven't missed it! *(Checks watch.)* And it's only two minutes late. *(Sticks out arm to stop it.)*
Robert	The 26 is due at 7:50, you know. That's the bus I catch.

- Have quiet music playing in the background of the Gospel reading at the point when Jesus comes and stands among the disciples – 19b-23 and 26b-29.

THIRD SUNDAY OF EASTER

Acts 2:14a, 36-41
Psalm 116:1-4, 12-19
1 Peter 1:17-23
Luke 24:13-35

Jesus explains the scriptures and is recognised in the breaking of bread.

All-age talk

Bring a game or piece of equipment which needs putting together and setting up properly before it can be used. This could be anything from a computer to a folding bed – it all depends on what is available and the interest area of the congregation. It needs to have a set of instructions to go with it.

Begin by introducing your item of equipment. We are continuing to look at the resurrection stories, when one person after another is astonished by amazing events. The congregation may well be astonished to see one of these brought into church for the sermon! Pretend that you are having a real problem with this thing because you don't understand it at all. You don't understand how to get it to work.

Have a primed helper who comes up at this stage and shows you the instruction leaflet. They tell you that if you read that it will tell you how the thing works and how to use it. Be surprised, but set to reading some of the instructions, without relating them to the equipment. They don't make much sense to you, and you get fed up. It's no good – you don't understand and it doesn't make sense.

Explain that this is rather like the way the two disciples felt as they walked sadly back home on the very first Easter Day. They didn't understand anything any more. They had great hopes about Jesus, but now he was dead, so their hopes were dead as well. They had heard about the women saying they had seen Jesus alive early that morning, but that didn't make any sense to them either. How on earth could someone be dead as dead and now be alive? It couldn't possibly be true!

Just then, as we heard in the Gospel just now, someone joined them and asked what they were so sad about. And when they told him, he started to show them how it actually did make a lot of sense. (Break off as the helper comes and offers to take you through the instructions and sort the equipment out. Accept their help and marvel as gradually, step by step, it starts to come together, and eventually works. Be excited about this and thank the helper. Then come back to the Emmaus story.)

Well, it certainly helps to have someone who really understands to help you when you are in a muddle! That's how those disciples felt when the stranger explained that it was all there in the scriptures (pick up a Bible) about the promised Messiah having to suffer and die before there could be new life. When they reached their home they invited the helpful stranger in to stay with them, and when their guest took the bread and blessed and broke it (mime this) . . . what do you think they suddenly realised?

It was Jesus!

And that is still what Jesus does. He walks along with us where we are walking. He helps us understand about God through the words of scripture (pick up the Bible again), he helps us make sense of life and its problems (stand beside the working piece of equipment), and (move to the altar) he makes himself known to us in the breaking of bread.

All-age ideas

- Have the Gospel mimed as it is narrated, using the centre aisle as the road and the sanctuary as the house, so that the breaking of bread is mimed at the altar. Have Jesus wearing an alb to link with our bread-breaking in Holy Communion.

- Use different voices in the reading from Acts, with the words of the crowd, 'Brothers, what shall we do?', displayed so that everyone can say them. (They could be on the weekly sheet, on a large sheet held up, or on an OHP.)

- Have a display of Bible reading notes and various Bibles suitable for different age groups, so as to encourage people to get to know the scriptures better and deepen their understanding.

FOURTH SUNDAY OF EASTER

Acts 2:42-47
Psalm 23
1 Peter 2:19-25
John 10:1-10

Jesus, the Good Shepherd, has come so that we may have life in rich abundance.

All-age talk

Using chairs, build a circular sheepfold, with a gap for the entrance. Ask for some volunteer sheep to go inside. Explain that this is what a sheepfold was like in Jesus' day, except that it was made of stones, not chairs. Is there a door? No, there isn't. That's because the shepherd himself was the door. Ask a volunteer shepherd to come and be the door of the sheepfold. (You could even give the shepherd a stick or crook from the Nativity costumes, and a shepherd's sling.) Why is this living door likely to be a good safe one for the sheep? Because the shepherd would hear any dangers, such as wolves, or bears, or sheep stealers, and take action to protect the sheep, using his staff or sling. (The shepherd can pretend to frighten off a dangerous wolf.)

Another thing about sheep is that they get very frightened by lots of things, but when they hear the voice of the shepherd at the door they know they can trust him, and they feel safe. They will even follow him when he calls them and leads them off to some good juicy grass. (The sheep can try this.) And then they will follow the shepherd back home at the end of the day. (They do this.)

Now why are we getting a lesson in sheep farming this morning? What has all this got to do with Jesus? Or us?

In the Gospel today we heard Jesus telling the people that he is the sheep-door. (And you know what that means, now.) He told them all about the sheep being safe when the shepherd is the door, and the sheep knowing the shepherd's voice and following him. (You know about that too.) But the people didn't have a clue why Jesus was talking to

67

them about sheep and shepherds. So they asked him to explain.

Jesus said he was trying to tell them something important about God. (Can anyone think what it was?) He was telling the people that they were a bit like sheep and Jesus was like the good shepherd who lies down in the doorway to keep the sheep safe. He was saying that God looks after us and defends us with his life because he loves us so much. He hates the thought of us coming to harm, and fights off evil. We can trust God's voice when he calls us, and follow him without any fear because we know God is always faithful and good and loving.

So whenever you are scared to face a bad problem, or bad ideas and temptations keep coming at you, stand there in the sheepfold behind Jesus, the sheep-door, and you will be safe. And whenever you are muddled about whether to do something or not, or whether to be selfish or not, listen out for the quiet calling of the Good Shepherd (you won't hear it with your ears, but you will know it in yourself) and follow him into the way that is right and good and kind and loving.

All-age ideas

- Include some model or toy sheep and lambs, or a shepherd's crook in one of the flower arrangements, which could make use of wild meadow flowers and grasses.

- If you have an OHP, find a picture of a shepherd and sheep and have it made into an acetate at the local office shop. Or use a projector to show a few slides of sheep on hillsides. These can be displayed during the singing or reading of Psalm 23.

- Consider making a parish photograph album, scrap book or a video which aims to capture something of the real Christian identity of your church community, based on the portrait of the Early Church given to us in Acts. This may well be a year-long or an ongoing project, and could include prayers and excerpts from special service sheets, as well as pictures.

FIFTH SUNDAY OF EASTER

Acts 7:55-60
Psalm 31:1-5, 15-16
1 Peter 2:2-10
John 14:1-14

Jesus is the Way, the Truth and the Life, through whom we can come into the presence of God for ever.

All-age talk

Ask two or three experts to come and explain the way they do whatever it is they are good at. (The actual areas of expertise depend on the interests of your congregation, but try and choose people from representative age and interest groups. The skill should be capable of being demonstrated in front of everyone, so it could be ironing, juggling, dribbling a football, doing a cartwheel or skipping, for example.)

First ask each one to explain it to you, placing them out of sight of everyone as they do so. Share with the congregation how it all sounds incredibly complicated, and difficult to follow, even though it is obviously expert advice. That's rather how it is with the Old Testament Law – everyone respects it highly and it's very good advice for living, but somehow we never seem to manage to follow the instructions or get the hang of them. They help us to know how to live a good life, but they don't change us so that we are able to do it. Some of the prophets had told everyone that one day it would be different. People wouldn't need those instructions any more, because they would already know, in their hearts, how to behave properly.

Let's find out if we can understand our experts any better if we can actually see them doing these clever things. (Invite them to demonstrate, one by one.) Ah, that's much clearer! We may not be able to do it ourselves, yet, but at least we have their example in front of us, to learn from and copy. (Someone might like to try copying one of the skills.)

When Jesus came, it was like being able to see God's way of living – in person. 'So that's what it means to love God and love one another!' people thought. 'So that's what God's love for us is like!' And even though we may not yet be able to do it very well, at least we have a wonderful example to learn from and copy.

If we're still full of bitterness about something that happened to us long ago, we can look at Jesus and copy his forgiving. If we're looking down on someone because they aren't as clever or rich as us, we can look at Jesus and copy his way of enjoying people and accepting them for what they are. If we are always worrying about clothes and possessions, we can look at Jesus and copy his simple way of living, and spend our energy cultivating the treasures that we can take with us to heaven. So Jesus is like a living 'Way' – he's a walking, talking Way to live.

In fact that's what Jesus called himself in our Gospel today; he said, 'I am the Way, the Truth and the Life'. With Jesus we go one better than having his example to copy – since the Resurrection we can have his life living in us! That would be rather like our experts being able to fill us with all that makes them able to do those clever things. Imagine what a skilled parish we would be if that were possible! We'd all be expert ironers, football dribblers, jugglers and cartwheelers! Well, I have to tell you that we can't do that. As humans we have to pass on our skills the hard way, by teaching and learning. But with Jesus it's different. He really can live in our lives, enabling us to love God and one another. All we need to do is invite him into our personal lives and our church, and be prepared to be gradually transformed.

All-age ideas

- On a wall or pillar display a very large speech bubble made of paper, on which is written: Lord Jesus, receive my spirit!

- Incorporate rocks and stones and a builder's trowel in one of the flower arrangements today.

- As people come into church give them a building stone shaped piece of paper on which they write their name. During the time of confession, or as an alternative form of intercession, ask everyone to hold their stones and pray in silence for their different areas of life commitments, such as homes and families, work, worries, hobbies, hopes and dreams, needs and thanks. Have these collected in baskets and then redistributed. Now everyone prays for the person named on this stone. Finally all the stones are fixed inside an outline of a church by the children, using glue sticks. Music can be played or sung while this is going on.

SIXTH SUNDAY OF EASTER

Acts 17:22-31
Psalm 66:8-20
1 Peter 3:13-22
John 14:15-21

The Spirit of truth, given to us, enables us to discern the living, risen Christ.

All-age talk

Start by displaying a fairly simple equation, such as $2x+3=x+10$, or $y(5+2)=21$, or $x+4=6$ (difficulty depends on your congregation), perhaps on a blackboard. Provide chalk, and ask someone mathematical to take us through the stages of solving the mystery of this unknown value of x or y.

When Paul was in Athens he saw an altar to 'the unknown god', and set about explaining to the people who this God was. It was as if the people had been calling God 'x'. Now when we tried to solve our x mystery, we worked it out, step by step, gradually getting a clearer idea of what x meant, until, in the end, it was quite clear to us (or some of us!).

That's rather like the way we can look at the beauty and order of our world, and all the physics and chemistry of it, and all the variety and colour and shape in it, and begin to work our way towards discovering what God is like. We can work out that he must be clever and thoughtful, and imaginative and faithful, for instance.

But with Jesus coming, and showing us exactly what God is like, it's more like this.

Set up the same equation as before, using solid shapes, like building blocks. Each x is a bag, filled with the correct number of blocks. We could still work out what x is, but if the bag is opened, we can actually see what it is. (Do this.)

With Jesus' life there in front of us through reading the Gospels, and through living in his company every day, we can have a very clear idea of what God is like. We can see that he is forgiving and totally honest and good, that he is responsible and

72

stands up for what is right, whatever happens to him and however much people sneer. We can see that he looks for the good in people and doesn't condemn them or give up on them. We can see that his love has been proved stronger than death.

If we put our faith in that God, whom Jesus has revealed to us in a new and clear way, and if we claim to love him, then we will have to start doing what he says. Who finds it easy to be obedient? Most of us find it very hard. We don't want to do what we are told; we want to do what we like!

Jesus says that the way you can tell if someone really does believe in him and love him, is by whether they are obedient to him, and obey what he says. That means listening to God and saying yes to him, whether it's what we want to do or not.

That is a *very hard* thing to learn, but it's worth learning, because being friends with Jesus is the best and happiest thing that could ever happen to us.

All-age ideas

- Have a group of dancers (these can be mixed ages and gender) to work on expressing in movement the truth that we are brought through the waters of death into new life, and given the guiding Spirit of Truth to lead us onwards. They could use waving silver and blue cloth or streamers to represent the flood water as they pass through. They need to make it clear that they are turning their backs on the old life, and going willingly into this 'drowning', from which they emerge, with the Spirit to hold their hands and guide them, first to an attitude of praise and worship, and then out, through the congregation. Suitable music would be something like *Amazing grace; Jesus, take me as I am; Let your living water flow over my soul* or *Lord, you have my heart.*

- If you have an OHP, make up an acetate which has in the centre: 'Our God is . . .', and invite people to tell you characteristics about God that

73

they know to be true. Write the suggestions up and then invite everyone, in their own time and order, to read out these truths – Our God is faithful, our God is forgiving . . . – so that there is a general noise of praising God for who he is. As the voices die away, finish by a single voice saying just the centre words: 'Our God is. Amen.'

ASCENSION DAY

Acts 1:1-11 or
   Daniel 7:9-14
Psalm 47 or Psalm 93
Ephesians 1:15-23 or
   Acts 1:1-11
Luke 24:44-53

Having bought back our freedom with the giving of his life, Jesus enters into the full glory to which he is entitled.

All-age talk

Begin by staging a Mexican wave, which runs through the whole church or assembly. Point out how it only worked so well because all of us as individuals were working together as a unit of energy.

Remind everyone of the events leading up to today, giving them a whistle-stop tour of Jesus' life, death, Resurrection and post-Resurrection appearances. Explain how the disciples needed that time to get used to Jesus being alive and around, though not always visible or physically present.

Now they were ready for the next stage in the plan. Jesus leads them out of the city and he gives them his blessing, telling them to hang around Jerusalem without rushing off to do their own bit of mission work. (Enthusiasm is wonderful but it can sometimes make us race off to start before we've got everything we need.) The disciples have got to wait because God is going to send the Holy Spirit to empower them and equip them for the work they will be doing. It will make it possible for the news of God's love to spread out through the world like our Mexican wave.

When Jesus had finished giving the disciples their instructions and his encouragement, we are told that the disciples watched him being taken into heaven, until a cloud hid him from their sight. Those are the only practical details we have, so we don't know exactly how it happened. But we do know that the disciples were in no doubt about where Jesus had gone, and they were full of joy and excitement as they made their way back to the city to wait for the Holy Spirit, as Jesus had told them to.

A lot of years have gone by since Jesus ascended into heaven – nearly two thousand years. But that isn't much if you aren't stuck in time as we are, and God isn't stuck in time. He's prepared to wait to give us humans the chance to turn to him in our lives, and we don't know the date when Jesus will return. We do know that in God's good time he will come back, and everyone will see his glory together, both the living and those who have finished the earthly part of their life.

In the meantime, we have been given the Holy Spirit, so that God can be with us in person every moment of our life, helping us and guiding our choices, steering us safely through temptations, and teaching us more and more about our amazing God. All he waits for is to be invited.

All-age ideas

- Any artwork or writing that the children have done on what the Ascension is about can be displayed around the building, and time given in the service to looking at it.

- Have a beautiful helium balloon at the ready. Write on it an Ascension message that the children would like to send. After the service two representative children can let the balloon float away.

- Children can wave white and yellow streamers during some of the hymns.

SEVENTH SUNDAY OF EASTER

Acts 1:6-14
Psalm 68:1-10, 32-35
1 Peter 4:12-14; 5:6-11
John 17:1-11

God's glory is often revealed in the context of suffering and failure in the world's eyes.

All-age talk

Before the talk, use the short sketch in the all-age ideas section.

Begin by talking about saying goodbye. The kind of goodbye it is depends on how well we know each other, whether we love or hate each other, and whether we are saying goodbye for a short time, a long time or for ever. Today in our first reading we were with the disciples as Jesus said goodbye to them. Since Easter we have been looking at various times when he had been meeting up with them after the Resurrection. Sometimes he had met them when they were all together, sometimes on their own. They would suddenly recognise him, or he would suddenly be there among them, and the disciples had begun to get used to Jesus being with them even when they couldn't see him with their eyes.

Now, here they are, all together with Jesus, and this is going to be their last goodbye to him as a person whom they see with their eyes, because he is going back to heaven. He tells them two things: (show a picture of rushing wind and flames) that they are going to be given power when the Holy Spirit comes upon them, and (show a picture of an empty speech bubble) that they are going to tell lots of people all over the world about the Jesus they know and love so well.

Then we are told that he was lifted up, while they watched, and a cloud took him from their sight so that they couldn't see him any more. So they stood there, peering up into the sky, rather like you do when you've just let a balloon go, and you watch and watch until you can't see it any more. What happened next?

They realised that two people, dressed in white, were standing next to them. 'Why are you standing here looking up into the sky?' they asked. They told the disciples that one day Jesus would come in the same way they had seen him go. But what they wanted them to know was that there wasn't any point in hanging around in that one place for a glimpse of Jesus, because he had gone on to the next phase, where he would be with all his friends, including us, all the time, not in a way that we can see, but in new ways. Just as real, just as much alive, but in a form which makes him free to be in all kinds of different countries and places and dates and times all at once!

What he said to the disciples that day, he says to us as well: we will be given power when the Holy Spirit comes upon us (show the first picture again) and we are going to tell lots of people about the Jesus we know and love (show the second picture).

All-age ideas

- *A goodbye sketch.* This works with either a number of different pairs of people, of different ages and gender, or one pair who keep changing style and props. They simply walk on, say goodbye (it can be a wordy or a one-word goodbye) and walk off, but in several different roles. Here are some suggestions:
  1. A mother and her son at his first day at school.
  2. Lovers at a station.
  3. Host and unwelcome visitor who has overstayed his welcome.
  4. Two friends after school.
  5. Daughter with well-loved elderly parent in hospital or nursing home.

- Have people reading the different parts in the passage from Acts.

- Incorporate some horse chestnut blossom in one of the flower arrangements. It is traditionally known as the candle tree, in flower to celebrate the Ascension.

PENTECOST

Acts 2:1-21 or
   Numbers 11:24-30
Psalm 104:24-34, 35b
1 Corinthians 12:3b-13
   or Acts 2:1-21
John 20:19-23 or
   John 7:37-39

With great power the Spirit of God is poured out on the expectant disciples.

All-age talk

Bring along an electrical appliance and, if necessary, an extension lead. Alternatively, have a torch or game powered by batteries, and keep the batteries separate at first.

Refresh everyone's memory of today's dynamic event, with the disciples praying and waiting on God, and the early morning experience of his power coming to them like a rushing wind, or flames, searching out each one of them and touching them with the touch of God.

It quite overwhelmed them, and left them fired up with excitement at what God is capable of doing in people. They were bursting to tell everyone else about it, and wanted everyone to share this sense of God actually living in them. It was quite different from knowing about God; it was even different from walking about in the company of Jesus. This was like being flowed through with new life that set them living, talking and working in a new way.

Show the electrical appliance you have brought. Explain what this thing is capable of doing, but point out that at the moment it can't do any of those things. It has everything in place to work in that lively way, but something is missing at the moment – it isn't linked up to the power supply. Would it help if the appliance knew exactly how electricity works? Not really. However much is known about electrical circuits and the power grid, that won't bring this appliance to life. What it needs is this. (Plug the appliance into the power supply and switch on.)

79

Now the thing springs into life, and all kinds of potential are activated. That's what it's like having God's Spirit living in us and flowing through us. It makes that much difference! Just think what our world could be like if we were all full of the power of God's Spirit. Just think what a difference it would make in the world if all those in churches today all over the world asked God, seriously and openly, for a fresh outpouring of the Holy Spirit!

So often we are like well-finished appliances or games, knowing all about God's power, but not wanting to have the power switched on in us, just in case. Just in case what? Our God is the true, living God of love and compassion and mercy. Which means that any power he sends to touch us and affect us, will be only and entirely good for us. God is longing for his Church to be 'live' with the active power of his Spirit; we may be in good working order, but we also need to have the power, so that we actually 'work'!

All-age ideas

- Bring out those flame-coloured banners, flags and streamers, to wave in worship during the hymns.

- Lots of flame and white colours in the flower arrangements, with the swirling sense of movement and power.

- Use shakers to start a sound of wind during the reading from Acts.

TRINITY SUNDAY

Isaiah 40:12-17, 27-31
Psalm 8
2 Corinthians 13:11-13
Matthew 28:16-20

*The mystery of God – Creator,
Redeemer and Sanctifier all at once –
is beyond our human understanding,
yet closer to us than breathing.*

All-age talk

Produce a jacket or sweater of a young child's size, and invite a much larger volunteer to get into it. (It should be obvious that they won't be able to, even though they try.) Agree that it is impossible to get Ben into Justin's jacket – he's simply too big to fit!

Sometimes we expect God to be able to fit into our human-sized minds. We start to think about God, and say things like, 'But how can he possibly be able to hear us all praying at once?' when what we really mean is that we know humans couldn't do that, so it must be impossible for God as well. Or we say, 'God *must* have had a beginning sometime, because *everything* does!'

When we do this we are holding out a small human shape (hold out the little jacket) and expecting God to climb into it. And of course he doesn't fit, because being God is much bigger and deeper and wider than being a human being. God is so great that he is always going to be full of wonderful mystery for us, however much we learn about him. As humans we cannot hold his nature and understand it, any more than this small jacket will hold a big boy like Ben.

So does that mean that we can't really know God? Not at all! Invite Ben and Justin to come up and shake hands, and say hello to each other. You could have Ben asking Justin some questions, so that everyone can see that both boys are able to have a conversation.

Just because God is God and you are human doesn't mean you can't be good friends. There are lots of people here today who talk with God every day (it's called praying) and know that he is the person they love and trust best in their whole life.

We have been given a lifetime to get to know God really well and live as his friends. Sometimes we waste that time, and sometimes we suddenly realise that nothing else is quite so important. Sometimes we don't bother to tell other people about our loving God, or we let our behaviour tell them that we don't think he is worth very much at all. And other times we feel such love for our God that we can't wait to let other people know about him. And then our loving behaviour tells them as well as our words.

Our God is wonderful and all-knowing. He is the maker of our universe and of us all, he is the one who came as Jesus to die for love of us and save us, and he is present with his people, living in us as the Holy Spirit. How could we possibly ever expect to completely understand a God as amazing as that!

God being so great that he is full of holy mystery should make us excited, not frustrated. Let's enjoy being friends with the God who is so amazing that no human can ever explain what he is really like! And let's lavish our worship on him; any god smaller, or knowable, wouldn't be worth worshipping anyway.

All-age ideas

- Have a length of lining paper on which are drawn several outlines of a Celtic expression of the Trinity, shown below. Provide green crayons and invite some people (they do not have to be children – adults would benefit from it just as much) to come and draw round the lines continuously, following their path of inter-relatedness so that they sense, rather than understand, the harmonious community of the One God. This could be done during the singing of *St Patrick's breastplate (I bind unto myself today)*.

- In the flower arrangements use evergreen for eternity, shamrock and clover leaves, and three colours blending in and out of one another to make a unified whole.

- Have a group of readers for the passage from Isaiah, so that, by use of several and single voices, and dynamics, they bring out the awesome wonder and sheer scale of God, linked with his concern for each one of us.

PROPER 4

Sunday between 29 May and 4 June inclusive (if after Trinity Sunday)

Deuteronomy
  11:18-21, 26-28
Psalm 31:1-5, 19-24
Romans 1:16-17;
  3:22b-28 (29-31)
Matthew 7:21-29

Wise listeners build their lives up on the strong rock of the word of God.

All-age talk

Set up some young children and an adult or two to build with Lego, building blocks or a variety of cartons in the aisle during the talk. Draw attention to the building they are involved with and explain that today we have heard Jesus advising us on a wise building policy in our lives. We are also concerned that we do as much as possible to ensure that our faith is passed on faithfully to our young children, and their children yet to come. Having them building here in front of us will serve as a memory jogger to remind us both of our life building, and our responsibility to the young ones entrusted to our care.

Let's look again at that verse from Deuteronomy about passing on our faith. We are not to expect our children to pick up the faith all by themselves – we are to talk to them about it in all kinds of situations, so that they get to realise that it is relevant and valuable, of great importance for the whole of life. What does that mean in practice?

- It means that our children will not see God as the firm, secure rock he is unless they see the adults around them trusting that rock and building their lives on it. They need to see adults living their faith, every day of the week.

- It means that if our children see the adults in their Christian community saying they believe in God, coming to church and behaving in ways which are selfish, prejudiced, unforgiving or without loving respect for everyone, they may get the impression that God is not strong rock at all, but sand; that he is not to be taken seriously.

84

Heaven forbid that we should lead any of our little ones astray by the inconsistency of our life.

- It means that we need to get over our embarrassment in talking about God, and chat about him with our children as we would talk about all the other things that are important and excite us.

- It means that we need to start praying aloud with our children, and praying daily with them, so they learn what it is to talk over everything with the loving God, sharing both the lovely times and the sad ones with him. We need to get back the habit of thanking God – aloud – for our food before we eat. Our homes need to become places where it is natural to pray. How else will our children learn to pray naturally?

Of course, this is not going to be easy, especially if we live in a community where only part of the family are believers. But that makes our church community particularly important. Children can cope with the fact that one of their parents believes and one doesn't. It is the hypocrisy of conflicting words and behaviour that confuses them. All our families need the support of the whole Christian community in the precious work of parenting. We are all part of that, whether we have young children ourselves or not.

So let us watch how we build. When we hear Jesus' words, let's really start acting on them, changing our behaviour and our habits to sing out those words in all we do. And then we shall be taking seriously our charge to nurture our little ones, and pass on to them faithfully the Gospel that sets us free to live abundantly, even through storms and floods.

All-age ideas

- In one of the flower arrangements incorporate bricks, a trowel and a spirit level.

- Act out the Gospel with bodies forming the houses being built on rock and sand, and others holding hands in a chain that swirls around as the storm and flood.

PROPER 5

Sunday between 5 and 11 June inclusive (if after Trinity Sunday)

Hosea 5:15-6:6
Psalm 50:7-15
Romans 4:13-25
Matthew 9:9-13, 18-26

Jesus' life of healing and compassion acts out God's desire for mercy rather than empty sacrifice.

All-age talk

Beforehand work with one or two people who don't mind acting in front of the congregation. They are going to say 'Hello' to one another in various different ways that mean:

- I was really hoping I wouldn't meet this person here.
- I have no respect for this person whatsoever.
- This person is of no interest to me at all.
- This person has a swimming pool and I'd like to be invited round, so I'll suck up to them.
- I'm really glad to see this person.
- I respect and love this person very much.

Begin the talk by getting the actors to say 'Hello' to one another in each different way, and each time follow their greeting with the interpretation, read like a label.

We all show what we think of each other by the greeting we offer one another. (Incidentally, does the way we offer the Peace tell the other person that they are really valued, or are we looking at someone more our type or more interesting while we greet some people?)

Today we have come to meet together as Christians for a reason. Why have we come here? We haven't come just to see our family or friends (though that is always nice to do!) and we haven't come just to play with the Noah's ark, or to get out of mowing the grass. We have come to greet our God in worship and to greet one another in his name. What kind of 'Hello' are we giving to God by our worship?

Perhaps we are hoping that we won't actually meet God here, in case he asks of us something we don't want to give. We glance in his direction, but don't want to make eye contact, so to speak. Today we are reminded that to worship God beautifully we need to COME TO GOD HONESTLY, JUST AS WE ARE. (Display this.)

Perhaps we nod in his direction, but have really got our thoughts on the people coming for dinner and whether the bathroom should be white or pale green. Or we are thinking more of the piece of chewing gum under the seat in front of us, or the behaviour of the young, or the middle-aged or the elderly, or how many candles need replacing. Today we are reminded that to worship God beautifully we need to GIVE GOD OUR FULL ATTENTION. (Have that written up.)

Perhaps we are here thinking God will notice and tick off our names for good attendance, so that when we die we will have a pre-booked place in heaven. We intend to join in with all the hymns and prayers in church, but for the rest of the week we plan to carry on with the real life in the real world, where Christian values are not actually practical. Today we are reminded that to worship God beautifully we need to KNOW THAT GOD IS NOT FOOLED, and MATCH UP OUR WORDS WITH OUR LIFE (or WALK THE TALK).

Our God is the God of compassion and healing. He does not want our empty words, dry habit worship or closed-up prejudice. He does not want pretence or hypocrisy. God loves us and delights in his people coming to meet with him in worship, Sunday by Sunday. Wherever we are in our spiritual journey he can work with us, and he will never turn anyone away who is genuinely seeking. But whether we greet him in worship with our faces scratched and bruised, as we lie sprawled in the dust of life, or whether we greet him as we stop for breath from running away from him, or whether we greet him timidly but bravely, what we must do is greet him honestly, openly and expectantly.

Suggest that, not out loud but in the silence of

their hearts, everyone says their own 'Hello' to God, honestly, openly and expectantly.

All-age ideas

- Act out the Gospel using the whole aisle, so that the calling of Matthew happens at the back of the church, the woman's healing in the 'street' of the aisle, and the healing of Jairus' daughter at the front. Suggest that people turn to face the action, or crowd round it, as appropriate.

- Following on from the Gospel, have a group of people improvising the call of Matthew, voicing the sub-script. By 'sub-script' I mean that the religious leaders can be talking together as they watch Jesus making friends with Matthew, before they decide to approach him and then voice their concerns to his followers.

PROPER 6

Sunday between 12 and 18 June inclusive (if after Trinity Sunday)

Exodus 19:2-8a
Psalm 100
Romans 5:1-8
Matthew 9:35-10:8
  (9-23)

Jesus sends his ambassadors out to proclaim God's kingdom and bring hope and peace of mind to the harassed and lost in every age.

All-age talk

Ask everyone to place their hand flat on their tummy. This is often the place where we can tell if we are anxious or stressed, because it feels 'uptight'. When we are at peace, and not tensed-up, this place is where we feel calm and relaxed, and contented. (In fact, one way of calming yourself down is to do what you are doing now, and breathe slowly in and out a few times.)

Recently we have been looking at what religion *isn't*. We've found that it isn't telling God he is Lord of our life and then behaving as if he is not important. And it isn't going through the motions of worshipping him without showing his love and compassion to other people.

Today we are looking at what religion *is*. It is all about being at peace with God. Ask for two people who are really good friends to come to the front, and talk to them about what it feels like to be with each other. How does being together make them feel? Do they feel worried about how the other friend will treat them? Would they trust their friend with a secret?

Best friends are good news. You are contented and happy to be with them, and are not worried all the time that you might say the wrong thing and offend them, or that they may start being nasty to you, so you need to be ready to hit them back if necessary. You know you can trust them with your secrets, and they won't laugh at you or think you are stupid. Even going through bad experiences

89

isn't as bad if you are both in it together, because you know you will help one another along.

Well, that's what being at peace with God is like, and it has the spin-off effect of making us deeply happy and calm inside – a feeling that, whatever happens, all will be well. We heard today how Jesus wanted everyone to know this sense of calm assurance and peace and joy in their lives. He knew there were lots and lots of people going around worried and lost, with no peace inside them because they were not at peace with God. And he sent his disciples off to tell them that the kingdom of God was coming very soon, and soon they would be able to have that closeness with God which would give them peace.

Between the two 'best friends' put up a very large piece of cardboard with the word 'Sin' on it. Sin shuts us off from God and from one another. It makes us think of God as our enemy instead of our friend.

We know that Jesus went on to die for love of us all, which knocked that block of sin away between us and God. (Knock the cardboard away.) So now we can all know that lovely closeness to God which gives us real peace and hope, not just when everything is going well for us, but also through the times of suffering.

All-age ideas

• Try this sketch to draw attention to the right attitude of those sent out to proclaim the good news of the Gospel of Peace.

Make a 'Take 1' clapper-board using card and a split pin. An assistant shows 'Take 1'. They will also need a carton full of the various items to be given out.

A new recruit is being prepared for a mission by a couple of people holding clipboards and ticking off items as they are given out. (Their lines can also be on the clipboard.)

Tony OK. We've got the necessary info and equipment for you ready now. Let's see . . . ah yes, overnight bag, complete with nightwear, toiletries (mouthwash included) and towel; mosquito net, insect repellent (this is the one with the unclogging nozzle), and lightweight complete Bible (with matching magnifying glass).

Margaret Yes, and here's your fully comprehensive insurance policy (it includes return of body to country of origin, if necessary), travellers' cheques, ID card, small change in each currency in case of emergencies, first aid kit and manual, visa card and PIN number – that's sealed, of course.

Tony Now you'll need these letters of introduction, all on headed notepaper, naturally, and our emergency number should you have any difficulties. Oh, and rations . . . dehydrated lasagne and chips, cranberry ice cream, and plenty of soya mince to keep you going if you're not offered anything better.

Margaret Right, there you are! And good luck!

Assistant Cut! *(She comes on with the 'Take 2' clapper-board.)* Take two!

Tony I say, you've got an awful lot of stuff there – it looks as if you're more interested in keeping yourself safe and comfortable at all costs than telling them the good news. How about getting rid of some of it? *(Takes bag away.)* Better to travel light, I think. Then they'll be able to see that you don't mind too much about personal comforts, and you'll have your hands free for healing and comforting other people instead of being weighed down with your own possessions all the time.

Margaret All this paperwork is a bit OTT, don't you think? You're supposed to be ready to go wherever God leads you, and if you've planned every detail of your life already how are you going to stay available? *(Takes the paperwork.)*

Tony Ah, that's better – there's only one thing you really need, you know, and it's this. *(Places a simple cross round neck.)*

Both So go in peace, to love and serve the Lord!

Missionary In the name of Christ. Amen!

- By the entrance door place a notice with *'Excess baggage here'* written on it, below which are dumped various large cases and bags.

- Involve everyone in the Exodus reading, with their words written out on the weekly sheet or shown on the OHP.

PROPER 7

Sunday between 19 and 25 June inclusive (if after Trinity Sunday)

Jeremiah 20:7-13
Psalm 69:7-10 (11-15),
  16-18
Romans 6:1b-11
Matthew 10:24-39

When we are willing to take up our cross with Jesus we will also know his risen life.

All-age talk

Today we have heard in the reading from Romans that we are to think of ourselves as dead to sin and alive to God through Christ Jesus. What does that mean?

Well, perhaps a few sleeping lions can help. Ask for a few volunteers to play 'sleeping lions' in the aisle, while you and some others try to get them to move. They have to remain as still as they possibly can. Point out that they have to think of themselves as 'asleep' to all those temptations to move which are going on around them. That is rather like us thinking of ourselves being dead to sin. We have to remind ourselves that sin is something which no longer concerns us or has any hold on us.

Ask a few people to say what noises there are in their home at night – any creaks or tickings or chimes. Then draw people's attention to the way we have no difficulty sleeping through these noises, because we know we don't have to worry about them. Some parents will have found that if it isn't your turn to get up and feed the baby you're quite likely to sleep through the crying. You are 'dead' to that sound because you know it isn't anything to do with you. And we are told that we are to think of ourselves as dead to sin.

But it isn't just being dead to sin – it's also being alive to God. What does that mean? Perhaps some people who like chocolate can help us here. Choose a few volunteers and tell them to stand with their backs to you and the congregation. When they think they can detect the presence of chocolate, tell them to raise their hand. Now, as you talk about the way

93

we can always hear what we want to hear, start to open a bar of chocolate, and even though there isn't much sound, and they have their backs to you, it probably won't be very long before they notice, either by hearing or smelling, or both.

That's like us being 'alive' to God. We are going to live as dead to sin, but expectant and interested as far as God is concerned. We will be so tuned in to God that we notice his still, small voice, recognise him in all we see and in those we meet, and live with our hearts and ears and wills turned in his direction all through every day, whatever is going on around us.

All-age ideas

• While the choir or congregation are singing *Take up your cross* (see Appendix, page 410, for words and music), have two people at the front of the church holding upright a large wooden cross. In the first chorus, three people walk slowly up to the front and kneel at the foot of the cross. In the first verse one of these people is given the cross and carries it, with some difficulty, around the church. By the next chorus they come back to the front and return the cross to those who were holding it. They now stand with these people while the cross is given to the next person for verse two, and similarly for verse three. With the last verse all five are standing facing the cross, holding it with both hands. At 'the cross can set me free' they all turn outwards with one hand extended. At 'nothing is stronger than the love of God' the extended arms are raised, and at 'I know that he loves me' they turn back to the cross. During the last chorus they all carry the cross high down the centre aisle.

• Before and after the prayer of confession, invite people to join you in saying 'Dead to sin *(with eyes closed)* and *(open eyes)* alive to God'.

PROPER 8

Sunday between 26 June and 2 July inclusive

Jeremiah 28:5-9
Psalm 89:1-4, 15-18
Romans 6:12-23
Matthew 10:40-42

As Christ's people we are no longer slaves to sin, but available for righteousness.

All-age talk

Bring along a kitchen knife, a pen or pencil, a can of paint spray and a £10 or £20 note. You will also need two signs, one saying 'Good' and the other 'Evil'.

Begin by observing that lots of things we handle every day can be used either for good or for evil. Ask for two volunteers to hold the signs, some distance apart, and go through each of the objects in turn, gathering from different people how each can be used. Take the objects to the appropriate notice for each suggestion.

Now ask a person to stand up. It's not only *things* which can be used for good or for evil; it's people as well. Stand the person beside the 'Evil' sign. In what ways can a person use themselves for evil? (Collect suggestions from people of all ages.) Stand the person by the 'Good' sign. In what ways can a person use themselves for good? (Collect suggestions.)

In our readings today we heard about how the false prophet Hananiah used his voice to encourage God's people to believe lies, and how Jeremiah wanted to use his voice differently – to build up God's people. We need to try and use our voices to encourage one another and help one another. We need to use our voices to tell out the truth, and not use the voices God has given to spread unkind gossip, or lies, or to be rude and unkind.

We heard Paul writing in his letter to the Romans that all the different parts of our bodies can either be offered to sin as instruments of evil, or offered to God as instruments of good. We've looked at our voices. What about our hands? Our minds? Our maleness or our femaleness? Our feet? Our ears? Suggest that during this week they make a point of

95

checking how they are using all the parts of their body, and seeing if they offer all those parts of themselves to God for good.

All-age ideas

- Have little posies of flowers scattered in various corners of the church. At one point, perhaps during a hymn, the children can be sent off to find these 'little acts of kindness', and everyone can say together, 'No act of kindness, however small, goes unnoticed by the God of love.'

- Display the objects used in the all-age talk with the 'Good' and 'Evil' signs and a large question mark shape in the middle, so that people are reminded as they go to receive communion, or as they go out of church. This could be on display for people to see next week as well, so they can check up on their week's focus and keep the teaching in mind.

PROPER 9

Sunday between 3 and 9 July inclusive

Zechariah 9:9-12
Psalm 145:8-14
Romans 7:15-25a
Matthew 11:16-19,
    25-30

To all who are weary with carrying heavy burdens in life, Jesus offers rest for our souls and unthreatening relief.

All-age talk

Bring along four bags or cases, labelled 'Worries', 'Guilt', 'Duty' and 'Wants'. Inside each wrap up heavy bundles, labelled appropriately. Here are some ideas:

Worries
What if it rains?; They might crash; She hasn't got enough money for that bill; He's in with a bad lot of friends; I might get it wrong and look silly; What if we get broken into?

Guilt
I'm so ashamed; God can never forgive me for that; I'll never be able to put that right; It haunts me every day; I'll never forgive myself.

Duty
I should drive myself even harder; I just grit my teeth and wait for life to be over; I'll do my duty even if it kills me; Day off? That would be lazy!

Wants
They've got one – I want it too; I wish I was rich and could buy whatever I liked; I want more freedom; I want to look like Leonardo DiCaprio; I'd be happy if only I had a . . .

Talk about how hard it is to struggle along carrying heavy shopping bags, or loads of kit and books for school, or a delivery of newspapers, or a supposedly portable laptop computer and printer. Who has ever found their load after school too heavy and given it to someone else (like Mum or Dad!) to carry home, so they can be free to run and play? We all find that carrying heavy loads makes our arms ache, and slows us down. We all enjoy it when we can put that heavy load down, and our arms start lifting up into the air, because they suddenly feel so light!

Today we heard Jesus giving us a wonderful offer. He said, 'Come to me all you who carry heavy loads and I will refresh you. Take my yoke upon you and learn from me, for I am gentle and humble in heart, and you will find rest for your souls. For my yoke is easy and my burden is light.' They are such lovely words to hear for any one of you who feels that you are lugging along heavy loads in your life. Let's look at some of the heavy loads we carry.

Struggle along with the four bags, and read their labels. These are some of the most common heavy loads we carry. What is inside them to make them so heavy? With the help of some volunteers open up each bag in turn. Different people can read out the kind of things that weigh us down so much. It's strange that even wanting things can weigh us down, but it's true. Whenever we are not at peace, we are carrying heavy loads. The good news is that Jesus says we can give those loads to him, so that we are free to play; free to live at peace; free to enjoy life again. (If there is space by a cross, or by the altar, have the bags placed there as you speak.)

When we are yoked, or joined up with Jesus, it is going to be much easier to carry the loads we need, and unnecessary to carry the ones that weigh us down so much.

All-age ideas

- If you have young people present, or the young at heart, play 'Sanctify' – one of the songs from the Delirious? album *King of Fools* – as part of the time of confession, or as an introduction to the reading from Romans, as it deals with the problem of wanting one thing and doing another.

- Gather two groups of children and two of adults before the service and teach them to do the playground chant, like this:

Two young people walk up as passers-by and stop to watch.

Children 1 We played happy music and you wouldn't dance!' *(chins up and arms folded)*

Children 2 Well, we played sad music and you wouldn't cry! *(chins up and arms folded)*

Adults 1 Look at him – eating weird food, fasting, teetotal – disgraceful! *(chins up and arms folded)*

Adults 2 Look at him – eating too much, drinking, spending time with sinners – disgraceful! *(chins up and arms folded)*

Young people carry on walking as they look back at the groups.

Young person 1 Bit childish, eh?

Young person 2 Yeah! *(raising eyebrows in 'oh heck' fashion)*

They walk on to the back of church.

They can do this just before the Gospel, or as part of it.

- Before or after the service have someone with a broom handle who can let some of the children and young people try out being yoked up with them, to see how the yoke helps them do exactly what the partner is doing, without effort.

- Use two voices in the reading from Romans to read the contrasting sections separately and the rest together. This will often mean splitting sentences, but that's fine, as it will reinforce the divided nature Paul is exploring.

PROPER 10

Sunday between 10 and 16 July inclusive

Isaiah 55:10-13
Psalm 65:(1-8) 9-13
Romans 8:1-11
Matthew 13:1-9, 18-23

Seed of God's word, sown in good soil, watered by his rain and warmed by his sunlight, produces a good crop of spiritual fruit.

All-age talk

You will need a seed tray filled with seed compost, some large-sized seeds, a dibber (to poke holes for the seeds) and a cloth bag of pearl barley. You will also need to arrange for a broom to sweep up the scattered barley after the talk. Have one large piece of paper to represent a rocky patch, and a few paper footprints to represent a stony path.

You might like to play a snatch of the *Gardeners' World* theme tune at the beginning, as you set out the seed tray and compost on a table and invite a couple of keen gardeners in the congregation to demonstrate planting. As the gardeners work, talk with them about why the seed planted like this is more likely to be successful than if we just shake the seeds outside.

Today we heard a story, or parable, that Jesus told, which was all about seeds being sown, and the best growing conditions. Of course, it wasn't just about seeds being planted and growing. Parables are stories with secrets inside, and the secret of this story is that it was really all about us, and how we respond to God's word when we hear it. This is how it works.

Where Jesus lived, it was very rocky, and the farmers had fields with bare rock showing here and there (put down the paper), and stony roads that went right through the middle (put down the footprints). They ploughed the earth in long furrows, like we did here in the seed tray, only much bigger of course, and then the person sowing the seed walked up and down the furrows sowing the seed

100

like this. (Demonstrate with your bag of pearl barley, scattering the seed to left and right.) The problem is that not all the seed goes in the nice soil you have prepared. When God's word is spoken, we are not always ready to accept it. Let's look at where some of those seeds have landed.

Involve a volunteer to look at the stony path and stand over any seeds they find there. Sometimes we read or hear God's teaching and we're more like a stony path than good soil. It just goes in one ear and out of the other, and we hardly notice what we've heard. We might sit here for the readings and our thoughts fly in, like birds, and take away God's message so we don't even remember what was said.

What about the rocky ground? (Send a volunteer there.) Sometimes we hear God's message and get really keen, and take on far too much far too early, so, like plants growing up on rocky soil, we haven't got good roots. We burn ourselves out and drop away.

What about the soil next to the rock? (Send a volunteer there.) Lots of weeds grow here, so there's a lot of competition for the seeds. Sometimes we hear God's message, but there are so many other things going on in our lives, which we consider important, that the really important message of God gets choked and crowded out.

But all the rest is in good soil. We are like good soil when we listen to God's teaching carefully, think about it and what it means, and then live with it. That way we shall certainly grow and produce a good harvest. Let's check this week that we are taking good notice of God's words to us, and giving him proper space and time, so that we grow in his love.

All-age ideas

- For one of the flower arrangements today include plenty of wheat, a bowl of seed and a loaf of bread. Entitle it with Matthew 13:23.

- Invite a group of people to write Bible references on small pieces of paper, enough for every person in the congregation to have one. As people come into church, or during a reflective time with music playing, people hand these out from baskets, as if they are sowing the word of God. Everyone can be encouraged to look up and read their text each day during the week. Here are some suggestions for texts: Matthew 11:28-30; Matthew 10:29-31; Matthew 10:39; Matthew 11:4-6; Matthew 9:36-38; Matthew 9:28; Matthew 7:7-8; Matthew 7:24.

• The Isaiah passage works well read chorally, with a group of different voices. Invite such a group to work with copies of the text, so that sometimes the voices are separate and sometimes together to bring out the meaning and the poetry.

PROPER 11

Sunday between 14 and 23 July inclusive

Wisdom of Solomon
    12:13, 16-19 or
    Isaiah 44:6-8
Psalm 86:11-17
Romans 8:12-25
Matthew 13:24-30,
    36-43

God's justice is always blended with mercy and loving kindness, so that we have real hope.

All-age talk

Borrow and bring along one of those toys (Polly Pocket or Mighty Max) which look like a plain box and hold inside a whole miniature world.

Show everyone the toy, and explain that today we heard another of those parables which Jesus told. Parables are a bit like these toys, because they are stories which have secret meanings inside. You need to open up the story to find the meaning. (Open the toy.) First of all, let's look at the story Jesus told.

If you have an OHP you can illustrate the story using cut-outs of weeds and wheat, and the evil enemy based on the pictures below, as these will show up in silhouette on the screen.

Remind everyone of the story, using volunteers to be the farmer sowing his seed (accompanied by music from *The Archers*), and the evil enemy creeping into the field at night to sow the weeds (accompanied by everyone doing a pantomime hiss). When the farmer finds that his field is sprouting loads of weeds as well as wheat, he is faced with a choice (hold a question mark in a thought bubble over his head).

All the servants say, 'Shall we pull the weeds out for you?' (Have this written on a speech bubble so everyone, or a small group, can say it together.)

103

The farmer shakes his head. (He does.) He knows that if he pulls all the weeds up now he might pull out some of the wheat as well, and he certainly doesn't want to lose any of his wheat. So instead he decides to let both the wheat and the weeds grow together until harvest time, when the weeds can be gathered up and burnt, and the wheat harvested and put in the barn.

That's the parable Jesus told. What's the secret meaning of it?

Here's a clue. The field is the world, and we can all see that in our world there is a lot of good, but also a lot of evil. Why doesn't God burst out of heaven and stop all the evil in the world straight-away, and punish the people who get away with doing cruel and terrible things?

The parable gives us the answer.

If he did that while life is still going on – while the wheat and weeds are still growing – some good might get lost or damaged. It is because God cares about us so much that he won't risk anything that would cause us lasting harm. There's time enough for punishment when the world comes to an end. Then all that is good and honest and kind and thoughtful will be gathered up safely for ever. All that is mean and selfish, cruel and greedy will be completely destroyed for ever. We can trust our God to know the right time to punish and the right time to hold back, because he always acts with love and mercy as well as justice.

All-age ideas

- Make a flower arrangement with wheat and weeds.

- The Gospel can involve the congregation reading the words of the servants and the disciples.

- The speech on mercy from Shakespeare's *The Merchant of Venice* would work well as an introduction to the time of confession, if you have someone with the gift of reading it well. If the reader is appropriately dressed in legal costume, the significance of merciful justice, compared with condemnatory judgement, is highlighted.

PROPER 12

Sunday between 24 and 30 July inclusive

1 Kings 3:5-12
Psalm 119:129-136
Romans 8:26-39
Matthew 13:31-33,
44-52

Jesus, the teacher, enables the ordinary, unlearned people to understand God's wisdom – the eternal laws of his Father's kingdom.

All-age talk

Bring along something that is precious and old, and something that is precious and new. Choose items which your congregation are likely to relate to. (It could be a well-worn teddy and a new Teletubby for a baby, for instance, or an old stained-glass window in the church and someone's new engagement ring.)

First introduce everyone to the old thing, pointing out why it is so treasured and important and valuable. In our faith there are also ancient things which we as Christians value and treasure, such as the stories in the Old Testament which teach us about our God (for example, creation, Noah's flood, the great escape from Egypt, and the teaching of the prophets), and God's law, the ten commandments given through Moses to the people to help them live well and in line with God's will. Although these are old, ancient things, they are precious to us because they help us get to know God and live as his friends. We don't just throw them out because Jesus has come. Jesus valued them himself, and told his followers to go on valuing them.

Now introduce the new thing, explaining why it is treasured, important and valuable. In our faith there are also new things which we as Christians value and treasure. With the coming of Jesus, we are able to have a completely new kind of friendship with God that had never before been possible. Through Jesus dying, rising and returning to heaven, we are able to have the gift of God's life breathed into our own lives. That means that every new morning of our lives there are new possibilities in our daily friendship with the living God!

Not only are we looking forward to the coming of God's kingdom at the end of all time – we can also enjoy living in it now. In our Gospel today Jesus gave us some ideas of what the kingdom of God is like. Here is just one of them.

It's like some treasure you might find in a field. (You could have an exciting-looking treasure box there.) You're so excited about this precious treasure that you go and sell everything else you have, just so you can buy the field and own the treasure. Let's think about that. If you found a diamond ring, would you go and sell your house and car and World Cup coin collection to get hold of it? Probably not. You'd only bother to sell your house and car and cherished possessions if the treasure you had found was worth far, far more than all the things you already had. Jesus is saying that knowing God in a loving friendship and living in him each day is actually worth far, far more than anything else you own.

I don't think many of us realise that yet. It's as if we dig up a treasure box, look at it and think, 'Oh, that's interesting – a box of treasure. I'll pop over and look at it sometimes.' Then we bury it again and go home to carry on living in the same old way without realising what we're missing out on. Next time you catch a glimpse of what God is really like, and how incredibly wonderful he really is, commit yourself to doing something about it, so you can enjoy that treasure of living in peace and love with him every day of the rest of your life.

All-age ideas

- Have an arrangement of a treasure box, spade and a sign against it which says, 'What is God worth to you?'

- Have different readers for each of the different examples in the Gospel.

PROPER 13

Sunday between 31 July and 6 August inclusive

Isaiah 55:1-5
Psalm 145:8-9, 14-21
Romans 9:1-5
Matthew 14:13-21

God feeds all who come to him hungry, and we, as the Church, are expected to share in that work.

All-age talk

Begin by asking people how they like to spend their pocket money. Invite representatives of all ages to join in this. Has anyone ever spent their money on something which has let them down, or been disappointing, so that they end up wishing they had saved their money? Ask a few people to share their experiences.

It may be that you have had to watch as someone you are fond of wastes their money. You can see that it's all going to end in disappointment, or even tragedy, but they won't listen to you, and all you can do is stand by and wait to pick up the pieces when it all goes wrong, without saying, 'I told you so'! It's our love for the other person that makes us ache to see them wasting their money like that; because we love them we want better for them than to be sad and disappointed by things that aren't worth buying.

That's how it is with our parent God, who loves us to bits, and aches as he watches as we spend not just our money but our time and our love on things which are not going to be good for us, or satisfying or rewarding. He wants better for us than that. God wants us to be aware of our need for his love and power in our lives, and to come to him for it, because he is happy to give it to us free.

Look at all those people in the Gospel story today. Why had they bothered to leave their towns and villages and walk miles out into the country? They bothered because they knew their need of Jesus and were prepared to 'spend' their whole day looking for him and listening to him, hanging

107

on his words. What did Jesus do? Did he let them down or disappoint them? No! He was there for them, ready to heal the sick friends and relations they had brought, ready to reassure them that God loved them, and teach them about how they could best please God in their lives.

And when their tummies started rumbling, and they knew physical hunger as well as spiritual hunger, what did Jesus do? He fed them! All he used was what they had. That's what he always uses. Are you a three- or four-year-old, ready for Jesus to use your life? Then that's what he'll use to make lots of other people really happy. Are you a seventy- or eighty-year-old, ready for Jesus to use your life? Then that's what he'll use to bring blessing and hope to lots of other people. And it's the same with all the rest of us in between.

What about our church? Is St Martin's ready to be used by Jesus? If we are, he will use us, and lots of people in this area will be blessed and given hope; if we aren't, and can't be bothered to go and spend time seeking Jesus out and listening to him, then he won't be using us and the people in our area will lose out.

Let's make sure that doesn't happen. Our job is to make ourselves available, and help give out to the people the gifts of God, so that all are properly fed.

All-age ideas

- Incorporate a lunch box of bread and 'fish' in a flower arrangement of water and harvest colours.

- Try this sequence of responses which are said by the whole congregation, divided into two halves:

  All   Our world is hungry for God. (*Both sides turn to face each other.*)

  Side 1   You feed them.

  Side 2   You feed them. (*Both sides face the front.*)

  All   We have only ourselves. (*Both sides face one another.*)

  Side 1   That is exactly what God needs.

  Side 2   That is exactly what God needs.

PROPER 14

Sunday between 7 and 13 August inclusive

1 Kings 19:9-18
Psalm 85:8-13
Romans 10:5-15
Matthew 14:22-33

God is faithful to us through all the storms of life, yet our faith in God is so very small.

All-age talk

If you know a juggler, invite them to come and juggle as part of today's talk. Failing this, give out some balloons to a group of older children and ask them to keep them in the air, in as controlled a way as possible, using hands, head, knees and feet.

As the juggler or children perform, draw attention to the way they need to concentrate and keep their eyes on the balls or balloons if they are to be sure of catching them under control. Notice how the moment they lose concentration, or lose balance, things go wrong.

Today we heard in the Gospel about some people in a boat, weathering a terrible storm. It was the disciples, and Jesus had sent them off home while he himself went off to pray on his own after he had fed all those five thousand people. He needed to be alone with his heavenly Father to talk that over, and give special thanks for all that had happened. The waves were churning, and the boat was rocking and the disciples were frightened – especially when they saw Jesus walking across to them. This was water, and you can't walk on that! We are told they thought Jesus must be a ghost, and they got more scared than ever.

Let's look at what Peter did next. He called out to Jesus, 'If it really is you, then tell me to come to you over the water.' Why did he say that? What was he doing? It sounds as if he was testing whether Jesus was real or not, like us saying to a friend, 'If you've really been up in space, show me a photograph to prove it', or 'If you really love me, how about helping with this washing-up'.

Jesus knows he isn't a ghost, and he takes Peter

up on what he's asked. 'Come on, then!' he says. There's no way out now! Peter concentrates on Jesus, like the juggler concentrated on the balls. He gets as far as climbing out of the boat, and he starts to walk towards Jesus, still concentrating on him, and then suddenly it all hits him. 'This is crazy! This is impossible! The water can't possibly be holding my weight! Rationally I know I ought to be sinking!' And as those doubts make him panic and lose his sight of Jesus, he does just that – he starts to sink and has to shout out in terror to Jesus to save him. And, of course, Jesus reaches out to him and gets him to safety straightaway.

Trusting Jesus is keeping ourselves concentrating on him and his love, underneath everything else that we do. Suppose you're buying some sweets. At the same time you're aware of Jesus and his love. What difference does that make? You will probably buy without being greedy, and you'll probably end up sharing what you get. Suppose you are travelling to work, and you've also got your eyes on Jesus. That will affect the way you drive, and the way you treat other commuters.

Today Jesus is saying to each of us, 'Yes, it is OK for you to put your total trust in me. Just keep that in mind and all the things which make you feel frightened and insecure will not let you sink – you can walk straight over them, confident in my love and power.'

All-age ideas

- Using music such as the storm in *Noye's Fludde*, have a group of dancers to whirl and leap around like a raging sea in a storm, and gradually calm to gentle movements and stillness. You could dress them in sea-coloured tabards, on the shoulders of which are sewn thin strips of blue and green. These will then fly out as they move. Otherwise they could wave large flags and long streamers of sea-coloured fabric.

- Involve a group to make some sound effects as a background to the reading about Elijah. Having read the passage through together, good ideas may well be suggested, but here are a few to start you off:

  Wind – breathing and shakers, getting louder and then softer.

  Earthquake – Drums, shaken tray or hardboard, large cartons being banged with wooden spoons.

  Fire – Crunching up cellophane, and plastic bags, and shakers.

  Still small voice – Very quiet triangle or shaker fading into silence.

PROPER 15

Sunday between 14 and 20 August inclusive

Isaiah 56:1, 6-8
Psalm 67
Romans 11:1-2a, 29-32
Matthew 15:(10-20)
    21-28

The good news of salvation is not limited to a particular group or nation but available for the whole world.

All-age talk

Ask everyone who is a Brownie to stand up. That means that everyone left sitting down is a non-Brownie. Do the same with various other groupings, such as Scouts, servers, the short-sighted or cocopops-eaters. Each time we become a member of a group, there are lots of others who are not included.

Remind everyone of the promise God first made to his friend Abraham, whose family the Bible traces right back to Noah. What was it that God promised to Abraham? God promised that (1) he would make his family into a great nation, and (2) all the people on earth would be blessed by this nation which was starting with Abraham. That's quite a promise! And because God always keeps his promises, it came true. Abraham's grandchildren and great-grandchildren and great-great-great-grandchildren did grow into a great nation of God's chosen people.

The people of Israel (as the nation came to be called) were rightly proud of being God's chosen people. Like the groups we had standing up, they thought of themselves as God's chosen, and everyone else was outside and not included. They called all the outsiders 'gentiles'. Probably most of us here are gentiles.

So much for the first part of that promise to Abraham: 'I will make you into a great nation.' But there was a second part, wasn't there? What was that? It was that *all the people on earth* would be blessed by the nation which God had started with Abraham. All through the Old Testament there were prophets like Isaiah who reminded the people of this bit of the promise. 'This is not just for you, remember,' they'd say. 'We are called to bring blessing to all the other people on earth eventually!'

It was true. Starting with the chosen nation, God wanted all the people on earth to have that special friendship with God which Abraham had. It isn't just for a few people, or for one particular nation, but for people of every age, country and time. It's for all the Brownies and the Scouts and the short-sighted and the servers and everybody else, because with God not one person is left 'on the outside'. God's loving is for everybody, everywhere, every time.

If that's how it is for God, then that's how it must be for us as well. We must make sure that in all our loving we don't leave people out. Think about that when you are playing or working in a team, or chatting in a group. Check whether there are people we deliberately avoid. Do we assume some people are not worth telling about Jesus? Would we rather some types of people didn't come to our church?

If God had thought that about us, most of us wouldn't be here. It's his love for us that brought us, and he has love for lots of others who need us to show it to them, and love them into the kingdom.

All-age ideas

- Give the church an international flavour today, with banners and flags representing different countries, and a globe or world map surrounded or dotted with candles.

- Spread the peace from a small group outwards today, as a symbol of God's kingdom of peace and joy spreading throughout the whole world.

- If there are people in the congregation who speak different languages, invite all of them to stand in a line and speak out 'Jesus is Lord!' in as many different languages as possible.

PROPER 16

Sunday between 21 and 27 August inclusive

Isaiah 51:1-6
Psalm 138
Romans 12:1-8
Matthew 16:13-20

The Church is the Body of Christ, built on strong rock of faith and energised by the living Breath of God.

All-age talk

Beforehand, ask a few people of different ages to provide you with a photograph of them when they were very young, and have these pictures duplicated, or shown on an OHP. Don't identify them, but say they are all members of the church community. When people have had a go at guessing the identities, ask the people to come to the front. This narrows the choice, and makes it easier to see who's who. We might have a hunch about someone, and can ask them directly. They will tell us whether or not we are right, and then we'll know for certain. (Invite people to do this.) Once we know the true identity, it's often easier to see the likeness!

In today's Gospel, Jesus knew that people had all sorts of ideas about who he was. Some ideas were close to the truth, some were wide of the mark, and Jesus always wanted his followers to make the discovery for themselves. Discovering something for ourselves means that we always remember it far better than when we have simply been told things. (People may remember discovering for themselves that fire burns, for instance, that cement hardens into a solid lump, or that overloading a computer can cause it to crash.)

No doubt Jesus sensed that the disciples had almost got to the point of discovering that he was not just their friend and teacher, but also the promised Messiah, the Son of God. This conversation, starting with what other people think, will help them tip over into that 'Aha!' of learning, that point when you suddenly know something and everything falls clearly into place.

114

It is Simon, the fisherman, who comes out with it for the first time. 'You are the Christ,' he says, 'the Son of the living God.' It must have been a bit like when you first say the words 'I love you' or 'I'm three'. It's the first time you have ever said it and as you say it, you know it is really true, and your life will never be quite the same again.

All-age ideas

- The Isaiah passage is beautiful, both in meaning and poetry, and this is brought out well if it is read chorally, with a group of voices of different tones. Think of it as soprano, alto, tenor and bass, and work through the passage together, deciding where the separate voices sound best, and where the strength of all voices is needed.

- In the Gospel, everyone can join in with Peter's confession of faith, or this can be used separately as a credal statement:

  Leader   Who do you say that I am?

  All   You are the Christ, the Son of the living God!

PROPER 17

Sunday between 28 August and 3 September inclusive

Jeremiah 15:15-21
Psalm 26:1-8
Romans 12:9-21
Matthew 16:21-28

As Jesus prepares for the necessary suffering of the cross, he is tempted, through well-meaning friendship, to avoid it.

All-age talk

You will need two lengths of bramble, and gardening gloves to handle them. If you can get hold of a length of chain as well, this would be excellent; otherwise, rope, or a paper chain will do fine.

Lay the two lengths of bramble to form a cross on the floor, explaining what you are doing for the benefit of those who will not be able to see this. Make the point that you are wearing protective gloves as the brambles are painful. Explain that the brambles represent all the suffering and pain of the cross. Ask for a volunteer to stand at the top end of the cross. This person represents all of us humans, chained up in all the sin and selfishness that stops us from living freely. (Chain their hands together.) Ask another volunteer to stand at the foot end of the cross, some distance from it. This person represents Jesus at the point of today's Gospel.

Last week we heard how Simon Peter was ready to speak out the truth he had realised about Jesus – that Jesus was the Christ, the Son of the living God. Jesus knew his friends had to be sure of this before they could cope with the next stage of the plan. Now that was in place, and it was time for Jesus to get his friends ready for what had to happen next.

Jesus couldn't just go on working in one part of our world, because he had come into the world to save all of us. That would mean walking a very painful road – the way of the cross. The pain of giving his life on the cross was the only way for Jesus to be able to reach us and set us free. He couldn't get

116

round it; he had to go through with it, even though he knew it would hurt.

Ask the person who is representing Jesus to take their shoes off and start walking towards the cross. Before they get there, stop them as you remind people how Simon Peter couldn't bear to think of his friend going through all that pain, and said, 'Never, Lord! This shall not happen to you!' But if Jesus had listened to him (walk round to the representative human in chains), we would never have been set free from the sin that imprisons us. Never. There would have been no hope for us any more.

(Go back to 'Jesus'.) The good and wonderful news is that Jesus loved us far too much to let his own suffering stop him from saving us. Today we won't make (Lawrence) walk barefoot over those brambles, but as we think of Jesus gladly stepping out to Jerusalem, where he knew he would meet terrible pain and suffering, let's thank him in our hearts for loving us so much that he was prepared to do it anyway (walk round to the human in chains) so that we could all be set free. (Set the person free.)

All-age ideas

- While the congregation sing quiet songs of love and worship, invite any who are carrying heavy loads in their lives at the moment, or who want to re-commit themselves to walking Jesus' way, to come forward for anointing with oil, given in the shape of the cross on their foreheads.

- Have the bramble cross placed on the floor near the altar so that people see it and are reminded of its meaning as they receive communion.

PROPER 18

Sunday between 4 and 10 September inclusive

Ezekiel 33:7-11
Psalm 119:33-40
Romans 13:8-14
Matthew 18:15-20

It is our responsibility to encourage and uphold one another in living by the standard of real love.

All-age talk

Ask a number of volunteers to get themselves into a line in order of size. When they have achieved it they can be applauded. Draw attention to the way they helped each other in the task, and showed one another if they were in the wrong place, whenever that was noticed. Because they were working on the task as a team, no one got terribly upset by seeing they were in the wrong place – they just moved into the right place.

Today's Gospel gives us all some teaching about helping one another to keep in order as we live as Christians. The good thing about being a Church is that we are all in the same team, God's team, and we can help one another along. But we're not always very happy to do this. The truth is that we are all going to make mistakes and be in the wrong place with God sometimes, so we need to get used to reminding one another and being reminded without getting too upset about it.

Let's look at what we mean by being in the wrong place with God. (Ask some volunteers to stand facing the cross.) Explain that when we are facing God we are living in his love, and whenever we don't live lovingly, we are turning our backs on God. (Ask the volunteers to turn and face the cross when you say something which is loving, or turn their backs on it when you say something which is unloving.) Here are some suggestions: telling lies, telling the truth, looking after someone, being friendly, grumbling about everything, making sure you get your own way, being generous in your giving, telling dirty or unkind jokes, being bossy and pompous, listening carefully, cheering someone up.

And this is the way we want to be as the Church, with all of us facing God's way. It's our job to help one another keep facing that way, and to help them turn round if they are facing the wrong way.

Supposing we are behaving in an unloving way, then, turning our backs on God? (Turn one of the volunteers around and make up the wrong behaviour they are involved in.) How can the rest of the church help?

In today's Gospel we heard what Jesus said: 'Go and take him to one side and talk it over with him.' (Let one of the volunteers tap him on the shoulder and lead him off a short way from the others, pretending to talk with him.) The point is that we don't always realise that we're in the wrong place, and it is kind to let one another know, so that we can do something about it.

We actually ought to be grateful if someone takes us aside and says, 'Look, I've noticed that you've got really snappy lately. Is anything the matter?' We may have thought we were hiding our worry very nobly, and it will help us to talk it over and recognise that we've been taking our problems out on other people. Or perhaps someone is kind enough to take us aside and say, 'I don't suppose you realise, but you never actually look at people when you are saying hello, and it makes them think you aren't interested in them.' Or 'Have you noticed that every time I say anything at all you contradict me? Have I offended you in some way?' Or 'I've noticed you are always nasty to Paul whenever Steven and you are playing, and that's not very kind. What do you think you could do to stop that happening?'

It may not be a wonderful feeling to know that our faults and failings are noticed, but if it's going to help us put things right, then let's practise being thankful instead of offended, and be ready to help one another up whenever we fall down.

All-age ideas

- Make the time of confession a chance for a real checking of any selfish or unloving habits we may have slipped into. Here is a possible form for this:

Leader How is it that we are called to live?

All We are called to love God and to love one another.

Leader In that case, let us think about the times we would prefer God to be closing his eyes or blocking his ears.
How would we prefer God not to see us doing?
(Silence for reflection)
What would we prefer God not to hear us saying?
(Silence for reflection)
What would we prefer God not to know us thinking?
(Silence for reflection)
God desires not the death of a sinner but rather that he may turn and live.

All O God, you see all things, hear all things, know all things, and we are ashamed of the unloving way we sometimes act, speak and think. Have mercy on us and forgive us, and enable us to put things right.

- Display three large signs or posters with an eye, an ear, and a thought bubble, and the words: *'Does God hear you speaking with love?' 'Does God see you acting with love?'* and *'Does God find you thinking with love?'*

Proper 19

Sunday between 11 and 17 September inclusive

Genesis 50:15-21
Psalm 103:(1-7) 8-13
Romans 14:1-12
Matthew 18:21-35

Forgiving is a natural result of loving, so it is not an option for us but a command.

All-age talk

First ask anyone who has never done anything wrong, *ever*, to raise their hand. Make it quite clear that doing wrong doesn't stop when you grow up, and it's a problem that we all have to deal with. In which case there's going to be another problem we need to deal with. What about when people do things wrong which hurt and upset us? It's bound to happen, and today we are given some very useful teaching from our Lord Jesus to help us with it.

Suppose someone lets you down, cheats on you, loses their temper with you and says some cruel unkind things, lets you down again, steals from you, makes you look stupid, and breaks something you've let them borrow. (Count on your fingers seven typical offences.) Peter goes to Jesus and says, 'Is seven times about the limit for forgiving someone? It seems fairly generous to me. You might as well give up on them after that, don't you agree? Or am I being a bit over-generous – more forgiving than is good for me?'

Jesus says, 'Actually, seven times isn't nearly enough! You need to keep on forgiving until you've lost count and just do it anyway.' And then he tells one of his stories to explain what he means.

Give a volunteer a sign to hold which says 'IOU millions'. The story is about a servant who owes loads and loads of money. He has a wife and children, and he's borrowed so much and has been using his plastic money facility so much that he's stacked up a huge debt to his master, which he can't pay off. The master calls for him (use another volunteer and give him a mobile phone or a smart jacket) and demands the money. The servant kneels down and begs (he does this) to be given more time to pay. The master feels sorry for the servant and lets him off the whole debt! Just like that! (Master draws a thick black line through the IOU.) How do you think the servant feels? (Collect ideas.)

Now that is what God has done for each of us. Ask them to think of all the things they've done wrong, perhaps which no one else knows about except them and God. Think of all the meanness, selfishness, pride, hypocrisy and so on that we have been forgiven completely by God. It's just as if we owed God millions of pounds (hold up the IOU) and God has drawn that line through it, setting us free from the debt.

So here is this happy, free servant, who finds a fellow servant owes him a few pounds. (Give another volunteer a sign with 'IOU a few pounds' on it.) And the same thing happens. The servant goes on his knees and begs (he does this) to be allowed more time to pay. But what does the servant do? He grabs him by the neck and shakes him (not too realistically) and has him thrown into prison until he pays up. What Jesus wants us to ask ourselves is this: Is it fair or right for the servant to behave like this? What do we think?

Next time we are not wanting to forgive someone, let's remember how God has treated us, and pass on that loving forgiveness time and time and time again.

All-age ideas

- The Gospel can be acted out, either by miming while it is narrated, or by different people taking the parts and saying their words.

- Place the cancelled 'IOU millions' sign near the altar where it can be seen when people gather for communion as a reminder of what God has done for us in releasing us from our sins.

PROPER 20

Sunday between 18 and 24 September inclusive

Jonah 3:10-4:11
Psalm 145:1-8
Philippians 1:21-30
Matthew 20:1-16

We have no right to be envious at the generosity and mercy God shows to others.

All-age talk

Today we are given some useful teaching on being grumpy and sulking, something most of us do from time to time. (Have one or two volunteers to give a really sulky, grumpy face.) Did they notice how sulky and cross Jonah was in our first reading? Perhaps some of them do the same in rows – remembering things that were said at other times and throwing them back at the person we want to upset, and saying, 'I *knew* it would end up like this! If you'd listened to what I said, this would never have happened!' We feel quite at home here! And if we're a loving parent on the receiving end of all the anger and resentment, which we know comes from a lack of understanding or experience, perhaps we can sense something of how God feels, loving this very hot-headed, angry person shouting at us, and knowing that our job is to stay calm, stay loving, and pick up the pieces once they've got over it.

What is it that makes us sulk, usually? (Collect answers.) Usually it's when we feel hard done by, as if we have been unfairly treated and been given a raw deal. That's how Jonah felt. He didn't think his enemies should have been let off being smashed to pieces. Why on earth would God want to take pity on that lot! He'd even got Jonah to tell them to sort their lives out, and the annoying thing was that they had listened, and changed the way they were living. But forgiveness for them was the last thing Jonah wanted. So he sulked. (Have the sulky faces.)

Jesus told a story about some sulking workmen, which we heard today. The ones who worked all day agreed their wage, and at the end of the day they got it in full. Why were they sulking? Because some other workmen, taken on much later in the day, were paid the same wage. So they sulked. And we often behave in the same way. (Sulky faces.)

God helps Jonah understand with the help of a nice olive plant which grows up to shade him one day and dies away the next. Of course, Jonah is fond of this plant and sad when it is destroyed. So then God can talk to him about the people of Nineveh. Just like Jonah and his olive plant (only more so), God loves the people of Nineveh and doesn't want them destroyed, so, of course, he tried to save them, with Jonah's help. And in Jesus' story the owner helps the workmen to understand why they are sulking. He asks them, 'Are you jealous because I am good to these people as well?'

We all need to understand that God doesn't split us up into some who are OK to be saved and some who aren't worth bothering with. We shouldn't get jealous or angry if Christians of another church or tradition seem to be having God's blessing as well as us, or if people who have made bad mistakes in the past are allowed to be part of our fellowship. If we are loving, like God loves, this will make us not sulky (sulky faces) but happy (happy faces).

All-age ideas

- On large notices or posters, stuck on the walls or pillars, display the qualities of our God which today's readings emphasise: gracious; full of compassion; slow to anger; of great goodness; rich in love.

- Mime the parable of the workmen while it is being narrated, or have a group act it, expressing the dialogue in their own words.

- At the time of confession, or just before the shared peace, suggest everyone prays silently for anyone or any group of people who make them angry or any areas where they feel hard done by. You may like to have music being played quietly while this goes on.

PROPER 21

Sunday between 25 September and 1 October inclusive

Ezekiel 18:1-4, 25-32
Psalm 25:1-9
Philippians 2:1-13
Matthew 21:23-32

God longs for us to die to sin and live, but it has to be our choice, too.

All-age talk

Bring along the details of a children's colouring competition, and also one of those junk mail promotional letters which tell you that you have already been selected as a winner.

Begin by sharing this exciting letter with everyone, reading out some of the blurb, and getting a volunteer to scratch any secret messages included. No doubt many of us receive these kinds of letters. When we do so, we have a choice: are we going to bin it (or preferably recycle it), or will we take them up on their wonderful offer and claim our prize? What we decide will depend on all kinds of factors, such as how busy we are, how desperate for winnings we are, how many previous disappointments we have experienced, and whether we actually believe them.

But one thing is certain. Unless we decide to return our reply slip, we have no chance of winning anything at all. It's the same with colouring competitions. A prize is offered and anyone has a chance of winning. But if you don't get your felt-tips or paints out and do the colouring, and send it off in time, you will have no chance of winning a prize, however good you are at colouring.

Today we are being reminded by God that he has great prizes and gifts for us, which he longs for us to enjoy. He wants to see us all as winners, happily receiving the gift that has been reserved specially for us. But . . . and it is a big 'but' . . . unless we choose to turn to God and take him up on his offer, we will have no chance at all of winning. If we choose wrong instead of right, evil instead of good, and self instead of God, we cannot have the joy and

125

peace and life that God longs to give us. We don't just get it anyway, however we live. Lots of people think that is what happens, but it isn't because God isn't like that. He is a God of goodness and love, truth and kindness. Do we want to go along with that? We have to choose it, then, and start doing something about it.

As soon as we choose it, God can give us all the help we need, and he will, because all he wants is for us to know complete and lasting happiness with him.

All-age ideas

• As people come into church give everyone a copy of the form shown below, and at the time of confession, or just after the talk or sermon, provide time for them to fill it in. Actually ticking the boxes emphasises their commitment, and the forms can be given with the offering and presented for God's work.

	YES	NO
Do you turn to Christ?	☐	☐
Do you turn your back on evil?	☐	☐

• Everyone can say these words from Philippians to one another, as words of encouragement. The men and boys could say it to the women and girls, and vice versa, or one side of the church could say it to the other.

It is God who works in you to will and act according to his good purpose.

It is God who works in you to will and act according to his good purpose.

PROPER 22

Sunday between 2 and 8 October inclusive

Isaiah 5:1-7
Psalm 80:7-15
Philippians 3:4b-14
Matthew 21:33-46

God does everything possible for our spiritual growth and well-being, but still we can choose hostility and rejection.

All-age talk

Bring along a watering can, secateurs, a gardening fork and some slug pellets. Show everyone these things and ask the gardeners in the congregation (both young and old) to explain to you what they are all for. Ask if anyone has been using these this year, and what has been grown and eaten by the congregation at All Hallows.

All gardeners can feel in good company, because one of the often-used pictures of our God is as a gardener. In our reading from Isaiah, God is imagined as a gardener planting vines in a vineyard – digging the ground, and getting it all ready, planting carefully, weeding and watering regularly, supporting the branches and pruning, and really caring for this vine so that it may bear a wonderful juicy crop of grapes. Gardeners are always fond of what they grow – that's why they'll go to any lengths to protect their plants from things like slugs and greenfly. We can imagine God caring like that (only more so) for his people, and wanting desperately to protect them from evil and sin.

But when this gardener comes to pick the crop of grapes which he has grown so carefully, he finds they are not delicious and sweet but bad and sour, and the lovely vineyard ends up all overgrown and wild. Like a gardener, God has looked for the good fruit of justice in his people but found only bloodshed; he has looked for the good fruit of righteousness and found only the cries of those who are treated badly. What kind of fruit does God the gardener find in us, in his Church, or in our society? Does what he finds in this church and this world put a smile on his face, or does he find instead sour fruit which makes him sad?

We all know the kind of thing that delights God. He loves to find such fruits as love, joy, peace, patience, kindness, goodness, gentleness and self-control. He loves to see justice, mercy, right living, purity and honesty. May this garden grow a bumper crop of such fruits, that will gladden the heart of God and bring blessing and healing to our town.

All-age ideas

- Incorporate grapes and secateurs in one of the flower arrangements.

- Have the parable section of the Gospel mimed as it is read. Use clear, unfussy and stylised movements. Have the owner at the back of the action, facing the congregation, with his hands on the shoulders of the son until he sends him off. As two farmers grab the son and throw him out of the vineyard, they both pull his arms so that for a moment the son is stretched as if on a cross, and at the back the owner assumes the same position. At verse 40 the group freezes in attitudes of hatred and rejection. As the owner approaches, arms by his sides, they turn and see him, cover or avert their eyes, and creep away.

PROPER 23

Sunday between 9 and 15 October inclusive

Isaiah 25:1-9
Psalm 23
Philippians 4:1-9
Matthew 22:1-14

We are all invited to God's wedding banquet; in accepting we must allow the rags of our old life to be exchanged for the freely given robes of holiness and right living.

All-age talk

As people come into church make sure that everyone is given a small picture or cut-out paper shape of a robe of righteousness, with this title on it:

Probably we have sometimes looked into our wardrobes before a party and decided that we have nothing suitable to wear. However jam-packed the wardrobe is, with all that extra junk stuffed in to keep it out of sight, we can't find anything we want to wear! Prepare to be impressed: the wardrobe space of today's teaching is quite something.

Mention the piece of paper they were all given when they came in, checking for any who have been missed and providing for them now. Everyone has been given a beautiful wedding garment! That's what used to happen when guests were invited to palaces. It was the practice for kings to provide thousands of guests with a suitable robe each from their vast wardrobes in which thousands of garments were kept ready specially for such occasions. (Dress a volunteer up in a clean white robe – a surplice is fine.) They had special servants to be in charge of those huge wardrobes.

129

In Jesus' parable of the wedding feast we can imagine all the poor and the dirty straggling along to the palace in their smelly rags, and the people in charge of the king's wardrobes fitting up everyone with a clean, beautiful robe to wear, before ushering them into the grand dining hall. No doubt they felt different dressed like this – perhaps they even walked taller and were more polite to each other than usual! Then the king comes in to inspect his guests. (Perhaps everyone sits up straighter, like you do when someone important walks into assembly.) He is glad to see the palace full of guests who have accepted his invitation, because the original guests had refused to come. Everything is light and warm and happy.

Suddenly the king finds a guest who has accepted his invitation but rudely refused to wear the proper clothes provided. He's still in the filthy rags he came in, and the king has him put outside in the darkness with those who had chosen to turn down his invitation.

What is Jesus teaching us in this parable? One thing is that God is very happy to invite all of us to the Church of Christ and feed us here with love and rejoicing. So we can be happy together in God's company and enjoy ourselves in our worship. The other thing is that if we say yes to God, we do need to let him reclothe us, and not expect to go on wearing the rags of bickering and fighting, lying and cheating, self-indulgence and lack of self-control which we came in. That's why we always start our worship by saying sorry to God, and hearing his forgiveness, letting him clothe us with robes of righteousness.

All-age ideas

- Suggest that in the time of confession people are given a time with quiet music or silence when they can hold their 'robe of righteousness' and give over to God any 'rags' they are still wearing.

- Have an arrangement of golden flowers set inside a treasure chest labelled 'Holiness'.

- Try this sketch in which a reporter is interviewing some of the guests:

Reporter	Well, I'm standing here in the great hall; it's filled with the warm glow of candle light, the smells of delicious food and the sound of crowds of people enjoying themselves. Quite a wedding feast! Excuse me, sir, may I interrupt your meal a moment and ask how you came to be invited to this banquet?
Guest 1	Yes, sure. I was trimming my hedge.
Reporter	Trimming your hedge?
Guest 1	That's right – crazy isn't it! One minute I was trimming my hedge, feeling hungry, and the next this servant from the palace comes along and says I'm invited to the king's banquet! It seems the original guests had turned it down. So I'm here with the wife and kids, and we've never enjoyed ourselves so much, isn't that right, dear? I've never been to a banquet before, but I tell you, I could get used to it!
Reporter	And here's a very senior citizen. Good evening, madam.
Guest 2	Eh?
Reporter	(Shouts) Good evening, madam! how are you liking the banquet?
Guest 2	Oh, it's wonderful, dear! Just wonderful! We're being so well looked after – and I've never felt so loved and honoured in all my life. Just think – me being treated like this! It makes me feel young and beautiful again.
Grandchild	You are beautiful, Gran!
Guest 2	What's that, my chicken?

131

Reporter   Well, as you can see, the atmosphere here is amazing – so much joy and happiness for so many people! And none of them bought a ticket. When the original guests turned it down, the king just had all these ordinary, poor folk invited and brought in from the streets and farms, and gave them each a wedding garment to wear so he'd have a full gathering to celebrate his son's wedding. And I must say, it's the most happy and extraordinary wedding celebration ever. I'm going outside now . . . it's dark and cold out there, and there's a whole lot of people who sadly don't realise what they're missing.

PROPER 24

Sunday between 16 and 22 October inclusive

Isaiah 45:1-7
Psalm 96:1-9 (10-13)
1 Thessalonians 1:1-10
Matthew 22:15-22

All leaders and rulers are subject to the ultimate authority and power of God, the living truth.

All-age talk

Unless the size of your congregation makes it far too expensive, give everyone a penny. Invite everyone to look at their coin. On one side there is a picture of someone's head. Whose head is it? It belongs to Queen Elizabeth II. She is there, just as Caesar's picture was on the coin Jesus looked at, because she is the Head of State and we are her subjects. In our country there are taxes to pay to make sure that everyone, both rich and poor, can have schools, roads and hospitals. There are laws to keep, so that we can all live safely and peacefully, and there are police to check that we keep the laws. Those who break them are sent to prison or charged a fine.

Each country works out its own way of organising all this, and some are fairer than others. Each country has leaders – people who are in charge – and the country Jesus lived in was ruled by the Romans.

Now invite everyone to hold their coin in the palm of one hand. This penny is not very big. It won't buy very much. It sits here in your hand, and your hand is here in this church building. It's only a very little part of all the space in here. As you hold your penny, your hand is surrounded not just by the space of this building but by the whole universe. Now God is greater than the universe, because he is the One who thought and loved our universe into being.

There's a huge, huge difference between the kind of power and authority human leaders have, and the kind of power and authority God has. We are to give to God what is God's. What is God's? Is there anything God doesn't know? No. Is there anywhere

God can't reach? No. Is there anything or anyone God doesn't care about? No. God is much greater and more wonderful than we can imagine, and he holds all creation in the palm of his hand, like you are holding the little penny in the palm of your hand.

No wonder we've all chosen to come and spend some time praising him this morning! God is worth everything we can ever give him.

Of course, we are to respect our leaders, and keep the laws. We are to be good citizens, just as our Christian rule of love tells us. But we also need to remember who is ultimately in charge, and put God first. We need to be prepared to make a fuss if any laws are passed which are against God's law, and we need to do what we can to help our leaders uphold the authority of the God who made us all.

All-age ideas

- Use the coins as a focus for prayer, praying for all leaders and rulers as we look at the monarch's head; for the world, as we see the roundness; for the blind and spiritually blind as we feel its edge; for the imprisoned as we see the portcullis; and for the rich and the poor.

- The second part of the Isaiah passage is very effective read chorally with several voices, sometimes singly and sometimes together, with music in the background such as Shostakovich or Sibelius.

PROPER 25

Sunday between 23 and 29 October inclusive

Leviticus 19:1-2,15-18
Psalm 1
1 Thessalonians 2:1-8
Matthew 22:34-46

We are to love God with our whole being, and love others as much as we love ourselves.

All-age talk

Hold a large edition of the Bible, and tell everyone that today we are all going to read the whole lot as part of our talk!

Explain that today we heard Jesus giving us a summary of the whole of the Bible, in a couple of sentences. (Reader's Digest can eat their heart out!) He was saying that everything in all the law and the prophets was an exploring and working out of this. (Have Matthew 22:37-39 written out large, and invite everyone to join you in reading it out.) There – we've read the Bible! Or, to be more precise, we have read the subject matter of the whole Bible, because everything in it is to do with what we just read – people learning to love God with their whole being, and their neighbours as themselves. It's the story of their learning, their mistakes and failures, and of God's great love helping us make the impossible possible. (Well worth reading the full-length version!)

Let's look at what it means to love others as we love ourselves. How do we love ourselves? Invite a couple of friends to come and help show us. Get one to stand behind the other, with the front person putting their hands behind their back, and the back person providing them with substitute arms by pushing their own arms through the front person's. Have someone offering them a wrapped chocolate which they eat, and give them a brush so they can do their hair.

All day long we look after ourselves like this, feeding and washing and scratching ourselves whenever the needs arise. Even if we don't admit to loving ourselves our actions show that we do. If we start getting too hot, our body kindly makes us sweat to cool us down. If we're threatened by the cold, our helpful body sets us shivering and raises our hairs to warm us up again. And if there's a real emergency (the children can make an ambulance siren sound), the body shuts down some systems and kicks in with others to keep us alive as long as possible. That's love for you!

So if we are to love others like that, we'll be attentive, looking out for one another's well-being and ready to help when we see someone in need. We'll be doing what we can to feed the hungry and look after those with problems. We'll scratch where it itches but not where it doesn't. We'll be ready to drop everything and be there for people if there's an emergency and they need us. We'll do everything we can to help them feel better and get through the difficult times.

And where does all this love come from? From our wonderful God, who made us all in the first place, and loves to see all his children caring for one another like this.

All-age ideas

- Sing this summary of the law to the tune of *London's burning* in a round with actions. Then the whole of the law is being celebrated in voice and action, just as people are doing in real life twenty-four hours a day around our planet earth.

  You shall love the *(hands on heart)*
  Lord your God with *(arms raised)*
  all your heart and *(hands on heart)*
  all your mind and *(hands hold head)*
  all your strength! All your strength!
      (show muscles in arms)
  And love your neighbour,
      (arm round neighbour on one side)
  and love your neighbour.
      (arm round neighbour on other side)

- Make decorated banners or posters, proclaiming the summary of the law.

136

ALL SAINTS' DAY

Sunday between 30 October and 5 November inclusive

Revelation 7:9-17
Psalm 34:1-10
1 John 3:1-3
Matthew 5:1-12

Lives that have shone with God's love on earth are filled with joy as they see their Lord face to face.

All-age talk

Today we are celebrating the festival of all the saints of God. Saints are God's close friends, and there are lots of them around, as well as all the famous ones like Mary and Joseph, Peter and the other disciples, Francis, Benedict, Clare and Catherine.

What makes a saint?

Suppose your car breaks down on the motorway, and, as you drive skilfully on to the hard shoulder, smoke pours out of the bonnet. At this moment there is no doubt in your mind about it – you know that you need the AA or the RAC to sort you out. Suppose you've fallen down in the playground and find you can't move your ankle without terrible pain. At that moment you know without doubt that you need some help from the teacher on duty and the first aid people in the school office.

Show everyone a large arrow on which is written 'We know our need'. As soon as we know our need that points us towards getting it sorted. (Have 'Get help' written on a large piece of paper or card.) But what if we don't know or realise our need?

Suppose you have got some spaghetti sauce on your chin and you are just going out to meet an important client, or a new boyfriend or girlfriend. If we realise we have the sauce on our chin (show the arrow), then we'll probably go and wipe it off. (Show the 'Get help' sign.) But if we aren't aware of the sauce on our chin (show a sign without an arrow which says, 'Don't know our need') then we won't do anything about wiping it off. (Turn the 'Get help' sign over so it's a blank sign.)

137

If we don't realise our need of God (show 'Don't know our need') then we won't go to him for the help we urgently and desperately need. (Keep the blank sign up.) But if we *do* realise how much we need God (show the arrow) then that will lead us to seeking God's help in our lives. (Turn over the 'Get help' sign so it shows.)

Saints are ordinary people like us who realise their need of God (show the arrow) and spend their lives close to him so that he can help them in all they do. (Show the 'Get help' sign.)

All-age ideas

- Play some music as a background to the reading from Revelation, and ask several people to read it chorally, preparing it prayerfully and deciding how their voices can best express the sense of the heavenly.

- Ask different groups and clubs to prepare banners celebrating different saints, so that the church is full of their witness and example.

FOURTH SUNDAY BEFORE ADVENT

Sunday between 30 October and 5 November inclusive
For use if the Feast of All Saints was celebrated on 1 November and alternative propers are needed.

Micah 3:5-12
Psalm 43
1 Thessalonians 2:9-13
Matthew 24:1-14

With God's light and truth to guide us, we shall be brought safely through to the end of time.

All-age talk

Place around the church such warning signs as, 'Wet paint' on a chair, and 'Wet floor' next to a bucket and mop. Ask a couple of volunteers to go round the church to find the signs and bring them to you. Warnings are very useful! What would we do if we saw the 'Wet paint' sign? Avoid sitting on the chair. That's useful because it means our clothes don't get spoiled. What would we do if we saw the 'Wet floor' sign? We'd make a point of walking carefully, instead of running, so that we didn't slip on the wet floor and hurt ourselves.

It's quite normal for prophets to speak out God's warnings to his people, and Micah is doing that in today's reading. He doesn't mind that his message is going to be unpopular, any more than Jesus minds speaking out the truth. That's because he knows that warnings from God may help people sort out what is wrong in their life, say sorry to God for it, and ask his help to put things right as best they can. He tells his hearers the things they need to sort out and change. If they listen, and really start to repent, or turn their lives around, they will be able to work with God to put things right. Otherwise, they will end up with their holy city being destroyed.

In our Gospel today we heard Jesus warning his disciples that Jerusalem was going to be completely destroyed, even before some of them had died, because people had taken no notice of all the warnings they had been given. Jesus was talking in about AD 32, and over the next forty years all those earthquakes, wars and plagues happened in the area. In

AD 70 the Romans stormed the city of Jerusalem and destroyed it completely, just as Jesus had foretold.

Warnings are useful, and we need to take notice of them. Some of us have been shown films to warn us about the dangers of smoking and drugs and AIDS, and we are warned each summer to protect our skin from sunburn. The captain on the *Titanic* was warned that too much speed could be dangerous. These warnings are there to help us, but we do need to listen to them and act on them if they are going to work.

It's just the same with our spiritual health and well-being. Show a torch and a ruler. God gives us his light to see by, and his truth to measure our lives by. If we become aware of God warning us about our attitudes or behaviour or our relationships, we need to take it on board and do something about it before it's too late.

All-age ideas

- Have a 'still life' of a lamp and a ruler as part of a flower arrangement, with the title 'Send me your light and your truth'.

- With a very slow drum beat in the background, or a tolling bell, have two or three people in different parts of the church stating the facts that link with the Gospel, like this:

  Narrator There will be wars and rumours of wars.

  Other voices Caligula. Claudius. Nero. At Seleucia, fifty thousand Jews are said to have perished. Caesarea. Sythopolis. Joppa. Ascalon. Tyre. Alexandria.

  Narrator There will be famines and plagues.

  Other voices The reign of the emperor Claudius marked by continual scarcity of food. All Syria affected. Plague in Rome kills thirty thousand people.

140

Narrator   There will be earthquakes.

Other voices Good Friday, Jerusalem. Across Judea. Crete. Rome. Apamea. Phrygia. Campania. Devastation in parts of Asia. Achaia. Syria. Macedonia.

Narrator   Beware of false prophets.

Other voices 1 John 4, verse 1. 1 John 2, verse 18. 2 Peter 2, verse 1. 1 Timothy 4, verse 1.

All   AD 70: Jerusalem falls to the Romans,

THIRD SUNDAY BEFORE ADVENT

Sunday between 6 and 12 November inclusive

Amos 5:18-24 or
  Wisdom of
  Solomon 6:12-16
Psalm 70 or
  Wisdom of
  Solomon 6:17-20
1 Thessalonians
  4:13-18
Matthew 25:1-13

We need to keep ourselves awake and prepared so that the Day of the Lord does not come to us as darkness rather than light.

All-age talk

Beforehand prepare some sticks with red paper flames stuck on the end.

Begin by asking who has ever been a bridesmaid or a page-boy at a wedding. Were any of them late for the wedding? Today we heard a parable Jesus told about some bridesmaids. Some were ready when they were needed, but some weren't.

Show the 'torches' which were used at that time. Material was soaked in oil and tied on to the end of sticks. When you set light to them they would burn well, so the bride and bridegroom, coming from the bridegroom's house in the evening of the wedding, could have their way lit by the bridesmaids' torches. (Have a bride and groom and some bridesmaids to show this, holding their torch sticks.) At least, they could if the bridesmaids had their oil with them.

The problem in Jesus' story was that half the bridesmaids hadn't checked their oil supplies, so when the bridegroom needed their torchlight, they were rushing off to buy more oil, and ended up being shut out of the wedding feast.

What is the hidden message in this parable? What is Jesus wanting us to understand?

He wants us to be ready, and have our oil supplies topped up, so that whenever the bridegroom returns, even if he takes longer to arrive than we were expecting, we will be there waiting, shining brightly in the darkness. Then the bridegroom can lead us all into the celebrations and the feast.

Fill the oil lamp and light it. God's Spirit is like the oil we need to keep us burning brightly with God's love. If we stop keeping ourselves 'topped up' by forgetting to pray and read the Bible each day, our lives will stop shining, just as the girls' torches went out. Then, if Jesus suddenly returns, unexpectedly, either at the end of time or in a situation where our bright Christian love is badly needed, we won't be able to help.

So Jesus is telling us to keep praying, keep listening and keep loving. That way, we'll be all ready whenever he needs us.

All-age ideas

- Have an oil lamp and bottle of oil with some bridal flowers and a veil as one of the flower arrangements today.

- Give out small squares of foil or shiny paper to everyone as they come in. At the time of confession, invite everyone to look at their 'mirrors' and imagine them reflecting back their spiritual rather than physical state. Play some reflective music while this happens, giving everyone space to recognise any areas which need bringing to God's love for forgiveness and healing.

- Invite a group of people to mime the parable in the Gospel as it is read.

SECOND SUNDAY BEFORE ADVENT

Sunday between 13 and 19 November inclusive

Zephaniah 1:7, 12-18
Psalm 90:1-8 (9-11), 12
1 Thessalonians 5:1-11
Matthew 25:14-30

The Day of the Lord will hold terror for the wicked and unprepared, but rejoicing for those living in God's light.

All-age talk

Beforehand place three boxes of different colours around the church. In the red box put five one-pound coins (cardboard ones are fine!), in the blue box put two one-pound coins and leave the yellow box empty.

We know that one day the world as we know it will come to an end. We know that life as we know it will finish. All the prophets and Jesus teach us in the Bible that there is going to be a Day of the Lord, when we will see Jesus in all God's glory, and all that is evil will not survive. That includes people. How we live now in our lives will affect what happens to us that day. We do need to know that.

When will it happen? We don't know the time or date; in fact, what we do know is that it will happen suddenly, without us having loads of time to change. That's why we need to live every day as if it were our last.

But God doesn't want us so scared of the last day that we can't enjoy life here. Jesus came to set us free from that fear, and, if we are walking through life as Jesus' friends, there is nothing to be frightened of, because it's only the evil and bad and selfish that will be destroyed; everything that is good and loving and honest will be gathered up safely for ever.

Jesus told one of his stories with secrets – parables – about making the most of all the gifts God has given us, and we need three people to help us with it. (Make sure that the third servant chosen has been warned beforehand that she will be told off in the story, and is confident enough to cope with that.)

In Jesus' story, a man is going on a long journey

and, before he goes, he gathers his servants together and entrusts his property to them to look after. (Give five coins to one servant and send her off to find the red box. Give two coins to another servant and send him off to find the blue box. Give one coin to the last servant, and send her off to find the yellow box.) The man went off on his travels, and after a long time came back home. He called the servants to him to settle accounts with them. (Call the volunteers together with the boxes.) Let's see how the first servant has got on. (She opens the box and counts out to the owner ten coins. Be very pleased. Everyone can clap.) What about the second servant? (He opens the box and counts out four coins. Praise and applause.) What about the third servant? Tell everyone how this servant told the owner she was too scared to do anything with her gift, so she just hid it as it was. (She gives it back.) The owner was not pleased at all because the servant had not made good use of the gift she had been given. (Tell the servant off, and thank all the actors for their help.)

We all have gifts God has enjoyed giving us. Some of us are good at being friendly and welcoming, some good at looking after animals, working out money, ironing, or thinking out solutions to difficult problems. Whatever our gift is, we need to enjoy using it and making the most of it for the good of everyone.

All-age ideas

- The Zephaniah reading works well read chorally. Work it out in a group of light, medium and dark voices, experimenting to find how best the voices sound together and on their own.

- As the passage from Thessalonians is read, a child is dressed in Roman armour.

CHRIST THE KING

Sunday between 20 and 26 November inclusive

Ezekiel 34:11-16, 20-24
Psalm 95:1-7a
Ephesians 1:15-23
Matthew 25:31-46

In total humility, at one with the least of his people, Jesus, the Messiah or Christ, reigns as King, with full authority and honour for eternity.

All-age talk

Bring along a crown and robe, some pretend bags of money, a dish of fruit and two fans on sticks as shown below. Drape some cloth over a chair.

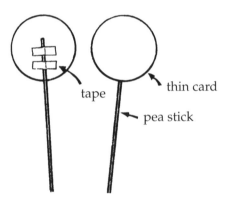

tape

thin card

pea stick

Tell everyone that today we are celebrating that Jesus Christ is King for ever. Ask a volunteer to come out and dress them up in the grand robe of very costly material, hand-embroidered by expert craftsmen, and the solid gold crown, studded with real diamonds and rubies. Sit the king on a grand throne covered in pure silk and made from finest marble, and provide him with some servants to stand around and wave him with fans, bowing before him. Give him bags of money on a table nearby, and provide a dish of fresh fruits for him to snack on between banquets.

Is this right? Is this what King Jesus is really like? No, it's all wrong! Although Jesus has been given all power and majesty and honour, and is King of all time and space, he is a very different sort of king. He lays aside his majesty (help the king up from his throne), lays aside his robe and his crown (take them from him), lays aside all wealth and comfort (the servants move the table), so that he can be one with us (he shakes hands with the servants) and live among us, caring for us, searching for the lost, and binding up the injured. (Thank the servant and the king for their help.)

Now if that's how our king behaves, then that's how we are to behave as well. If we worship and honour a Servant King, who doesn't greedily look after his own needs all the time but makes a point of looking after other people's needs, then that's what we have to do! Our wealth and treasure will be in loving service, wherever we're needed. That's how Jesus will recognise us as his people, when we get to the gate of heaven.

All-age ideas

- Have the crown and robe and the other props near the altar as people come up to communion, with the title 'The Servant King'.

- Have the parable mimed during the Gospel. To help everyone understand that the sorting is checking existing citizenship of the kingdom, give all the 'sheep' a cross on their foreheads, which the king looks for as they are chosen and welcomed.

YEAR B

FIRST SUNDAY OF ADVENT

Isaiah 64:1-9
Psalm 80:1-7, 17-19
1 Corinthians 1:3-9
Mark 13:24-37

Be alert and watchful;
keep yourselves ready.

All-age talk

Beforehand prepare a large sun shape from yellow paper and a large cloud from grey paper. First show everyone the sun. If this is showing in the sky during the summer, what can we tell about the best clothes to wear? Now slide the large grey cloud over the sun, so that the sun is hidden. What might it be wise to take with us if we are going out in this weather? We are very good at reading the signs in the weather to help us keep comfortable.

We read lots of other signs as well. At traffic lights, or at the top of scary water chutes, we know that red means stop and green means go. We know by the special music when *The Simpsons* or the news is about to come on. We know by the smell of cooking that dinner is nearly ready.

In today's Gospel, Jesus tells us to keep alert and check the signs which will tell us when he is going to come to earth again. This time he won't be coming as a tiny baby, but full of God's glory and in great power, riding on the clouds of heaven. It will be such an amazing event that it will rock the whole cosmos – the whole of nature will be shaken. Jesus tells us that the sun will be darkened, and the moon will lose its light, and stars will fall from heaven. This is something that every being will notice, both those who are alive on earth at the time and those who will have already died. Jesus tells us that even he doesn't know exactly when it will happen, but it certainly will take place, and we will all need to be ready for it, whether we are still alive here or already dead.

So how can we make sure we are ready? How can we read the signs?

150

The best way of making sure we stay ready is by keeping our eyes open – our spiritual eyes. That means keeping in touch with God on a daily basis. We need to get into a habit of praying, not just once a week on Sundays, but all times of every day. A good way of remembering, and getting ourselves into such a habit, is to get in touch with God every time we check our watches, or every time we put something to eat in our mouths.

Sensible sailors or hill walkers will check the weather forecast every time before they set out, so they are prepared. We need to check with God his will and guidance every time before we make decisions or spend money. Then our faith will be living and active, growing as we grow, and keeping us alert and available, so that whenever Jesus comes again in glory we shall be ready to welcome him with joy.

All-age ideas

- This response can be used at the time of penitence:

  Lord, we are sorry for the days we hardly speak with you at all.

  Lord have mercy.
  Lord have mercy.

  Lord, we are sorry for the times we refuse to follow in your way.

  Christ have mercy.
  Christ have mercy.

  Lord, we are sorry for the opportunities we miss for serving others in humility.

  Lord have mercy.
  Lord have mercy.

- Direct people to look at the cross as a sign of God's generous, self-giving love, and think about a spiritual 'new year' resolution at this beginning of the Church's year. This can be done either in a time of silence or accompanied by quiet music, which could be played on organ or piano, with a music group or choir, or from a tape or CD.

SECOND SUNDAY OF ADVENT

Isaiah 40:1-11
Psalm 85:1-2, 8-13
2 Peter 3:8-15a
Mark 1:1-8

John the Baptist prepares the way for the coming of the Messiah by helping the people to realign their lives.

All-age talk

Bring in a washing-up bowl with some water in it and a mop. Produce a mug or two which you were using earlier and explain how these are dirty and need washing up. You hope the mugs won't be too embarrassed by being shown dirty like this in full view of everyone. They are very particular mugs and prefer people to see them clean.

We are often a bit like that. We like people to see us when we're proud of what we are like and what we are doing. We don't like it much if someone catches us screaming at the dog, telling or living a lie, or being lazy or greedy. Usually we try to cover up the things we do which we aren't proud of. Perhaps we'll make out it's someone else's fault that we're late or grumpy; perhaps we'll think up good excuses for wrong behaviour. We get so good at this that often we believe our cover-up stories and stop noticing that instead of pretending we're clean-living Christians, what we actually need is a good, thorough wash.

The people who came to hear John the Baptist were just like us. There were things in their lives which were wrong and selfish, and they had become used to making excuses for themselves till they were quite content to live with their bad habits and carefully groomed images. But John got them thinking. And as they thought about their real selves and what they were really like, they suddenly started to realise that they were like dirty mugs which needed a good wash. If they were washed clean, they could be free from all the pretending and cover-ups, and just be themselves again.

John told them it was quite easy to do – they just

needed to name all those big and little sins aloud to God without hiding them, and choose to turn their back on that way of living. He said he would dip them right under the water in the river as a sign that their lives were being washed clean.

(Ask for a volunteer to come and wash up the mugs.) For some of them it must have felt very humiliating to do that in public, especially if they had groomed their images so well that they had kept their sins well hidden. And it must have been such a relief for others, who had worried about their sin for years and years, to have it washed away at last.

When they were all washed clean, like our mugs, without any need to hide from God or each other any more, John told them something very important. This washing was just the beginning; soon someone was coming who would be able to plunge them deep into the depths of the Holy Spirit, so they would be completely surrounded and filled with the loving God. And the person who would make that possible was coming very soon.

During Advent we can get ourselves ready for Jesus' coming to us, just as they did. We can look at what we are really like; how we really behave with others; recognise the parts of us that are real enough but we hope others won't see. Anything we find which needs washing away we need to confess to God, tell him how sorry we are about it, and the way we have made excuses, and choose to turn our backs on that way of living. You can talk to God on your own or go to your priest or minister and pray with them, especially if you feel you need some help with changing. But however we do it, we all need to come to God regularly for thorough washing, and he is the only one who can make us clean and free.

All-age ideas

- During the time of confession, gather everyone around the font and use a jug to dip in and pour water while the prayer of confession is said.

- Use today as an opportunity for everyone to renew their baptismal promises.

153

THIRD SUNDAY OF ADVENT

Isaiah 61:1-4, 8-11
Psalm 126 or Canticle:
  Magnificat
1 Thessalonians
  5:16-24
John 1:6-8, 19-28

In Jesus, God will be fulfilling the Messianic prophecies about the promised Saviour.

All-age talk

Talk about the buying of Christmas presents and take out a list you've been making of all the Christmas jobs and how far you have all got with them. At this stage of Advent some people have probably got all their presents bought, wrapped and hidden, while others have hardly begun.

Before Jesus had been born, the people of Israel had been waiting ages and ages for God's Saviour to come and save them. Every young woman would pray that her baby might be the Messiah, just as her grandmother had done before her. Through all the terrible crises of national life, the prophets had kept alive in the people of Israel their calling to be God's people. One day, the prophets all said, God would actually come in some way to be really 'with them' personally. They were to keep themselves ready and watchful for when that happened.

(Take out another 'list', and unroll it. On this are written the checkpoints from today's Isaiah reading.) The prophets even gave them a kind of 'Christmas' or 'Messiah' list of things to look out for in God's chosen one, the Messiah, or Christ. They would be able to recognise the Messiah when he came because these are the things he would do:

• tell the good news to the poor

• comfort the broken-hearted

• set free those feeling imprisoned

• announce the time when God would show his merciful judgement

154

- give people clothes of praise and joy to replace their sadness
- be fair to everyone
- make what is right grow strong
- put wrong things right

Now who do we know who did come and do those things, and is still doing them now? Jesus! And when was it that Jesus came into our world? At Christmas. So all their waiting and hoping was worth it. And anyone who wasn't sure could check with the Christmas (or 'Messiahmas') list and see for themselves. And so can we.

All-age ideas

- Have the Isaiah passage read with a group of voices, people of different voice tones speaking different sections. Work the best way out for your group by gathering to read through the whole passage and talking about it first, so their understanding will be reflected in the reading. Try out suggestions and be prepared to adjust them if they don't sound right. Each person can mark their parts on a copy of the passage.

- Mime the Gospel reading, but have the conversation section learnt so the actors say their own words.

FOURTH SUNDAY OF ADVENT

2 Samuel 7, 1-11, 16
Canticle: Magnificat
  or Psalm 89:1-4,
  19-26
Romans 16:25-27
Luke 1:26-38

God's promised kingdom, announced both to King David in ancient times and to Mary by the angel Gabriel, will go on for ever.

All-age talk

Bring in something to show which you thought would last you a long time, but hasn't (like a pair of shoes or a felt-tip pen), and something else which you didn't think would last at all and it has (like a paper bookmark or a jar of Marmite). Talk about these and the way some things, like great cathedrals, are built to last for hundreds and hundreds of years, while other things, like newspapers or toilet paper, are not designed to last very long at all.

King David was wanting to build a temple for the glory of God which was a strong, permanent structure, rather than a temporary tent. And God told David that his ideas for the kingdom were far more long-lasting even than a strong building; God's idea was for a kingdom of love and peace that lasts not just for a long time but for ever and ever and ever. And Jesus would be the king. The angel Gabriel was sent to Mary to tell her all about it.

'You are going to have a child, Mary,' said Gabriel, 'and he's going to be the king of a kingdom that will last for ever.' The angel even told Mary what to call her child when he was born. (Show a large notice with the word 'Jesus' on one side of it.) He was to be called Jesus.

Names are important, and they often have a special meaning. Pick out some of the names in the congregation and look up what they mean in one of those 'your baby's name' books. The name Jesus has a meaning as well. It means 'Saviour: the one who saves' (show this written on the other side of the Jesus sign). Through King Jesus, God was coming to save his people.

When Jesus, the Saviour King, was born at the first Christmas, that was just the beginning! God's kingdom is still here today, and it's still growing.

All-age ideas

- Have the children holding Christingles around the altar during the Eucharistic Prayer.

- Set out the passage from Romans on a sheet for everyone to read, like this:

Men/boys	Now to him who is able to establish you, by my Gospel and the proclamation of Jesus Christ,
Women/girls	according to the revelation of the mystery hidden for long ages past,
Men/boys	but now revealed and made known
Women/girls	through the prophetic writings by the command of the eternal God,
Men/boys	so that all nations might believe and obey him –
All	to the only wise God be glory for ever through Jesus Christ! Amen.

- Place a globe or a world map near the Advent candle wreath.

CHRISTMAS DAY

Isaiah 62:6-12
Psalm 97
Titus 3:4-7
Luke 2:(1-7) 8-20

Jesus Christ, the world's Saviour,
is here with us, born as a human baby.

All-age talk

Ask a few volunteers to take the microphone (or shout) and wish everyone a happy Christmas. We've all spent the last month preparing everything – the food and drink, the surprises, the gifts, the decorations – so that we can make a good job of wishing our loved ones a really happy Christmas.

What are we wishing them when we say 'Happy Christmas!' to them? Collect some ideas of what we want for them. They will probably include lots of good wishes directly linked with partying and family celebration. We choose this particular day to wish people those good things we might want for them every day of the year.

Why is the festival of Christmas such a good time to wish people wonderful things in their life? (Arrange for someone to be given a lighted candle at the back of the church at this point, which they carry up to you.) All those things we wish those we love are to do with wanting their lives to be bright and shining, well lit and beautiful in every way. And today, Christmas Day, we are celebrating a life shining with God's glory, which has come right among us. Jesus, the promised Christ, has been born.

So we are right to wish everyone a happy Christmas. What better way to celebrate God's great love for us all than by wishing everyone we meet the light of loving in their lives! Don't let it stop at the ones in your family or circle of friends. Wish it (and mean it) even to those you don't always get on with; wish it to those you hardly know, like the bus conductor, the toll collector at the road tunnel, the other people walking their dogs this afternoon and anyone else you should meet. Pray for them and wish them the light of God's blessing in their lives as you spread the message – Happy Christmas!

All-age ideas

- Have lots of candles around the church today, ensuring that they are really safe. Try nightlights on window ledges and/or along the front edge of the altar. Have some of the children holding candles around the altar at the Eucharistic Prayer. Or give every family a candle, which has been alight during worship, to burn at home each day of the twelve days of Christmas.

- Dress the children up to mime the Gospel, in a series of 'stills'.

- Give out bells, shakers and streamers to be shaken and waved all over the church in the aisles during the Gloria and in a lively carol.

First Sunday of Christmas

Isaiah 61:10-62:3
Psalm 148
Galatians 4:4-7
Luke 2:15-21

Just as the angels said, a Saviour has been born for us.

All-age talk

Bring along a pot of jam, some toffee or fudge, a skipping rope and a camera. Talk about the importance of getting the timing right when you are making jam or toffee, skipping or taking a photo. Invite experts from the congregation to describe that 'right moment' and how you know when it's there and don't miss it. Sometimes we do miss the right moment and end up with solid stuff that won't spread and tastes of burnt saucepan, our legs tangled up in the rope, or a photo of a giraffe's bottom.

Saint Paul talks about Jesus being born 'when the time was right'. That particular date in history – whenever it actually was – fitted in perfectly with God's rescue plan. And so he acted, and what we call Christmas happened: a baby was born who was God's own Son, and would grow up to show everyone what God is really like, in the language of being human, which we can all understand.

God is very good at knowing the right time to act. We can always trust him with that. Often he will bring things together in a way and at a time which brings blessing to many people rather than only one. Those who are older can look back over their lives and see how this has been true. We might have prayed for something to happen and got fed up with God not seeming to answer for ages. But later on we can see that the time of waiting perhaps helped us, or allowed something else important to happen, and God's timing turned out to be for the best.

Sometimes we don't understand God's sense of timing and would much prefer him to take our advice! Perhaps we are still feeling let down by

God over something which we so wanted and has never happened. We need to remember that it is the God of all eternity that we worship, and it may be that we shall only understand when we get to heaven. We are a bit like bewildered pets at the vets who find their owners bringing them along to have a stranger poke needles into them: we don't understand and just know that it hurts.

Jesus himself was not born into a comfortable home with an efficient maternity hospital just down the road. The family had to escape to another country before he was two years old, because King Herod wanted him killed. But still the time of his birth was right.

What God did was provide his Son with a human family to love him and look after him. When couples who love one another take on that commitment of marriage, and raise their children together, through all the inevitable strains and stresses, they are giving newborn children a wonderful, Godly gift. And as the Christian family here, we are all given one another to look after and be looked after by. Whatever our age, sex or marital state, we are all children together, born into God's family and enjoying God's own parenting, which is one thing in life we can really trust.

All-age ideas

- Organise a collection today of money and/or supplies for those who are without family support or homes to live in.

- Use the script on page 412.

- Gather everyone around the crib, making sure the children can see, for this short litany:

  Lord of heaven and earth, laid in the hay,
  Jesus, our King, we worship and adore you.

  Word of the Father, crying as a baby,
  Jesus, our King, we worship and adore you.

  Dressed in glory, wrapped in baby clothes,
  Jesus, our King, we worship and adore you.

SECOND SUNDAY OF CHRISTMAS

Jeremiah 31:7-14 or
  Ecclesiasticus
  24:1-12
Psalm 147:12-20 or
  Canticle: Wisdom of
  Solomon 10:15-21
Ephesians 1:3-14
John 1:(1-9) 10-18

The Word made flesh at Christmas was always with God, always expressing his creative love.

All-age talk

Start by giving everyone one minute to find out from and share with someone else something that went really well, or was really funny, or was a complete disaster over this Christmas. One thing all humans have always loved doing is talking together! Toddlers, children, young people, middle-aged and old people all love a chat. Even babies talk, in their own way. What would we do without the telephone, especially if we can't get out like we used to. With e-mail we can chat to people all over the world, and with television, radio, magazines and newspapers people can chat to us about anything and everything. Ground control can direct astronauts in space, pilots can be talked down to a safe landing, and surgeons can talk their students through complicated heart operations. Politicians can shout their ideas to crowds of people, and friends can whisper their secrets. All of this is the magic of words.

Why do we talk about Jesus as the Word of God?

Whenever we use words we express ourselves. Jesus expresses God, not in a speech bubble but as a human being like us, so that we can understand God in a better way than ever. God has always expressed himself, of course, so the Word of God has been there as long as God has – for ever. God *said*, 'Let there be light!' God *said*, 'Let there be stars and plants and animals, fish and birds.' God *said*, 'Let there be people in our likeness to look after the earth.' So it was the Word of God which spoke those things into being through love.

Then, at Christmas, the Word of God actually took shape itself – human shape. And his name was Jesus, which means 'the one who saves us'.

All-age ideas

- For the Penitential rite:

  The shape of God's Word is a loving Saviour; how loving are the words we speak?

  Lord, have mercy.
  Lord, have mercy.

  The Word of God is willing to be vulnerable and accessible; how high are the walls we build?

  Christ, have mercy.
  Christ, have mercy.

  In humility, the Word of God lays aside his glory; how important to us are the things we possess and desire?

  Lord, have mercy.
  Lord, have mercy.

- On the walls or pillars, have speech bubbles with the following sentences in:

  Let there be light.
  Let the earth produce growing things.
  Let us make human beings in our image.

  In one speech bubble have a picture of the infant Jesus.

THE EPIPHANY

Isaiah 60:1-6
Psalm 72:(1-9) 10-15
Ephesians 3:1-12
Matthew 2:1-12

Jesus, the promised Messiah, is shown to the Gentile world.

All-age talk

Consider using the suggested sketch in the All-age Ideas just before the talk. Have a number of masks, based on the pictures below, to put on some volunteers, which alter the way we see them and act towards them.

Vicky

Sydney

With the first volunteer, explain that Vicky is feeling really fed up because her Christmas tokens were stolen before she got round to spending them. (Aah!) Have everyone making a 'ding dong' doorbell noise. It's the football squad coach! Quick, Vicky chooses to put on the bright, happy mask! (Help her on with it.)

With the second volunteer, explain that Sidney's feeling really fed up because his Christmas tokens went through the wash by mistake and are now a hard crusty blob. (Aah!) The doorbell rings again. (Ding dong.) It's someone Sidney doesn't know, and they're wearing the colours of a team Sidney doesn't support! Quick, where's that angry 'What on earth do you think you're doing here?' mask? (Help him on with it.)

We all have lots of masks which we keep by the door. Sometimes it's right to wear them, and helps us get out of a bad mood faster. But sometimes we forget what is mask and what is real, and that's not so good.

For some people we are always on our best behaviour, showing them how kind and friendly we are, how ready to help and forgive them. With others we want to show them that although we're doing our grudging best to be polite, it's a real effort and we'd far rather we didn't have to have anything to do with them. Some people we're happy to welcome to church, some we hope will never come, at least not to the same church as us! Sometimes we're not very good at welcoming people who look different, wear different clothes or speak with a different accent from ours. We make it quite clear to them that they are outsiders.

But today we hear that God led these strangers all the way to Bethlehem, specially to show them his baby Son! We hear that King Herod pretended to make them welcome. And we hear that at Jesus' home they really were made welcome. God wanted these 'outsiders' to be among the first to meet his Son because Jesus had come into the world for everybody, and not just for the Jewish people.

As Christians, we need to remember that the good news of the Gospel is for everyone, and not just those like us. So today we ask God to turn us into people who are happy to welcome outsiders, without needing any masks to pretend.

All-age ideas

- This short sketch explores the idea of Jesus coming for the whole world.

  (Joseph, Mary and the baby Jesus are at the front of the church. The wise men walk up the aisle towards them and knock on a 'door'.)

  1st wise man   Excuse me, is anyone there?

(Joseph comes to the door)

Joseph	Bit late for visiting, isn't it? What do you want?
2nd wise man	Our navigation lights only work at night, I'm afraid. *(Points up to the star)* Is there a baby king here at all?
Joseph	You must be joking – does this look like a palace? Go and annoy some of your own lot – we're a respectable Jewish household here. *(Slams door. Wise men shrug, look at their presents and turn away.)*
3rd wise man	I thought it was too good to be true – a Saviour for the whole world. It's not for us, then. We're not included, obviously. *(They walk away)*
Mary	What was all that, Joseph?
Joseph	Oh, a bunch of star-gazing weirdos. You should have seen their ridiculous clothes! I didn't let on about our little Jesus, though. Got to protect him from all those prying Gentiles, haven't we!
Producer	CUT! What's happening? That's not the script! It didn't happen like that at all! *(Turns to wise men)* Come on, you lot! God wouldn't have got you seeking just to have you turned away!

(The wise men turn and walk back up the aisle. As a narrator reads Matthew 2:10-11, they mime the actions, and Joseph and Mary embrace them.)

- Have gifts of burning frankincense, gold and myrrh brought at the offertory, while the appropriate verses of *We three kings* are sung.

166

THE BAPTISM OF CHRIST: FIRST SUNDAY OF EPIPHANY

Genesis 1:1-5
Psalm 29
Acts 19:1-7
Mark 1:4-11

Through the Holy Spirit, Jesus is affirmed at his Baptism as God's beloved Son, and we too are given the Spirit of God which affirms us as God's adopted daughters and sons.

All-age talk

Bring along a pair of wellington boots which fit you, or arrange beforehand for a volunteer to bring their boots and do the actions as you talk.

Stand the boots together where they can be seen, and explain that these boots (being very keen, conscientious boots) want to walk wherever you go. (Walk about and watch the boots, still sitting there and not moving.) They are trying very hard, but they don't seem to be getting anywhere, do they? Perhaps they need a bit of encouragement. (Some of the children can encourage the boots from a distance!)

Poor old boots – they'd love to be walking where you walk, but they just can't manage it. Why not? Because they haven't got you inside them!

Climb into the boots and see the difference. Suddenly they are able to walk around wherever you walk. They can even jump with you, run with you and dance with you! And all because they have you in them.

Now what has a keen pair of boots got to do with our Bible readings for today? In the reading from Genesis nothing happened, nothing was drawn into life, until God's Spirit made creation happen. And in the Acts of the Apostles we heard about some people whose lives were changed when they received the Holy Spirit, just as our lives can. We can know lots about Jesus and what he did on earth and what he said, and that can make us very keen to live like him – in a loving, generous, honest way. But unless we ask God to be in us, getting to know him as a person, rather than a set of facts, or a bit of a history lesson, we'll be like the boots on their own, wanting to move with God, but not able to do it on their own. (As you say this, take off the boots and put them on their own while you move around.)

As soon as we ask God into our life, his Spirit comes and moves in us (put the boots on again), and that makes it possible for us to go wherever God wants us to go, and act as God wants us to act. The Spirit of God which was seen settling on Jesus when John baptised him in the river Jordan, settles on all of God's children as they put their faith and trust in him.

So let's not waste our time trying hard to do good things *for* God like a pair of boots without any living feet in them. Instead, let's invite the Spirit of God every day to come and fill us, so God's life is *in* us, and can let us dance through life with praise, walk beside those who need our help, and stick to the right path all the way to heaven.

All-age ideas

- Decorate the font with blue and white flowers, shells and stones, and have posters or banners nearby expressing the Spirit of God, with the words: 'Come, Holy Spirit, fill my life!'

- Renew baptismal vows, and recall our own baptism, with everyone marking a cross on their foreheads with their thumb as they say, 'I turn to Christ'.

- Invite everyone to pray silently and fervently during the administration of communion for the Holy Spirit to come and fill them and the whole Church with God's life. Encourage everyone to continue that prayer wherever they are each day at midday. If every person did that in every parish using this book, that's a huge crowd of praying people, all focused on asking for more of God in our lives!

SECOND SUNDAY OF EPIPHANY

1 Samuel 3:1-10
   (11-20)
Psalm 139:1-6, 13-18
Revelation 5:1-10
John 1:43-51

Jesus, the Christ, unlocks the mysteries of God.

All-age talk

Bring along one of those locked secret diaries, or a locked briefcase or file. Who usually has the key to the secret thoughts and ideas inside here? Only the one who wrote them. To use e-mail, or a hole-in-the-wall cash dispenser we need a special pass-word or number to make sure that our secrets are safe and no one else can get at them unless we give permission. Only we ourselves have the key, and the authority.

Only God has access to God's own secret thoughts. He chooses to make some things known to some people, but there's no way his thoughts are all left wide open for anyone to see and understand at a glance. Is there any human person you can think of whom you really know completely? We can't even fully understand another human person, let alone the mind of the all-powerful living God!

The only person who could have the key and be authorised to open God's thoughts up to us would have to be someone who was both human and God. But *is* there anyone who fits that description? Who is it? It's Jesus! Jesus is authorised and worthy to open up God's heart to us because he is both God and human. And he spent his life doing just that.

All-age ideas

- Cut out the letters for 'What God is like' and stick them on the underside of a sheet of lining paper. (Make sure you place the words back to front.) During the talk the youngest children can be given crayons and asked to scribble all over

169

the lining paper, so that gradually the colouring reveals 'What God is like'.

- Have the reading from 1 Samuel acted out with a young child and an elderly man, either miming it or saying their own words, with a narrator holding it all together.

- There is a children's version of Psalm 139, *Father God, you love me,* on page 413.

THIRD SUNDAY OF EPIPHANY

Genesis 14:17-20
Psalm 128
Revelation 19:6-10
John 2:1-11

Signs of glory lead us to believe in Jesus as Lord and Saviour.

All-age talk

Prepare beforehand a teddy with an envelope containing a picture of a married couple (from the congregation) tied to its arm; a plastic jug of water with a picture of a Bible stuck on to the outside; and a Bible with a red bookmark, on which is written 'John, chapter 2, verse 11'. (The married couple need to be provided with empty wine glasses.)

Explain that in this Epiphany season we are following signs, just as the wise men followed the sign of the star, and today we are all going on a journey.

Take everyone on a sign-by-sign journey, starting by inviting a couple of very young people to go to the children's corner and find a teddy with a message round his arm. (Have someone primed to place teddy with his message in the right place just before you start the talk.) When they return, they can open the envelope and find a picture of a married couple in the congregation. (These people are primed, of course.)

Another child can take the picture and match it up with the actual married couple, who are led by the child to the front. They are each holding an empty wine glass. Greet the couple and remind everyone that we've been hearing in the Gospel today about a wedding that Jesus went to in a place called Cana. Why are their glasses empty? Because in our story the wine had run out! Send another child to look for a jug of water (which should be placed somewhere fairly obvious). While the child pours water into the wine glasses, remind everyone of how Jesus had changed the water at Cana into the very best quality wine. (Let

171

the couple take a sip and check that our water is still water. It probably is!)

No wonder people were amazed at what had happened. It pointed them to look at Jesus in a new way; he had authority over things like water! Look again at the jug and point out that it has a picture stuck on the side – another sign for us. Ask a couple of older children to see what it is. The picture is of a Bible with a red bookmark in it. Invite these children to find a Bible with a bookmark. (It has been placed somewhere fairly obvious, such as on the lectern.) When they bring it back they can read out the verse indicated on the bookmark: John 2:11.

The miracles that Jesus did when he was walking this planet about two thousand years ago were signs that led people to realise that he was not just a good human being, or a clever preacher: he was none other than the Son of God.

There are signs of God's love all over the place today as well – in answered prayers, in the courage we get to do what we know is right, even though we're scared, in the peace and reassurance we are given sometimes, and in the grace which enables us to do impossible things, like forgiving our enemies, or giving up an addiction. What all the signs point to is a very real, very powerful God of love.

All-age ideas

- Have some arrows taped to the floor and walls which have Bible references or quotes on them – for example, John 1:14, John 2:11, John 14:6, John 14:11, John 18:37, John 20:8.

- Have the passage from Revelation read chorally by a group of children, women and men. Make copies of the passage for everyone and work through it together for meaning, each person highlighting the sections they are to read. Sound effects from large trays or sheets of heavy card and shakers can be added.

- Have one of the flower arrangements expressing a marriage reception, with white ribbon, a bottle of white wine and a couple of glasses, for instance.

172

FOURTH SUNDAY OF EPIPHANY

Deuteronomy
  18:15-20
Psalm 111
Revelation 12:1-5a
Mark 1:21-28

Jesus displays all the signs that mark him out to be God's chosen One.

All-age talk

Strike a match and light a candle. Talk about how useful fire is to heat up food and cook it, to keep us warm, melt steel and make steam to generate power. But fire is very powerful, and so it can be very dangerous. Show a picture or a model of a fire engine, and enlist the children's help in talking about what happens when fires get out of control, and how the firemen fight the dangers. We need to have a healthy fear of fire to keep us safe.

God is very powerful. When you think of the power needed to create fire and oceans, ranges of mountains and galaxies of stars, you can't help but be a bit fearful at the thought of getting in touch with such a powerful person.

We are sensible to stand in awe of this great Being, on whom we depend for everything, including life itself. We are right to respect the Lord of life, and think carefully before we speak to him, and give him our full attention whenever we pray. We are right to humble ourselves in his presence and behave well during church services. God sees everything we do and knows everything we think, both the things we are pleased about and the things we are secretly rather ashamed of. Sometimes we behave as if God is more of an easygoing pet than the Lord of the entire universe. We need to take God seriously and recognise that he is very powerful indeed.

(Pick up the candle again.) But that great power of God is only part of the story. Just as a candle is a person-sized fire, which we can hold and which gives us light, but doesn't frighten us like a house on fire, so Jesus is the way we can approach the great creative God in person.

173

All-age ideas

- Have phrases describing God's power written up on the walls and pillars.

- Have the Gospel read by a group of people taking the different parts.

PROPER 1

Sunday between 3 and 9 February inclusive (if earlier than the Second Sunday before Lent)

Isaiah 40:12-31
Psalm 147:1-11, 20c
1 Corinthians 9:16-23
Mark 1:29-39

The good news about God is far too good to keep to ourselves.

All-age talk

Begin by having the following read out, or having it printed on the weekly sheet. It is an extract from *The Solitaire Mystery* by Jostein Gaarder.

'Tell me about Rainbow Fizz,' I said.

He raised his white eyebrows and whispered, 'It has to be tasted, my boy.'

'Can't you tell me what it tastes like?'

He shook his old head in despair.

'A normal fizzy drink tastes of orange or pear or raspberry – and that's that. That isn't the case with Rainbow Fizz, Albert. You taste all those flavours at the same time with this drink, and you even taste fruits and berries you've never been near with your tongue.'

'Then it must be good,' I said.

'Hah! It's more than just good. You can taste a normal fizzy drink only in your mouth . . . first on your tongue and the roof of your mouth, then a little bit down your throat. You can taste Rainbow Fizz in your nose and head, down through your legs, and out through your arms.'

'I think you're pulling my leg,' I said.

'You think so?'

The old man looked almost dumbfounded, so I decided to ask something which was easier to answer.

'What colour is it?' I asked.

Baker Hans started to laugh. 'You're full of questions, aren't you, boy. And that's good, but

175

it's not always easy to answer. I have to *show* you the drink, you see.'

Talk about how hard it is to describe something so wonderful that it is impossible to imagine; the only way Albert is really going to find out how wonderful Rainbow Fizz is, is to experience it for himself.

Today's reading from the prophet Isaiah is a bit like this. The prophet is doing his best to describe to us how wonderful God is, but God is simply so incredibly amazing that we find it almost impossible to imagine. There's only one way to find out, and that is to experience God for ourselves. If you ask anyone who has become aware of the great, loving God working in their life, they'll agree that there really aren't any words to describe how wonderful and amazing he is. They just know because they've experienced him in action.

In the Gospel we heard how Jesus had been busy healing lots and lots of people at the house of Peter and Andrew, where he was staying. It started with Peter's mother-in-law, who had a bad fever and was very ill, and Jesus made her better. After she'd made them all supper, full of new energy, no doubt, crowds of visitors came, all wanting Jesus to heal them as well. So he did. Through Jesus, God was working right there in those people's lives, and making them more free and happy than they had ever felt before. It was so exciting to see! We can imagine how happy it made Jesus to see these people suddenly realising at last how wonderful God was! He couldn't wait for everyone else to find out.

Well, people are still finding out that our amazing God can set us free to live happy and joyful lives doing good and standing up for what is right and true. And how are they going to discover God? Only if those of us who have found out already how wonderful he is are prepared to tell them about him, and introduce them to him!

All-age ideas

- Try this wine tasting sketch:

Presenter Good morning, everyone, and welcome to today's pick of the bottles with our expert wine taster, Jelly Golden! Good morning, Jelly, it's nice to have you with us again for today's tasting.

Jelly Golden Gosh, yes, we've certainly got some super tastes here. Let's start with this delicious red – just look at that glowing, ruby colour. You can almost smell the sunshine through the glass, can't you?

Presenter If you say so, Jelly. Shall I pour some out for you?

Jelly Golden *(Sniffs it)* Mmm! Wonderful aroma . . . warm summer days with a breath of a breeze . . . and just a faintest hint of honey. *(Tastes it)* Oh yes, it's so rich and mellow . . . I can taste loganberry, plum and, yes, strawberry as an exquisite aftertaste, all blended wonderfully in the grape. My word, it's really sun-packed . . . utterly delicious! It must be late summer 1992, and if I'm not mistaken, it's from that little valley a few kilometres north-west of Nuits St Georges. Here, you've simply got to try some for yourself! It's the only way to know how magnificent it really is!

Presenter OK, if you recommend it so highly, Jelly . . . Cheers!

- Use music as an introduction to the Isaiah reading and a background to it. Depending on the tastes of the congregation you could try part of Dvořák's *New World* symphony, some of Karl Jenkins' *Adiemus*, or a tape of natural sounds.

PROPER 2

Sunday between 10 and 16 February inclusive (if earlier than the Second Sunday before Lent)

2 Kings 5:1-14
Psalm 30
1 Corinthians 9:24-27
Mark 1:40-45

Jesus wants to heal us to wholeness, and to him no one is untouchable.

All-age talk

Invite a volunteer to run up the aisle as if they really want to win a race. Then ask them (or another) to run as if they aren't much bothered whether they win or not. Everyone can pick out the differences in the two performances.

Paul tells us to think of our lives as Christians being like running in a race we are determined to win. What will that mean? We'll be taking our following of Jesus very seriously, and trying very hard at it, practising it every day and building up our stamina. We'll be like 'professionals' instead of wishy-washy drifters. And we'll be getting better and stronger as we practise. If we don't bother, and don't take it seriously, we won't make much progress.

Today in the Gospel we are given another example of what it means to be a follower of Jesus. Let's look at how Jesus behaves with the man who has leprosy. Then we can practise living like that, as we try to follow Jesus.

But first, what does it mean to be a leper? (Lepers and leopards both have spots, but there the similarity ends, so make this clear!) Leprosy is a skin disease. When people get leprosy, they first find they lose the feeling in a finger, or a bit of the foot, and gradually the skin turns very white in patches. It is a bad illness, and people die of it if they don't get the medicines which can cure it. In Jesus' time, lepers were sent off to live on their own because they were thought of as 'unclean'. No one else was allowed to touch them. If they did, the law said they would become unclean as well.

So what did Jesus do? There was the leper, knowing Jesus had the power to heal him, but not sure that Jesus would want to have anything to do with someone as unclean as he was. And there was Jesus, so much wanting the man to be healed that he did something very shocking. He reached out . . . and *touched* the leper! Jesus wasn't afraid of the law saying he would be unclean; he just knew that this man, who had been untouchable for years, more than anything needed to feel touchable again. We know what happened – the man's skin was made better straightaway, so he could go and show the priest and have it all made official; he was no longer unclean.

As Christians, we are followers of Jesus, so now we know a bit more about how we must try to live. We must try wanting the best for people, and we must try not to shut people off or have nothing to do with them just because they are poorer than us, or richer than us, ill, smelly or just different. Even if other people avoid them, as Christians we must never think of anyone as unclean or untouchable, because God made and loves every one of us.

All-age ideas

- Have some information displayed on leprosy aid, and have a collection for this important work. For more details contact: The Leprosy Mission, Goldhay Way, Orton Goldhay, Peterborough PE2 5GZ.

- Act out the Gospel, with the healed leper going down the aisle, telling individuals and groups in the congregation all about it at the end.

- Following the Gospel, try this mime. An 'untouchable' moves around in a group of people, who shrink away from him whenever he comes near, and turn their backs on him when he asks for their help. Then Jesus moves behind one of the group and gradually their actions fall in step with Jesus'. This time, when the untouchable comes near, Jesus stretches out his hands towards him, and so the person he is shadowing also reaches out. Through this touch, the untouchable realises he is accepted, and the others gradually come closer, losing their fear.

PROPER 3

Sunday between 17 and 23 February inclusive (if earlier than the Second Sunday before Lent)

Isaiah 43:18-25
Psalm 41
2 Corinthians 1:18-22
Mark 2:1-12

The Son of Man has authority on earth to forgive sins.

All-age talk

Start by explaining that you have a list of hard things to do, and you are going to ask everyone which they think is easiest of two options. They can have a moment to think or confer, and then a show of hands should indicate their communal decision. Here are the options:

1. Learning to ride a bike, or learning to talk.
2. Earning money, or saving your money up without spending any.
3. Doing something brave, or doing something thoughtful.
4. Talking non-stop for an hour, or being completely quiet for an hour.

In today's Gospel we heard Jesus ask a similar question. Remind them of the circumstances – the crowds, the paralysed man let down through the roof, Jesus telling him his sins are forgiven, and the scribes, knowing that only God can forgive sins, horrified that Jesus has done what only God can do. This was his question – which is it easier to say to the paralysed man: 'Your sins are forgiven you' or 'Stand up, take your bed and walk'?

Let's try and work out an answer. First we need to make a few things clear. Who is the only one who can forgive sins? It's God. And what about a paralysed man suddenly being able to get up and walk home – who's the only one able to do that? Once again, it's God. So in a way, Jesus is saying to the scribes, 'Is it easier for me to act like God, or to act like God?' And what would be the answer to that? There'd be no difference; both are a natural way for God to behave.

The man's body was paralysed – that meant he couldn't make it move freely. When Jesus healed him he was free to move about again. It's like that when our lives are jammed by sin and guilt about bad things we've done in the past. When God forgives us completely, he unjams us, so we are free to live happily again.

All-age ideas

- Have a choral reading of the Isaiah passage, with sound effects from such things as a rainstick, sand in a plastic bottle, small bells, and handfuls of rice sprinkled on to a drum or tambourine skin (rice and drum are both in a shallow bowl).

- Have the Gospel printed out, with movement directions, so everyone can join in. Jesus and the scribes know who they are beforehand. The scribes stand in a group a little apart from the congregation, and Jesus stands in the centre of the crowd. At verse 2 everyone moves out from their seats into the aisle. In verse 4 everyone looks up, and their eyes follow an imaginary bed as it comes down at Jesus' feet. Jesus says the words to the imaginary paralysed man, and the scribes pull their beards and look offended. Jesus looks over to them and says his words (verses 8-11). As the narrator reads about the man getting up, all the crowd gasp in amazement and say together their words in verse 12.

181

SECOND SUNDAY BEFORE LENT

Proverbs 8:1, 22-31
Psalm 104:24-35
Colossians 1:15-20
John 1:1-14

Christ is the image of the unseen God.

All-age talk

Bring with you a few Mr Men books – *Mr Muddle*, *Mr Bump* and *Mr Chatterbox*, for instance – and invite the children to help you explain to the adults why they are called those names. Point out how they look just like their names and their characters. In those stories we put shapes to ways of behaving. Meeting the characters helps us understand what it's really like to be muddled, accident-prone or extra chatty.

Our readings today look at the same kind of idea. To help us understand more about what God is like, we meet aspects of his nature as characters. We are introduced to Miss Wisdom and Mr Word.

Miss Wisdom shows us how wise God is. It isn't just a question of knowing lots of clever things (though God is all-knowing). Miss Wisdom is described as being beautiful, happy, and excited by all the loveliness of creation, enjoying it almost like a good friendship. So we now know that God's nature is like that.

Then, in the Gospel reading, written by John, we meet Mr Word. We are told he's been around as long as God has. From his name we would expect Mr Word to be telling us something, as that's what words do. And we'd be right, because that's exactly what Mr Word does. Mr Word is a person whose life tells us exactly what God is like. (Show a large version of the picture below.)

He's a bit like a human speech bubble – which God himself is speaking. And although we may not usually call him by his name of Word, we do actually know him already quite well. He is Jesus, God's Mr Word, who was born as a baby at Christmas, and lived on earth loving, healing and teaching, very wisely.

All-age ideas

- Display slides of the world's richness and beauty with music, as an act of thanksgiving.

- Lay down a long stretch of lining paper in the aisle and invite the younger children to draw and colour all the lovely, good things that live and grow and swim and fly in the world. (They could do this during the readings.) Have this laid down on the floor for everyone to reflect on as they come to receive Communion.

Sunday before Lent

2 Kings 2:1-12
Psalm 50:1-6
2 Corinthians 4:3-6
Mark 9:2-9

God's glory shows.

All-age talk

Bring along something that gets transformed when the light in it is switched on, such as an illuminated globe, table lamp or OHP with a picture on acetate. Or people can look at the church's stained glass windows.

First show it without being lit up, and then switch on to show the difference. When it is lit up we can see patterns and colours that we may not have seen before. Today we heard in our Gospel reading about a time when three of Jesus' friends saw him 'lit up', and it really did help them to see him in a new light.

We're none of us used to that kind of thing happening, so it all sounds rather strange to us. Let's imagine ourselves that morning, climbing up a steep, rocky mountain path with Jesus leading the way, and Peter, James and John struggling to keep up behind him. We're all panting a bit, and sometimes pieces of stone and grit get stuck in our sandals. We might see a lizard or two sitting in the early sun, and hear the wind in the grass.

When we reach the very top, we can see all around us, with the lake and the little villages far below. It's like being on top of the world. Jesus has come up here to pray. He knows that he needs to get away from the crowds sometimes to spend time quietly with his Father in heaven. We all need that, too.

Peter, James and John suddenly realise that Jesus is looking different. He seems to be shining – Mark says 'dazzling' which is like when you look into the sun and have to screw up your eyes because it's just too bright to look at comfortably. It's as if they're looking at the presence of God

184

himself, here on the mountain. And Jesus isn't alone, either. As if he's in heaven, rather than standing on the mountain grass, two other people are talking with him, and we recognise them from history. One is Moses, who led the people out of slavery in Egypt and gave the people God's ten commandments, and the other is a prophet from long ago called Elijah; both very holy people.

It's actually very frightening – all so holy and full of glory, and so unusual. It's then that the cloud comes over, and I think Peter, James and John have shielded their eyes from all the brightness. They hear a voice speaking out of the cloud, and they somehow know that it is God speaking. What is it he's saying? 'This is my beloved Son: listen to him.'

That's Jesus he's talking about! And we've just seen with our own eyes that Jesus wears God's glory – we just haven't been allowed to notice it before.

When the disciples look up again the brightness has passed, and their friend Jesus is standing there on his own, looking quite normal. On the way down the mountain path he tells them not to say anything about what they have seen and shared until he has risen from the dead. Peter, James and John don't really understand yet that Jesus will have to suffer death before he is glorified.

But we know what happened, don't we? And perhaps it helped Jesus' friends, when the first Easter Day came, and they met Jesus alive again that evening, to see how God had been glorified even in the dark sadness of the cross, because even there Jesus had been shining with love for us all.

All-age ideas

- Have lots of candles everywhere today, grouped together, on window ledges, surrounded by flowers, and, if it is a Communion service, held by the children around the altar during the Eucharistic prayer.

- For the time of penitence:
  You laid aside your glory to set us free.

185

Lord have mercy:
Lord have mercy.

Obediently you went to the cross.

Christ have mercy:
Christ have mercy.

Your shining love shows up our selfishness.

Lord have mercy:
Lord have mercy.

FIRST SUNDAY OF LENT

Genesis 9:8-17
Psalm 25:1-10
1 Peter 3:18-22
Mark 1:9-15

After his Baptism Jesus is led by the Spirit into the wilderness before returning to proclaim God's kingdom.

All-age talk

Bring with you a compass, and a chart showing that there are six weeks before Easter Day.

Explain that in six weeks' time it will be Good Friday and Easter Day, when we will all be celebrating Jesus rising to new life that lasts for ever, after being put to death on the cross. That's such a very special, important thing to celebrate that the Church decided we all need a few weeks to get ourselves ready for it. Time to think carefully about what it means to be a follower of Jesus. Time to sort our lives out a bit. Draw attention to the change of colour in church – purple is quite a serious, thoughtful colour, to match our serious, thoughtful mood in these next six weeks, which are called Lent.

Why *six* weeks? We are told that when Jesus had gone to the river Jordan and been baptised by John, he went straight off into the desert hills, to spend forty days, getting ready to tell everyone the good news of God's kingdom. He didn't get ready by reading lots of books and doing lots of homework, or talking to lots of people. He got ready by living very simply, even going without food, and letting God lead him into the areas he needed to think about. He wanted to spend time finding out what God really wanted him to do with his life.

So, as the Church, we're going to do the same. Today is the day we all set off into the desert for six weeks. What do you think we'll need to take with us? Produce various items of combat gear, and mountain-walking clothing and equipment. Then kick it all away. We're not going to need any of this. All we need is one thing – a compass. What does a

187

compass do? It helps you walk in the right direction. We need a special compass that always points us in God's direction.

Explain that you happen to have just the compass we need, and produce a cross – a wall-hanging one is about the right size so that people can see it easily. This is a special compass for us to take into the desert of Lent with us. Hold the cross flat. It points us always towards God's love, and at the same time it points back at ourselves. We can't pretend in this desert. We've got to be honest to God about who we are and how we are thinking and feeling. That's the only way the compass will point us in the right direction. Are we ready for the desert of Lent?

The first step on our journey is to agree to live more simply for a while, and go wherever God takes us. We can spend this week doing that, remembering to use our compass every day.

All-age ideas

- At this time of recommitment, invite everyone to close their fists and think of all the things they would hate to have to give up. Thank God for them all, recognising that we are not owners of anything, but stewards. As they feel ready to, invite everyone to open their hands slowly to God, with all that is in there open to be used in his service of love. As they do so they can say, silently, 'Here I am, Lord. I offer you my life.'

- For the credal statement consider using the baptismal promises, with everyone gathered around the font to remind them of their baptism.

- Construct a rainbow of God's promise for people to walk under as they come into church. This might be a paper archway fixed with Blu-Tack above the doorway and painted by the children.

SECOND SUNDAY OF LENT

Genesis 17:1-7, 15-16
Psalm 22:23-31
Romans 4:13-25
Mark 8:31-38

A commitment of faith has far-reaching implications.

All-age talk

Bring along some advertisements which proclaim special offers which look absolutely wonderful bargains, and completely good news, but when you read the small print you find all sorts of extra bad news which makes the bargain not quite so fantastic as it first sounded. (For example: '£50 OFF! – when you spend £300'; 'Children go free! – but only if you travel after 10 o'clock and buy two full adult fares'.) Of course, those who designed the advertisement hope that by the time you've read the small print you are so keen to take them up on the offer that you will be prepared to go along with the extra requirements.

Jesus is never like that with us; he is always completely open and honest. Jesus always gives us both the good and the bad news, gently but firmly, because he loves and respects us. That's why we know that we can trust him absolutely. (At this point you could have two people doing the conversation in the All-age Ideas.) If someone is always saying how wonderful we are, even when we know very well that we have not been at all wonderful, we can't really trust that they are telling us the truth. But if someone tells us the bad news when it's bad and the good news when it's good, then we know we *can* trust them to be honest with us.

In today's reading from Mark's Gospel, we find the disciples expecting something that can't happen. They are thinking that, as Jesus is the Messiah, he is one day going to lead an army to drive out the Romans from their country. Jesus takes the risk of them rejecting him, and being angry and disappointed, rather than lead them into false hopes.

189

In effect he's saying, 'OK, so you know I'm the Messiah, but I'm afraid I'm not going to be the kind of Messiah you're all expecting. It's not going to look like a great victory at first – it's going to look like complete failure.' Jesus tells them he's going to be killed, all as part of his work as Messiah.

And Peter can't bear to hear this 'bad news'. He tries to shut it out and to persuade Jesus that he must be mistaken. Sometimes we do the same. Perhaps Jesus nudges us to give something up, or change something in our lives, or make friends with someone we don't want to, and we spend a lot of time and energy pretending not to hear, or pretending that God must be mistaken. He isn't mistaken; he's just being lovingly honest with us, and we take it as bad news because we don't want to hear it as the truth.

We've reached the second week of Lent, our thoughtful time in the desert. Let's use the coming week to take notice when Jesus nudges us, and go along with what he suggests, even if it means giving up something we like doing.

All-age ideas

- Use this form of confession:

  Forgive the lies we live and the truth we hide;

  Lord, have mercy,

  Lord, have mercy.

  Forgive our fear of speaking out
  for what we know is right;

  Christ, have mercy,

  Christ, have mercy.

  Forgive us seeing only what we want to see
  and hearing only what we want to hear;

  Lord, have mercy,

  Lord, have mercy.

- This conversation sketch shows how we like people to be honest with us – unless they say something we don't like!

Jasmin and Mel are in a dress shop. Jasmin is trying various clothes against herself.

Jasmin What about this, Mel? What d'you think?

Mel Yeah, that's cool.

Jasmin Or this one?

Mel Yeah, great!

Jasmin There's this one as well . . .

Mel Yeah, fantastic!

Jasmin Oh, go on, Mel, they can't all look brilliant. Tell me what you really think.

Mel OK. I think they all make you look old.

Jasmin *(cross)* Oh, nice! I thought you were my friend! *(walks out of shop, calling back to Mel)* Anyway, you've got as much fashion sense as a woolly vest!

Mel *(shrugs)* Thought she wanted me to be honest.

THIRD SUNDAY OF LENT

Exodus 20:1-17
Psalm 19
1 Corinthians 1:18-25
John 2:13-22

God's wisdom may shock us. Jesus, obedient to God's Law and fulfilling it, dies a death which, according to the Law, makes him cursed.

All-age talk

Begin by asking for some volunteers to read the following conversations.

1. Mum: David, it's time to stop playing and go to bed now.

   David: Oh, but Mum, I'm much too busy!

2. Dad: Turn that music down, Gary!!

   Gary: But I like it, and it needs to be loud!!

3. Hilda: George, it's time you gave up smoking.

   George: But, Hilda, it's my decision, and none of your business.

4. Fred: Now, Mother, you need to wear a hearing aid.

   Mother: What's that, Fred?

   Fred: A HEARING AID! YOU NEED TO WEAR ONE, MOTHER.

   Mother: No, I don't – I can hear perfectly when people bother to speak up properly!

All through our lives we're supposed to be obedient, and all through our lives we prefer to do as we like!

Today we're on the third week of our desert journey together through Lent. And we're going to look at what it means to be obedient, and why it's a good thing to work at, even though we all find it so very difficult to do what we're told.

Scatter the ten commandments, written on pieces of card, over the aisle, or stick them with Blu-Tack on to pillars.

192

In our first reading we heard the ten command-ments – ten useful rules to help us live God's way. These rules were given to the people through Moses, the great leader who had led the people out of slavery in Egypt. They've all been in the desert for quite a long time, learning to be God's people, like we are through Lent. And then God gives them the Law, which they are told to obey. They are still good rules, and when Jesus came he didn't say, 'Listen, everyone, now I've come you don't need to bother with all those commandments any more!' Jesus insisted that he had come not to destroy the Law but to fulfil it, to fill it full of God's love.

So Jesus summed all the rules up in two parcels. Produce one bag labelled 'Love God' and another one labelled 'Love one another', and sort out the first four commandments into the first bag and the second six into the second bag. That makes them easier for us to carry around in our heads (hold a bag in each hand), but we need to remember what's inside each bag, and take them out to look at from time to time, like we've done today.

So Jesus thought it was good to be obedient. He was obedient to his heavenly Father, even when that turned out to mean he had to die on the cross! The reason he was obedient was because he really understood why it was important.

If we understand the reason for being obedient, we're much more likely to try and do what we're told. If Fred's mother really understood how diffi-cult it was becoming for the family to talk to her without her hearing aid, she'd *want* to wear it. If Gary really understood how hard it was for his Dad to concentrate on his work with the music so loud, he'd *want* to turn it down a bit.

In other words, obedience is all to do with acting out of love. As we get to understand and love God better, we shall find we are more and more keen to do what he wants us to.

All-age ideas

- Use the first reading as an extended form of penitence, encouraging everyone to get to know the commandments by adding visual clues. (These might be a large number one; a blank piece of paper; a cardboard speech bubble with 'Keep it clean' written on it; a calendar page with Sunday circled in red; a bunch of flowers with a label reading, 'To Mum and Dad'; a gun; a wedding congratulations card; a swag bag; a file clearly labelled 'Lies'; and a thought bubble with 'If only . . .' written on it.)

- Have two voices to read the commandments alternately, with someone holding up a finger as each is read, till all ten fingers are held up. In their places, everyone can follow this counting off process as a focus. After each commandment, pause for reflection before everyone says, 'Lord, have mercy on us'.

- If the commandments are permanently displayed in church, draw attention to them; if not, have them written up and displayed on walls and pillars for today.

FOURTH SUNDAY OF LENT: MOTHERING SUNDAY

Exodus 2:1-10 or
  1 Samuel 1:20-28
Psalm 34:11-20 or
  Psalm 127:1-4
2 Corinthians 1:3-7 or
  Colossians 3:12-17
Luke 2:33-35 or
  John 19:25-27

God provides comfort in all our troubles and sufferings.

All-age talk

If you have stained glass windows, direct people to look at these during the talk. If not, bring a picture or poster which is full of contrasting colours, or have such a picture or photograph made into an OHP acetate and project it.

Draw everyone's attention to the different colours that are used, asking them to pick out their favourites, to pick out some of the darks and some of the lights. Perhaps there are also different textures involved.

Explain that family life is rather like this – a whole picture made up of bright and dark colours, of happy and sad times, angry and contented times, worrying and relaxed times. Ask for examples of these from everyone, so that our own colourful picture starts to take shape.

It isn't just us on our own who are making these family works of art – it's us and God together, and we go on making them all through our lives. Whenever there is a whole lot of dark, sad colour, God will brighten it for us with the rich, warm colours of his comforting love.

All-age ideas

• Families or households can bring the offertory and collect people's gifts, welcome people into church and lead the intercessions.

195

- As the offerings are presented, and the gifts of bread and wine placed on the holy table, ask everyone to hold hands remembering that they too are part of the offering. The president can then use these words:

  Blessed are you, Lord God of all creation.
  Of your goodness we have ourselves to offer,
  fruit of the womb and available
  for your service.
  Blessed be God for ever.

- Either of the Old Testament readings can be mimed by a family while it is read by a narrator.

- For the intercessions, suggest that people form themselves into small clusters, and pray in those groups for one another's families, for the local schools and for the homes in the streets the group members live and work in.

FIFTH SUNDAY OF LENT

Jeremiah 31:31-34
Psalm 51:1-12 or
  Psalm 119:9-16
Hebrews 5:5-10
John 12:20-33

Through Christ's death, full life would come to people of all nations and generations.

All-age talk

Bring with you a box of assorted sweets or chocolates, and invite a couple of volunteers to choose one. Ask them why they chose it (there may be no reason at all) and whether they are happy with the choice they made.

All our life long we are faced with making choices. Sometimes the choice isn't that important; if you make a mistake and choose a chocolate which isn't a favourite, you haven't lost out much. But sometimes the choices are more important. Invite a couple of car owners to talk about their choice of car and whether they are happy with their decision. Ask a student which A levels they have chosen to take, or which degree course, and a child what they have chosen to do for a birthday treat.

Sometimes we have to choose even more important things than that! Let's look at a very hard choice Jesus had to make, which we heard about in today's Gospel. Jesus knew that he was alive on earth for a very important mission – he was here to save the world, and he really wanted to do that, because he loved the people. But there was a problem. He also knew that saving the world was bound to land him in terrible pain and danger, more pain and agony than anyone has ever faced before or since. It would involve taking on himself all the sin and evil of the world, and going on loving right through it.

So he had the choice – to go ahead with saving the world, taking on the suffering as part of the deal, or to avoid all that appalling suffering by opting out, in which case the world would have no hope of being saved.

And it wasn't an easy thing to choose. Everything human in him screamed out against going through the pain of it all; but everything divine in him pleaded for love and compassion, and selfless giving whatever the cost.

We know what Jesus chose. Love won, and he chose to go through hell, giving up everything, including his life, just so that we could be set free to live.

All-age ideas

- As a form of Confession, provide everyone with the words of Psalm 51 and play a recording of it (*Miserere* by Allegri) so they can have a time of meditation and sorrow for sin before the absolution. For children use a larger print and this simplified version:

O God, have mercy on me
because you are loving.
I know about the things I have done wrong
and cannot forget them.
Please wipe out all my wrong doing.
Wash away my guilt
and make me clean again.
Give me back the joy that comes
when you save me.
Keep me strong by giving me a willing spirit.

- Use music as a background to the reading from Jeremiah – such as the slow movement from Mozart's *Clarinet Concerto*, or *The Swan* by Saint-Saëns.

Palm Sunday

Liturgy of the Palms:
Mark 11:1-11 or
  John 12:12-16
Psalm 118:1-2, 19-24

Liturgy of the Passion:
Isaiah 50:4-9a
Psalm 31:9-16
Philippians 2:5-11
Mark 14:1-15:47 or
Mark 15:1-39 (40-47)

As the Messiah, Jesus enters Jerusalem, knowing that he rides towards rejection and death in order to save his people.

All-age talk

Beforehand make two large, clear signs, one saying, 'Hosanna! Blessed is he who comes in the name of the Lord!' and the other, 'Crucify him!'

First remind everyone of the way the crowds had welcomed Jesus as he rode into Jerusalem on a donkey. They were all giving him the red-carpet welcome, throwing down greenery and their coats for the donkey to walk on, and waving palm branches as flags, cheering and singing. One of the things they shouted was from one of their traditional songs, which we know as Psalms: 'Hosanna! Blessed is he who comes in the name of the Lord!' (Everyone can shout this as loudly as possible.) It meant they were welcoming Jesus as the new King David; they were really excited, expecting Jesus to become their king and throw out all the Romans so they would be free again. They thought they really wanted God's kingdom.

Sometimes we are like the people in this crowd. We get all excited by Jesus, and promise to work with him, and feel ready to do anything to help the kingdom come. 'Let your kingdom come! Let *your* will be done!' we pray, and we really mean it. We work hard at our praying, and do our best to be loving and honest in the way we live. We give God the worship we know he deserves, and we give of ourselves simply because we are filled with love for him.

199

In today's Gospel we heard what happened to Jesus on Good Friday. It makes us very sad to hear what happened to our friend, and we might find ourselves thinking that we wouldn't have left him alone like his friends did; we would have been there for him; we would at least have prayed with him and not fallen asleep in the garden.

But the crowd remind us of something rather nasty. They weren't singing 'Hosanna!' any more. They were shouting, 'Crucify him!' (All shout this.) And although we wish it wasn't true, we all know there are times when we do that as well. Those times when we know very well what is the right and loving thing to do or say, and we want Jesus out of the way so we can be as unkind and dishonest as we like. It's hard work having Jesus there when we don't want to be loving, or humble, or obedient. At those times we don't much like his kingdom. Every time that happens we are joining the crowd which shouted, 'Crucify him!'

Let's remember that, and pull ourselves together when it next happens so that, instead, we shout with our lives, 'Hosanna! Blessed is he who comes in the name of the Lord!'

All-age ideas

- Involve the whole congregation in the reading of the Passion, giving individuals and small groups their parts to read and having the words the crowds say held up on placards, or shown on a screen using an OHP.

- If you are having an outdoor procession, make it a festal one, with children shaking instruments and waving greenery or streamers, and everyone singing songs they know well and won't need words for. Consider inviting the local schools to take part, and possibly a real donkey.

- Use Psalm 118 with the congregation joining in the refrains (His love endures for ever) and a 'cheerleader' calling the other sections.

EASTER DAY

Acts 10:34-43 or
  Isaiah 25:6-9
Psalm 118:1-2, 14-24
1 Corinthians 15:1-11
  or Acts 10:34-43
John 20:1-18 or
  Mark 16:1-8

Jesus is alive; Love has won the victory over sin and death.

All-age talk

Bring along a hot cross bun, a chocolate Easter egg, an ordinary hen's egg, and one of those fluffy Easter chickens.

Ask a volunteer to take the first object (the hot cross bun) around the church so everyone can see what it is. As they go, explain that these buns remind us that because God loves us so much he was prepared to live among us in person, and go on loving us even when he was arrested, tortured and killed on a cross. It's in Jesus' life, and in his experience on the cross, that we can 'taste and see that God is good'.

Now for the next object (another volunteer does the rounds) which is . . . a hen's egg. The egg looks as dead as a smooth oval stone, but we know better. We know that if the egg is fertilised, and kept warm by the mother hen, that hard shell will start to crack, and into the world will climb . . . (a volunteer takes the chick around) a fluffy yellow chick, full of life! So the egg reminds us that what looked dead and hopeless on Good Friday (when Jesus' dead body was taken down from the cross, and it seemed he had failed as a Saviour) was actually full of new life, because on the third day after that, Jesus broke out of death to be alive for ever!

And so our last object (a volunteer walks the chocolate Easter egg around) is what we all enjoy having on Easter Day – chocolate Easter eggs. They're always bright and colourful, fun and delicious, and that's because Easter Day is party time for Christians! Today we celebrate the fantastic truth

201

that Jesus Christ is Lord – Love has won the victory over evil and death for ever!

All-age ideas

- Consider having a sunrise Easter morning service, followed by shared breakfast. Beginning in the darkness and witnessing the light building during worship is such a powerful image of resurrection that it seems a pity to miss out on it!

- Encourage people to make their own miniature Easter gardens and bring them to church on Easter Day.

- Fill the church with flowers and candles to celebrate – perhaps different groups and clubs could undertake an arrangement each, or work on an Easter banner. Ideas for banners: 'Love is stronger than death'; 'Jesus is alive!'; 'New life'; 'He is not here, he is risen'.

Second Sunday of Easter

Acts 4:32-35
Psalm 133
1 John 1:1–2:2
John 20:19-31

Our faith in the risen Christ is bound to affect the way we live.

All-age talk

Bring with you some items of clothing which alter the way you move when wearing them, such as a pair of flippers, a pair of very heavy boots, a pair of binoculars and a pair of very high-heeled shoes.

Invite volunteers to demonstrate that when they are wearing (or looking through) these, it changes the way they walk. The changed way of moving is all part of wearing them.

It isn't only clothes and footwear which change our way of going about; it's our thoughts and feelings as well. If we've just won a match, if the person we love has just realised they love us as well, if the mortgage rate has gone down, or if we've just been fed and changed, then the whole day looks rosy and happy, and we'll pass on our feel-good factor in the way we react to those we meet. On the other hand, if the cat's been sick on the new sofa, you've lost your spelling list and know you haven't learnt the words, if the 7.27 is half an hour late, or you're hungry and your bottom feels damp and sore, then those feelings will probably make you less friendly and forgiving, and far more grumpy!

When we look at today's picture of life in the early Church, we're struck by how much love there seems to be in the community. Something is making these people happy to look after one another instead of fighting and arguing, and happy to share everything instead of looking after number one all the time. So what is making them like this? It must be something very good and very powerful!

It's all to do with them knowing something. They *know* that Jesus is alive and among them, so

203

they are living in Jesus' company all the time. Jesus being there changes the way they live.

Now for a big question we all need to ask ourselves. Would anyone guess, just from looking at how we think and speak and behave, that we *knew* Jesus was living here among us?

He is, so it should show!

All-age ideas

- As part of the Confession, or immediately after the all-age talk, have someone knocking loudly on the outside of the church door. Then in the quietness, someone says:

    If the risen Jesus knocked on the door of our church, would we be happy to let him in? *(Pause for reflection)*

    If he knocked on the door of our home, would we want to let him in?
    (Pause)

    What would he be glad to find?
    (Pause)

    What would he be sad to find?
    (Pause)

    (The door is knocked again)
    Come, Lord Jesus, we welcome you among us!

- Cut out the letters of 'LIFE' from foil and stand candles along them where people will see them as they come to receive Communion. During the reading from 1 John, someone lights these candles, which remain burning for the rest of the service.

THIRD SUNDAY OF EASTER

Acts 3:12-19
Psalm 4
1 John 3:1-7
Luke 24:36b-48

Having redeemed us by his death, Jesus can offer us the forgiveness of our sin, which sets us free to live.

All-age talk

Bring along a dry stick and a growing plant with fresh shoots.

Easter is all about a different, richer sort of life which we can now have, thanks to Jesus going through death for us. It's a bit like the difference between this dry stick (show it) and this one which is full of life and growing (show it).

In today's Gospel we heard that Jesus comes into the locked room where his frightened disciples have met (display a number 1), and puts their minds at rest, so they aren't terrified, even though they are open-mouthed at God's power. Then (display a number 2) Jesus explains things to them so that they begin to understand that Jesus had to die and rise again, and lastly (display a number 3) he commissions them, sending them out to set everyone free to live this way (the shooting plant) instead of that (the dry stick).

We may not have noticed, but there are lots and lots of dry sticks like this walking around. Dry stick people are often disguised. Because they are only interested in money, possessions or following their own wants, they often look attractive, with the latest everything to wear, smear on their face, drive or play. But a look into their eyes will show you that they are hard and dry as people, without any real joy, and may well be full of worries and anxieties, guilt and fear. Many of these dry sticks really know that this way of living is 'second best' but don't know how to get fully alive, or are frightened that God would say they were beyond his help.

Today is great news for all dry sticks! In going through evil and death without love slipping, even for a split second, Jesus has won for us all the victory over the sin and evil which dries us up and stops us living God's full life. All any dry stick needs is God's forgiveness; as they admit to themselves and to God what they are really like, and how they are cut off from him, his forgiveness starts to work on them, turning them into vibrant, warm, joy-filled people, happy to be living God's full life, and no longer bullied and caged by things that don't matter.

All-age ideas

- Use a song such as *Purify my heart* as everyone calls to mind the areas in their lives and attitudes where repentance is needed, and *I'm accepted, I'm forgiven* as God's forgiveness is pronounced.

- On a long piece of lining paper, have a dead-looking twig drawn. During the talk, or the intercessions, the younger children can stick on green leaves (pre-cut) so that this dead branch is given new life. The title of this could be: 'Dear friends, we are now God's children' (1 John 3:2).

FOURTH SUNDAY OF EASTER

Acts 4:5-12
Psalm 23
1 John 3:16-24
John 10:11-18

'I am the Good Shepherd and I lay down my life for the sheep.'

All-age talk

Gather all the young children in the aisle and get them doing sheepy things like eating grass, drinking from a stream, sitting and chewing, and bleating. Place a few older children around the edges of the building to be wolves and bears, sheep-watching and hoping for a chance to eat one of the lambs. They can howl sadly as they wait, or growl. One person is a good shepherd, keeping an eye on the flock, and watching out for any signs of wolves and bears.

The wild animals are waiting for the shepherd to go for a break, or doze off, because that's when they might get a chance to grab a lamb or sheep. But this shepherd loves his sheep, and that means he isn't going to give the wild animals any opportunity to attack the flock. He's ready to defend them with his life, if necessary.

Now swap the shepherd for a hired hand. Here's a different flock, with a different shepherd, further up the valley. The wild animals have gathered here now, and they're still waiting. (Howls and growls.) A couple of wolves start to come closer, but this shepherd doesn't frighten them away – he just runs away! The wolves get more confident. They're getting dangerously close, and the sheep are all huddled together, when that good shepherd walks up, with stones in his catapult, and the wolves back off quick!

Thank the sheep and wild animals for their help, and explain that Jesus is like a good shepherd, who cares for us and looks after us, protecting us from evil. He loves us, so he isn't going to let us down, and is even ready to lay down his life for his sheep.

207

In fact, as we know, Jesus did just that – he was ready to lay down his life to set us free.

All-age ideas

- Have a simple cut-out of a sheep on white paper for everyone and give these out as people come into church. Use them as a focus in a time of prayer, as an alternative form of intercession. First people write their name on their sheep, and hold it as they pray for people in need of Jesus' shepherding in their own families, in this country and in the world. Then swap the sheep around by collecting them and distributing them again. Now everyone can pray for the person named on the sheep, knowing at the same time that they are being prayed for themselves.

- Incorporate a crook and sheep or lambs in one of the flower arrangements, using meadow flowers and grasses.

FIFTH SUNDAY OF EASTER

Acts 8:26-40
Psalm 22:25-31
1 John 4:7-21
John 15:1-8

To produce fruit we need to be joined on to the true vine.

All-age talk

Cut six long strips of green crepe paper, or lengths of green string. Also prepare ten cut-out bunches of grapes from coloured paper.

Begin by suggesting that if you came in and said you were a pair of curtains, everyone would probably tell you to pull yourself together. But in our Gospel today we find Jesus saying, 'I am a grape vine.' Obviously he wasn't really a grape vine, was he? So what on earth did he mean?

To help us understand, we're going to make a kind of grape vine. Ask one volunteer to hold a green string in each hand, and two others to tie the strings round their waists. They can now hold four strings between them, and four others can tie these round their waists. Now for the fruit. Each of the last four people can hold a bunch of grapes in each hand (eight altogether) and the other two bunches can be stuck with a loop of sticky tape to the fronts of the second two volunteers.

In just a short time, and with just a few people, we've grown quite a big vine and ten bunches of fruit! Just imagine how much fruit there would be if everyone here was joined on the vine.

Jesus said he was the true vine and his Father was the gardener, looking after the growing and helping the vine branches to produce as much fruit as possible. Obviously these branches are only able to produce their fruit if they're joined on to the vine, because all the life-giving sap feeds them and if they're cut off they don't get anything to keep them alive.

Jesus was really saying that if we want our lives to produce fruit like love, joy, peace, patience,

209

kindness, goodness, faithfulness, gentleness and self-control (stick these labels on the grapes), then we have to make really sure that we're joined up to Jesus and in touch with him. We need his life in us all the time. We need to keep in touch with him every day!

All-age ideas

- Include some vine leaves, or vine-like plants, and grapes in one of the flower arrangements today.

- Just before the Peace, ask everyone to hold hands like a vine, with the end person in each 'chain' holding on to a processional cross, held centrally in the church. As everyone stands like this, the following words are said: 'I am the true vine, my Father is the gardener. Apart from me you can do nothing.' You can then go straight on to 'We are the body of Christ . . .'.

- Pray particularly for church mission links today, including any updates and specific prayer concerns, photos and maps. Have an airmail open letter for people to add their encouragement and send it off today.

Sixth Sunday of Easter

Acts 10:44-48
Psalm 98
1 John 5:1-6
John 15:9-17

We are to love one another as Jesus loves us.

All-age talk

Begin with the sketch in all-age ideas, which looks at the difference between servants and friends.

Invite everyone to spot the differences. Also ask those involved in the sketch what differences they felt. The kind of things which might come up are the sense of involvement and belonging which friendship gives, compared with the distance and lack of co-operation in servants; the difference in how they feel valued, and what response is acceptable.

Point out that Jesus said he was no longer thinking of us as servants but as friends. That means we are people he is happy to talk things over with, co-operate with and involve in the work. There is going to be companionship and perhaps some good-natured teasing. Above all is the sense that we are in this together, and enjoying one another's company.

Another thing Jesus said is that we are to love one another in the way he loves us. So how is that? How does Jesus love us? Collect people's ideas; here are some that occurred to me:

- as friends
- with affection
- treating us seriously
- understanding us
- with honesty
- with forgiveness
- ready to put himself out for us
- with faithfulness
- consistently

Is this how we are treating other people? Or is it how we treat the people we like? As Christians we

211

don't have the option to choose certain people to treat with God's love, while behaving how we feel with all the rest. We can't claim to love God and then decide that some people aren't worth treating with respect or understanding.

Of course it isn't easy to love one another like this. Lots of people are difficult to love in God's way – perhaps we are, ourselves! But when we look at how amazingly God treats us, copying his way of loving is the very least we can do. And the often surprising thing is that putting ourselves out and making the effort to live God's way is very rewarding, and makes us feel much happier inside.

All-age ideas

- This sketch can be used to introduce the talk. Write two titles on sheets of paper or slate boards, which are walked around the church before each section, so everyone can see them: 'The Servant' and 'The Friends'.

The Servant

The employer is talking on his mobile phone, pacing up and down, with a file open. He's sorting out some complex problem. The office cleaner comes in with feather duster and starts cleaning.

Mr King   *(Into phone)* Quite . . . Quite . . . But look at these figures on page 24 . . . *(catches sight of Marg the cleaner)* Marg, get me a strong coffee. And a doughnut or something. *(Returns to phone)* Yes, these figures should have warned us . . . Well, the point is what can we do about it now?

(Marg reappears with coffee and doughnut.)

Marg   Coffee, Mr King. It's strong. And a doughnut. *(Puts them on desk)*

Mr King   *(Still on phone, listening and making 'mm' noises. Motions with hand for Marg not to interrupt him as he's busy.)* Sorry, Steve, say that again . . . the schedules systematically reduced what? . . . Oh, I see. Yes, of course. So what are you going to do about it?

(Marg continues dusting.)

Mr King   *(Still on phone)* Marg, get me the February file – it's there on my desk. *(Talks into phone)* It seems to me we can possibly get ourselves out of this mess, Steve. I've just had an idea.

(Marg brings the February file to Mr King.)

Marg   The February file, Mr King.

Mr King   *(Takes it without thanking her and starts looking in it. Into phone he says)* Yes, here it is! I'm looking at these figures for the second week of February . . .

(Marg goes back to the dusting. The desk phone rings.)

Mr King   Answer that, Marg.

Marg   *(Picks up phone)* Hello, Mr King's office. Well, he's very busy at the moment, in an important meeting . . . Oh, I've no idea, I'm only the cleaner here. I just do what I'm told.

The Friends

Norman and Pete walk up to a bench and sit down. They put their rucksacks down.

Pete   Phew! That was quite a climb, wasn't it. What a view, though, eh?

Norman   Marvellous, isn't it. *(Pause)* Anyway, you were saying about your inter-view . . .

Pete   Oh yeah, that's right. So we've got to decide whether to move or not, basically. And that's a big decision to make.

Norman   How does Sheila feel about moving? She settled here, isn't she?

Pete	Yes, it would be quite a wrench for her, but you know Sheila, she's willing to give it a go if she feels it's what God wants for us.
Norman	Funny, isn't it. This time last year, there you were just made redundant, and no hopes for the future, and now this new door seems to be opening for you. I'm really happy for you, Pete.
Pete	Thanks, Norman. Well, you've been a good friend through all this – it's always good to talk things over with you. Shall we be on our way then? *(They get up and walk off.)*
All four characters	I no longer call you servants, because a servant doesn't know his master's business. Instead I have called you friends.

• As an alternative form of Intercession, try these prayers with a repeated response:

In our homes, at work and at school
help us to love one another.

In what we think and speak and do
help us to love one another.

When there are arguments
and when we disagree
help us to love one another.

When we are tired and not feeling our best
help us to love one another.

Every moment of every day,
whether it's easy or hard,
help us to love one another.

ASCENSION DAY

Acts 1:1-11 or
  Daniel 7:9-14
Psalm 47 or
  Psalm 93
Ephesians 1:15-23 or
  Acts 1:1-11
Luke 24:44-53

Having bought back our freedom with the giving of his life, Jesus enters into the full glory to which he is entitled.

All-age talk

Prepare a large cardboard arrow pointer, and have the following things ready to use as signs: a Nativity play manger or a doll wrapped in swaddling clothes; a pair of sandals; a cross; a lit candle.

Explain that today is called Ascension Day (which means 'going up' day). Why is it called that? Because we are remembering the day when Jesus went out to a hill with his disciples this time after Easter, and they watched him returning to heaven. We are told that it looked as if Jesus was going upwards, not so much up into the sky as out of their sight. It was the last time Jesus was seen on the earth.

In a way, today is like being with the disciples on the top of a hill. If we look down one way (point the arrow backwards) we can look back to when Jesus first came to earth, as a newborn baby. (A volunteer takes the baby or crib to stand as far as possible behind the arrow, but where they are still visible.) We're not just looking back to last Christmas (which does seem quite a long time ago!) but right to when Jesus was actually born. From our Ascension hilltop we look back to Jesus' life, and all the travelling around he did. (The sandals are taken behind the arrow, but closer than the crib.) Jesus walked from town to village, healing the sick, teaching and loving the people. We can look back to the cross (the cross is brought behind the arrow, closer than the sandals) which Jesus' love brought him to, and we can remember what a great victory over evil was won there. And we can look back to that first Easter morning (the lit candle is brought close

215

behind the arrow) when death couldn't hold the Lord of life any longer, and Jesus burst into fuller life than ever.

(Turn the arrow to point upwards.) So today marks the end of Jesus' time on earth, tied to a time and a place, and we are celebrating his triumphant return to heaven, having won the victory and defeated the power of evil for us.

(Turn the arrow to face forwards.) From today's Ascension hill we are also looking forward into the future. And what do we find in the future? Among other things, all of us, sitting in this church in this year, with our lives transformed and filled with joy because of our faith in the living Jesus!

All-age ideas

- Decorate the church with clouds cut from white paper and crowns cut from gold wrapping paper.

- After the narrative of the Ascension is read, have a group of people who walk forward as if following Jesus, while music plays. They kneel in worship and then all raise their eyes slowly upwards, till they are staring at the sky. They hold this position for a few moments, and then stand up, amazed and suddenly smiling at one another. As they turn to walk joyfully down the aisle, they shout above the music: 'Let the kingdom come! In every time, in every place, let the kingdom come!' (Suitable music: 'Morning' from Grieg's *Peer Gynt* Suite.)

SEVENTH SUNDAY OF EASTER

Acts 1:15-17, 21-26
Psalm 1
1 John 5:9-13
John 17:6-19

Although now hidden from our sight, Jesus lives for ever, and in him we can live the Resurrection life even while we are on earth.

All-age talk

Prepare two short straws amongst a few full-length ones. Begin by asking for volunteers. Let all those who have offered come out but explain that as you only need two we'll choose by the fairest way – each pulling a straw from your hand. Those who pull the short straws will be the ones chosen.

Label these two Matthias and Joseph, and remind everyone of the problem the disciples had – there had been twelve of them and now there were eleven. Why wasn't Judas with them any more? Because he had helped get Jesus arrested, and afterwards gone and taken his own life.

So Peter organised the believers to choose a replacement for Judas. Who would they choose? If we were going to choose, what kind of person would we look at? What would that person have to have done?

(Collect the ideas, and re-read verses 21 and 22.) Well, there were two possibilities, Matthias and Joseph, both good people, and both having been with Jesus all through his ministry. So how are they to choose? They did it in two stages:

1. They prayed, asking God to show them the one he wanted.

2. They used the straw method, like we used.

In effect, they had decided not to take on the choosing themselves, but felt it was so important that they should leave it entirely up to God's leading. And the one who drew the short straw was Matthias. That didn't mean that God liked Matthias

217

better; it was just that God had another important job for Joseph, and knew that Matthias was going to be most useful for this one.

Although Jesus has ascended into heaven, and we can't see him here any more, he's very much with us *all* the time. When we have difficult decisions to make and important, scary things to organise, we don't have to do them alone. We can do what the disciples did, and keep in touch with God, wanting only what God wants and asking him to show us what that is. We can practise wanting what God wants at all kinds of times, just by saying in our hearts, 'Let your will be done!'

All-age ideas

- The mime suggested for Ascension Day could be used today instead.

- Consider using *The Message* for the reading from 1 John 5.

- Play some quiet, reflective music (either live or recorded) while everyone sits for a few minutes, opening themselves to God's possibilities for them and choosing to commit themselves to their calling as Christians.

PENTECOST

Acts 2:1-21 or
   Ezekiel 37:1-14
Psalm 104:24-34, 35b
Romans 8:22-27 or
   Acts 2:1-21
John 15:26-27;
   16:4b-15

The Holy Spirit of God is poured out in power on the expectant disciples, just as Jesus promised.

All-age talk

Cut flame shapes from red and orange paper (shiny paper is specially good), and have these given out to everyone as they come into church.

Remind everyone of how the Holy Spirit came, with the noise of a gale-force wind (the noise of which they can try making), and looking like fire which split up into flames resting on each of those in the room. (Everyone holds up the flame they have been given, so there are flames all over the church.) That was how it seemed from the outside.

Inside each person, what was going on?

- (Display an exclamation mark.) The disciples were stunned by this display of the power of God. God meant business, and was clearly way outside their control. God was in charge.

- (Display a red rose or a red heart.) They suddenly knew, at first hand, what God's love really meant. They felt full of it, and it made them very happy and excited. They wanted to tell God all about it!

- (Display an empty speech bubble.) They wanted to tell other people all about it too. They wanted everyone to know God like this, because they knew how wonderful it was. And God's love in them made them want to share the good news, rather than keep it to themselves.

God is still pouring out his Holy Spirit on people, every day. Wherever anyone seriously wants to have the powerful love of God living in them, the Spirit will come and fill them.

Often we don't really want God that close. This

may be because we are scared of God being really powerful; but we forget that with power which is full of love and goodness we don't need to be afraid. Mostly we just aren't bothered enough to take God seriously. The disciples were spending all day in God's company, waiting and hoping for the Holy Spirit to come. How much time do we spend focusing our attention on God?

If we want something really badly, it fills our thinking all the time. Suppose we really want a computer, or to be a ballet dancer, or to drive a car. We'll be reading all the advertisements and the magazines, spending out on lessons and working hard at them, making sure we're in touch with the experts and so on.

So if each of us, and all of us as a church, are impressed by today's reading, and serious about wanting a fresh outpouring of the Holy Spirit, what can we do?

We can really want more of God in our lives. We can want that when we wake up, all through the day, and when we lay our heads down on the pillow at night. We can want it so much that we start listening to God and getting our lives ready to receive his gift. We can put God at the centre, instead of somewhere squeezed in at the edge.

And God will come to us, filling us with his Holy Spirit, and transforming our lives.

All-age ideas

- Give the children red, orange and yellow streamers to dance with in one or two of the hymns, or the Gloria.

- Make posters or banners with flame shapes of paper stuck on and words describing the life of the Spirit, such as love, joy and peace, power and gentleness.

- Arrange to have a parish party or picnic, so that the fellowship of the community is enriched. Suggest that everyone wears something flame-coloured.

TRINITY SUNDAY

Isaiah 6:1-8
Psalm 29
Romans 8:12-17
John 3:1-17

The mysterious and holy nature of the one true God is beyond our understanding, but it is both communal harmony and individual personality, Father, Son and Holy Spirit.

All-age talk

Prepare either an OHP acetate or a very large cut-out triangle, as shown.

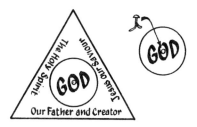

Also have three equal strips of card and three paper fasteners, or bring three equal strips of a large-scale construction toy, with the appropriate nuts and bolts – basically any three things which can construct a triangle.

Start by asking a volunteer to help by making a triangle from the separate strips. As they work, do a commentary on the progress, observing the sides move in all directions until that final join, at which point the triangle is a strong shape, with each two sides holding the other firm. It's such a strong shape that it is used in building – bridges, towers, pylons, roof rafters, for example.

Why on earth are we looking at triangles in church today? Explain that today we are exploring the nature of God. Will we be able to end up by bedtime knowing all about God, then? No! Human brains aren't big enough to cope with understanding our great God completely, any more than your hamster can understand completely what it is to be human.

But as your hamster gets to know you and

221

become your friend, little by little he will understand more about you, as much as a hamster can.

So, back to the triangles. Perhaps they can help us understand a little bit more about the great and powerful God of love. (Show your triangle.)

We've seen how strong one three-sided shape can be. Suppose for a minute we look at the threeness and oneness of God as a bit like this triangle. We know that there is only one true God, and here we have one triangle. We know that God is our Father and Creator, Jesus our Saviour and the Holy Spirit. (Turn the triangle round as you refer to each side.) Whichever aspect of God we focus on, we are always looking at God in all his truth and fullness.

And there's another thing. The Son always directs us to see the Father and the Spirit; the Father always directs us to see the Son and the Spirit; and the Spirit always directs us to see the Father and the Son. (Turn the triangle round as you refer to each side.)

Of course, our God is far, far more than a mathematical shape – the God of love and glory is much more than a triangle! But the way a triangle works can help us understand a little more of how, for God, it's no problem to be one God, who is also Father, Son and Spirit. It's as natural for God to be like that as it is for us humans to be able to be in one place and think about being somewhere else, both at the same time.

All-age ideas

- Have music as a background to the Isaiah reading, starting with just the music, and imagining it all as you read it. The natural gaps between ideas and pictures will be filled with the music and enable those who are listening to sense the vision rather than just hearing about it.

- The Gospel can be read as a conversation, with Nicodemus arriving as the narrator describes this.

- The children can wave green streamers in one of the hymns today – not as a performance, or for anyone to see, but simply as part of their own worship offering.

PROPER 4

Sunday between 29 May and 4 June inclusive (if after Trinity Sunday)

1 Samuel 3:1-10 (11-20)
  or Deuteronomy
    5:12-15
Psalm 139:1-6, 13-18
  or Psalm 81:1-10
2 Corinthians 4:5-12
Mark 2:23-3:6

Jesus has the words of eternal life – he sheds light on a right attitude to the Law.

All-age talk

Bring along a piggy bank and some money to put in it. Some people keep their treasure safe in one of these, adding to it each week. (Drop some more money in.) Sometimes people will get an ordinary jar and fill it up with coins, so that soon it's full of treasure. The pot or jar is often very ordinary – it's the treasure inside which makes it special. People in Roman times used to use clay pots to keep their silver jewellery safe – archaeologists have found them, still guarding their treasure!

In one of the letters Saint Paul wrote, he said he thought we were all a bit like clay pots holding special treasure. As people we're just ordinary, but we've got something as Christians which is extraordinary – real treasure. It's being friends with God through Jesus which changes our lives from being ordinary to extra-special, because we're actually holding in us the love of the living God.

What does that look like?

We saw a bit of what it looks like in today's Gospel. Jesus notices a man whose arm is withered and shrunk so he can't use it, and immediately his heart goes out to that man, and more than anything he wants to set the man's arm free to wave and lift things, touch and hold things. His love for the man makes Jesus sad for him having to struggle, and he sets about mending him.

What Jesus doesn't do is look at the man and think, 'Ah yes, a man with an arm which doesn't work. But it's the Sabbath, so that's too bad; he'll

223

have to stay like that – I'm not going to break the rules and heal him today.'

Well, of course he wouldn't think like that, because you can't be full of God's love and yet shut off your compassion. What Jesus did was the Godly, loving thing – he used his power of healing and set that man free, there and then, rules or no rules. And that offended the teachers of the Law. They had become so keen to keep the Law that they'd actually blocked God's light out, and couldn't see that Jesus was keeping the real spirit of the Law completely – love God and love one another.

So here we are as ordinary human pots, holding in us the light of God, and that's going to affect the way we live. We'll have to reach out in love and mercy to those around us, and that might mean we end up offending some people. But who cares? If we're living God's way, then we won't be offending God, and if living that way makes us unpopular sometimes, we'll be in very good company.

All-age ideas

- Collect the offering today in earthenware pots, such as unglazed flower pots.

- Have a flower arrangement expressing God's love and mercy, using warm colours and gentle, delicate foliage. Label it 'Jesus displays God's love and mercy'.

PROPER 5

Sunday between 5 and 11 June inclusive (if after Trinity Sunday)

1 Samuel 8:4-11 (12-15)
  16-20 (11:14-15) or
  Genesis 3:8-15
Psalm 138 or
  Psalm 130
2 Corinthians
  4:13-5:1
Mark 3:20-35

Anyone who does God's will is considered a close family member of Jesus.

All-age talk

Whether we live on our own or with others, most of us have family; we may not see them that often, or we may see them every day. Some of them may no longer be alive, but they are still our family. Mothers and fathers, stepmothers and stepfathers, parents-in-law and children-in-law, sons and daughters, grandchildren and grandparents, aunts and uncles, brothers, sisters and cousins, are all family. We share the same genes (and sometimes the same jeans).

In every family there is something called a family resemblance – a family likeness. (Some family members may be willing to demonstrate this likeness.) The DNA within our families shows up right across the generations; in my family there's the Morris nose, the Rackett musicality, and the Orme stubborn determination, for instance!

In our Gospel reading today, Jesus says something rather amazing. He's sitting teaching, surrounded by a closely packed circle of faces, people from all kinds of different families and backgrounds, with all kinds of different looks and personalities. They are there because they sense that in Jesus they can get closer to the true, living God than they've ever been before. They are so keen that they are hanging on every word Jesus speaks, listening to him intently.

And as he looks around at them sitting there, and sees in their eyes their love of God, Jesus happily counts all of them – and everyone else who does the will of God – as members of his close family. He is saying that any of us, however ordinary or damaged, whatever natural family we belong to, or are separated from, are close members of Jesus' family! So you can think of yourself as closely related to Jesus. And that makes all of us in the Church part of the same family, distinguished by the family likeness of doing God's will – living the loving way.

All-age ideas

- As a form of confession:

  Father, there have been times
  when we have seen your will but failed to do it.
  Lord, have mercy.
  Lord, have mercy.

  Jesus, there have been times
  when we have behaved more as your enemies
  than members of your close family.
  Christ, have mercy.
  Christ, have mercy.

  Spirit, there have been times
  when we have ignored your prompting
  and preferred to live selfishly.
  Lord, have mercy.
  Lord, have mercy.

- If you are using the reading from Genesis, have it read by a group of people, so that the different voices are clearly brought out.

PROPER 6

Sunday between 12 and 18 June inclusive (if after Trinity Sunday)

1 Samuel 15:34-16:13
   or Ezekiel 17:22-24
Psalm 20 or
   Psalm 92:1-4, 12-15
2 Corinthians 5:6-10
   (11-13) 14-17
Mark 4:26-34

From small beginnings, and by God's power, the kingdom of heaven grows.

All-age talk

Ask everyone to look at the mustard seeds they were given when they came into church (*see* All-age Ideas), and have a couple of tall people (or children on chairs) to stand back to back, spreading their arms out. In Israel, where Jesus was living, mustard seeds often grow as big as this, and local people will even use the mustard branches for firewood, so that tiny seed really does grow into a spreading tree, and all the birds love to sit in the shelter of its branches. The mustard plant provides spicy flavour, fuel and shelter.

Why did Jesus talk to the people about mustard? He often used things that were all around to help describe spiritual things which can't be seen. Perhaps there was a shady mustard plant right there where they were sitting, and some of its seeds scattered on the ground.

Anyway, Jesus said that the way God's kingdom grows is a bit like the way a mustard seed grows. It starts off very little, and gradually grows very big. The little seed may be an act of kindness you do which makes someone think to themselves, 'I wonder! She's become a Christian, and it seems to be changing her for the better. Perhaps there's something in this Jesus person after all!' Or perhaps you're the one in the office who insists on honesty, even if you'd gain from being less than honest, and someone notices and starts thinking. Or perhaps someone notices that you aren't that impressed by the labels people are wearing, even though you're cool.

227

The little seed of God's kingdom is someone opening themselves up a tiny bit to the possibility of God being real and active in their lives. Gradually it grows in them. Perhaps they begin to ask more questions about God, perhaps they read some Bible stories or start coming with you to church sometimes. Then they start to pray! Now that little seed can really begin to grow, because God can lead the person step by step as they get in touch with him more and more. Sometimes the kingdom of God grows gradually as they pick up teaching week by week, or look at God's world with new eyes. At other times there's a sudden growth spurt. Perhaps a verse of scripture hits home and they realise how their life needs to change, or they suddenly sense God real and close to them in a time of sadness or joy.

Perhaps over a few years, or a lifetime, that little seed has grown in the person until they are so full of God in their life that they are standing tall and strong in faith, and many come to them, now, for spiritual help and comfort, like the birds coming to the mustard plant's spreading branches.

How is the growing of God's kingdom coming on in us? Is it still a tiny seed, full of hope but not yet developed very much? Has it just started to sprout, putting out roots and shoots? Is it not growing very much at all at the moment, or has it recently had a big surge of growth and is excitedly stretching upwards and outwards in the knowledge of God's love and forgiveness? Or is it already tall and strong, providing spiritual shelter for others, scattering other seeds all around, and happy to be full of God's life?

What a world it would be, with churchfuls of people in it, in whom the kingdom of God was growing strong as mustard trees! It could happen. The people could be us.

All-age ideas

- Have bowls of mustard seeds and invite people to take one as they come in. They can plant their mustard seed when they get home.

- If you are having the Samuel reading, have it mimed alongside the narration, with Samuel shaking his head as each young man files past, and a younger child being called down from the hills (or the balcony if you have one!) to be anointed king.

- If practical, include some mustard plant in one of the flower arrangements.

Proper 7

Sunday between 19 and 25 June inclusive (if after Trinity Sunday)

1 Samuel 17:(1a, 4-11,
  19-23) 32-49 or
  1 Samuel 17:57-18:5,
  10-16 or Job 38:1-11
Psalm 9:9-20 or
  Psalm 133 or
  Psalm 107:1-3, 23-32
2 Corinthians 6:1-13
Mark 4:35-41

What kind of person is this? Even the wind and waves obey him.

All-age talk

If practical, arrange for a couple of people to bring their (well-controlled) pet into church this morning. If this isn't possible, interview a couple of pet owners.

Look at the animals and talk to the owners about what they like to eat, and how they like to play. Then ask them about how their pets behave when they are frightened or feel threatened, and how they calm them down.

It isn't just pets who get worried, angry and upset – it's humans as well. Today we heard about a time when Jesus' friends were so frightened they were panicking, and we saw how Jesus calmed them down. Remind them that Jesus was actually asleep, and the disciples woke him up to tell him to start worrying! With the stormy waves pitching the boat up and down, and the water coming in over the side it was beginning to look like a *Titanic* situation, and there was Jesus fast asleep in the bottom of the boat!

Sometimes we do that, too, if life seems very scary, and everything seems to be going wildly out of control. We scream out to Jesus, demanding that he notices and *does* something, instead of being so calm about it all. It's almost as if we want him to panic as well.

Jesus, once he's been thoroughly shaken awake, doesn't seem to be caught up in the excitement. But he can see that it isn't only the disciples who are churned up – it's the weather as well. And perhaps he sees here a good way to help the disciples understand more about who he is. The disciples are so scared at the moment that they can't take anything in. So instead of calming them down, Jesus calms the wind and the waves. As the howling wind eases and settles quietly again, and the pounding waves flatten back to a gentle lapping around the battered boat, the disciples calm down as well. In this lull they recover themselves and stop panicking.

What does Jesus do next – wait for their applause? Go back to sleep? In fact we find he now starts teaching them, because they are now calm enough to listen. He talks to them about trusting God, even in the middle of raging storms.

Often in life we will find that when we have invited Jesus into our boat – into our life – we don't get so thrown by all the stormy problems (things like quarrels in friendships, loved ones moving away, financial problems, pressure and stress at work). And if we're panicking about them so much that we can't hear Jesus helping us to weather the storm, then often we'll find we're given a breather – a bit of space – where things are calmed down long enough for us to realise that, with God in charge, we don't actually need to be terrified.

All-age ideas

- As an introduction to the talk, try this eye-opener to the wonder of God:

   Voice 1 The highest waterfall on earth is Angel in Venezuela, where the water plunges down 979 metres. The River Nile in Africa is 6,695 kilometres long. At its greatest depth the Pacific Ocean is 11,034 metres deep.
   What a universe.
   What a God!

   Voice 2 Adult salmon in the open sea find their way by rivers and streams and up waterfalls, to the actual pool they

hatched in, years before.
What a universe.
What a God!

Voice 3   Our Milky Way galaxy is one of thousands of millions of galaxies, all appar-
ently rushing away from one another
at tremendous speeds. The nearest
neighbour star to our solar system is
24 million million miles away.
What a universe.
What a God!

• During the reading of the Gospel, some of the
children can interpret the mood of the sea by
moving a length of blue fabric, first gently, then
increasingly stormily until Jesus' calming of the
waves, to which they quickly react, restoring the
gentle calm once more.

PROPER 8

Sunday between 26 June and 2 July inclusive

2 Samuel 1:1, 17-27 or
   Wisdom of
   Solomon 1:13-15;
    2:23-24
Psalm 130 or
  Psalm 30 or
  Lamentations
   3:23-33
2 Corinthians 8:7-15
Mark 5:21-43

God's power can reach even into death and draw out life.

All-age talk

Make a circle of chairs near where you are talking, or a circle of rope – something which is clearly visible.

Explain that this circle is like our life here on earth. How do we get into it? By being born. (Invite a couple of people to make their way in.) While we're here what do we do? We eat, play, work, talk, make friends (and perhaps some enemies), watch TV, learn things and so on. (Everyone can add to the list.) Invite the people in the circle of life to mime some of those things as they are suggested.

How do we get out of the circle of life? By being born backwards? We get out of this life by dying. (The volunteers make their way out of the circle.) Point out that they're not in the circle any more, but they're in a huge space, much bigger than they might have imagined, if they'd only ever known life in the circle. And outside this space is the whole outdoors, stretching outwards and upwards, and full of light and colour, better than anything we could imagine if we'd only ever known the circle as 'life'. Just as the circle isn't the only place, so this earthly life isn't all there is to complete life – Jesus told us that life after our death can be full, rich and wonderful; and it's Jesus who has made that possible for us.

Remind everyone of the story in today's Gospel, about a twelve-year-old girl dying. Everyone is specially sad when a young person dies, because they haven't had a chance to live very long here and enjoy our world. But Jesus brings that young girl back to life again. It's as if from inside the circle of life he calls to her on the outside and she comes back in again, completely better, and hungry. He could do that because Jesus *is* life. When she next died, perhaps after a long and happy time on earth, she closed her eyes on earthly life and heard Jesus calling her name again into life – but this time from heaven, into the life with Jesus that lasts for ever.

When we get to the point of our death, Jesus will be there, calling us out into that life, and welcoming us. And because we know his voice, from a lifetime of prayer, we'll be very happy to move towards it and find him, waiting for us there.

All-age ideas

- Act out the Gospel for today, either miming it as it is narrated, or preparing it with spoken parts. These can stick to the actual Gospel translation or people can express the meaning in their own words.

- As a reflective time of penitence try this dialogue:

   Left side If we were praying for rain, would we bring our umbrellas?

   All Forgive us, Lord; we place limitations on what is possible with you.

   Right side If we pray for others, are we ready to be part of the answer?

   All Forgive us, Lord; we mark off boundaries where your kingdom is not welcome, because it makes demands on our time.

   Play some reflective music during which the following is said:

   Voice 1 Come, Holy Spirit and draw us into full life.

   Voice 2 Come, Holy Spirit and melt our hearts of stone.

   The music continues, or have a period of silence before the reassurance of God's forgiveness.

PROPER 9

Sunday between 3 and 9 July inclusive

2 Samuel 5:1-5, 9-10
  or Ezekiel 2:1-5
Psalm 48 or
  Psalm 123
2 Corinthians 12:2-10
Mark 6:1-13

If we are not ready to listen to the truth, we will not hear it.

All-age talk

You will need a sieve – either a culinary or a gardening one. Also some appropriate thing to sieve – such as flour or earth.

First talk about the way we tend to hear if someone offers us a second chocolate biscuit, a raise in our pay, or a special discount, but not if we're being told to clean out the rabbit, work late, empty the washing machine or make a dental appointment. As the saying goes, 'There's none so deaf as those who won't hear'.

Explain that what our minds do is to sieve information which comes in through the ears and the eyes. Produce the sieve and start sieving so that everyone can see this process in action. The holes are a particular size so that everything is sorted automatically. Big lumps are not wanted, so they won't fit through the holes. Fine flour or earth can get through quite easily. The rest only gets through if we process it a bit first (breaking it down to a suitable size) and if it can't be broken down (like stones in the earth or a free sticker in the flour) then it doesn't get through the sieve at all.

In just the same way we are selective about what we hear, and mostly that is very useful to us. It stops us turning into nervous wrecks by the daily news items, for instance.

But sometimes we try to keep out what God is trying to make us hear. Just because it may mean us changing something in our lives, we treat it as a threat, and shut it out, when really it is helping us to get rid of a way of thinking or behaving which is not healthy to us or others, physically, mentally or spiritually. What we need is to have 'God's Word'- shaped holes in our sieves, so that God's Word can always get through.

All-age ideas

- As a response to the all-age talk, suggest that we trace the cross on our ears and eyes (or do this to one another) as a sign that we really want to see and hear what God is telling us, whether it is comforting or challenging.

- Cover the base of a flat sieve with paper which has a cross cut out of it. Place this where people will see it as they come to receive Communion, or as they leave the church, and label it: 'Lord, may we hear and receive your Word'.

- In the Ezekiel reading, mime the prophet walking about trying to tell people good news. Each in turn starts to listen, but some shrug and shake their heads, getting on with what they were doing before, and others look affronted or angry, and deliberately turn their backs on the prophet, folding their arms and sticking their chins in the air.

PROPER 10

Sunday between 10 and 16 July inclusive

2 Samuel 6:1-5, 12b-19
   or Amos 7:7-15
Psalm 24 or
   Psalm 85:8-13
Ephesians 1:3-14
Mark 6:14-29

Those who speak out God's will are bound to be vulnerable to rejection and abuse.

All-age talk

As everyone comes into church give them a length of thin wool or string and a paper clip.

Begin by inviting everyone to fix one end of the wool or string into the paper-clip so that they have made a plumb-line. Explain that this can be used to check whether things which are supposed to be upright are as straight as they should be. (They can try out their plumb-lines on the pews and chairs around them, and some volunteers can check other uprights in the building.)

Suppose we were to find that one of our upright walls was actually leaning over – would it be useful to know that? Yes, because then we could get in the workmen and pay them to put it right.

Suppose we just got angry and offended at being told our wall wasn't as upright as it should be? We could tell the person with the plumb-line to go away and not talk about it to us any more. That way we could go on pretending our wall was upright, and we wouldn't have to pay to put it right. But if we did that, the upright wall might go on leaning more and more until in the end the whole building crashed down in rubble.

Plumb-lines for checking how straight and upright things are can be very useful indeed. Being told where things aren't as upright as they should be can also be very useful indeed.

One of the things prophets do is draw our attention to places in our lives or our society or our church community which are leaning dangerously and are nowhere near as upright as they should be.

237

How do people react to being told? We heard today how the people shouted at the prophet Amos to go and leave them alone. They didn't want to hear, because they didn't want the bother of putting things right. We also heard about John the Baptist, who had shown King Herod and his new wife where their life wasn't as upright as it should be. How did they react? By throwing John into prison where they couldn't hear him, and then having him put to death so he couldn't speak out God's truth to them any more. They didn't want to hear it because they didn't want to put things right.

How good are we at hearing God whispering lovingly into our hearts about the places in our lives that should be standing tall and upright but are instead leaning a little, or leaning dangerously? Do we thank him for showing it to us so we can quickly put things right again, or do we get sulky or angry and pretend we haven't heard?

All-age ideas

- On upright pillars or walls stick strips of coloured paper with Bible verses on them which emphasise the importance and joy of living upright lives in God's love and strength. Here are some possible verses: Psalm 85:10 – Love and faithfulness meet together; Psalm 24:1 – The earth is the Lord's and everything in it; Psalm 32:11 – Sing, all you who are upright in heart; Psalm 112:2 – The generation of the upright will be blessed; Proverbs 3:32 – The Lord takes the upright into his confidence; Ephesians 1:4 – He chose us in him before the creation of the world to be holy and blameless in his sight; Matthew 22:37-39 – Love God and love one another.

- Have someone dancing during one of the hymns or times of praise and worship.

Proper 11

Sunday between 14 and 23 July inclusive

2 Samuel 7:1-14a or
   Jeremiah 23:1-6
Psalm 89:20-37 or
   Psalm 23
Ephesians 2:11-22
Mark 6:30-34, 53-56

Like a good shepherd, Jesus sees the needs of his people and always responds with love.

All-age talk

Bring along a crowded diary or calendar, and other gadgets for coping with busy lifestyles, such as a computerised notebook, a laptop, mobile phone, alarm clock or fax message.

Ask a few children to walk up and down pretending to be talking on their mobiles or driving their cars, while you talk about the way we can now continue our office work walking along the High Street or on the train. We can send messages by e-mail or fax so that they get there almost immediately. All this enables us to spend more and more of our time being fully at work if we happen to have a job, with increasing pressure and decreasing space in our lives. People have either far too much work than is healthy or none at all, and leisure activities often have to slot in some frantic physical activity to compensate for all the physically inactive work of brain and adrenaline. Advertisements shout at us to buy this, choose that, look like them; the newspapers and magazines advise us what to think and how to behave, and often we believe their lies. We are like a scattered flock of sheep racing in different directions, without knowing where we are or where we are going.

(Stop the children and have them sit down very still wherever they are.)

Today we heard in the Gospel about Jesus' busy ministry of teaching and healing, listening and encouraging. When he and his disciples had been hard at work for days, and were really tired and drained, they'd get into a boat to sail across the

239

lake for a bit of peace and quiet – only to find all the crowds had run round the edge of the lake and were already there waiting for them! Jesus didn't send them away and tell them what the office hours were, or put them on hold. He didn't ask Peter to change course and sail off somewhere else instead.

Instead, Jesus saw the lost and struggling lives, the need for reassurance and practical, wise teaching, the longing for healing and wholeness, and the hearts attracted to God but needing help to find him. And seeing all that, he loved them, with the deep affection of God's love; he climbed wearily out of the boat and fed them with the teaching and comforting they so badly needed. From stories like this of Jesus' ministry we know with certainty that God never ever turns any of us away. None of our needs or wounds or sorrows are hidden from him. Whenever we run around the lake to be there waiting for him, he will step on to our beach and minister to us, because he loves us. Like a good shepherd he is concerned for our well-being and leads us carefully and safely through time into the eternity of heaven.

All-age ideas

- Have a time of peace and reflection after the talk, where people can simply be still and settle themselves in God's loving company. Music is helpful at such times – possibly the music group singing *To be in your presence*, or a recording of Beethoven's *Pastoral Symphony* (No. 6) – the song of thanksgiving after the storm, for instance.

- Read the Gospel while walking around the church so that it is read on the move.

- Consider a parish away-day for some relaxation and spiritual refreshment together.

PROPER 12

Sunday between 24 and 30 July inclusive

2 Samuel 11:1-15 or
   2 Kings 4:42-44
Psalm 14 or
   Psalm 145:10-18
Ephesians 3:14-21
John 6:1-21

Out of God's riches, a great crowd is fed and satisfied from a small offering of food.

All-age talk

If you have an ancient building you can direct people to look at how steps or pews are worn away by generations of people simply walking on the step or holding the end of the pew. Or you could show a well-used copy of a Bible, worn out and falling apart just by being handled and read every day. (It is said that Bibles which are falling apart are read by people who are not.) You could show an old and well-loved teddy, threadbare through daily loving.

Each step, each picking up of a book, each cuddling of a bear is in itself only a slight action which we can't imagine would do much. But day by day, over the years, the effect of all those little actions starts to show quite dramatically. Little actions turn out to be very important. Even a smile can spread wider than we might think. There's an old children's poem about that:

> Smile awhile, and when you smile
> another smiles, and soon
> there's miles and miles of smiles
> and life's worthwhile
> because you smile!

Today we heard about one boy and his packed lunch. What was the point of him offering that when there were so many thousands of people to feed? Perhaps we think he might as well have just eaten it himself! But look at what happened when, instead of that, the boy wanted to offer what he had to share. Jesus used it. He blessed the gift that was offered and then all the people were fed, with some left over.

Those who have been God's friends for a long time will have noticed that God is very good at giving us more than we asked for, and giving in ways we hadn't thought of! But he does need us to offer what we have, whether that's time, money or talents and skills. Basically what we have to offer is ourselves. And when we do that, God can use the rest of our life here in ways we haven't even thought of, blessing people who perhaps we haven't even met yet, and may not meet till heaven. If we offer ourselves at the start of every day, then every day can be used for some wonderful good that wouldn't otherwise happen.

All-age ideas

- Have written on the day's handout, or displayed on a board or OHP, the words from John 6:14 – 'This must be the Prophet who's to come into the world!' Ask everyone to turn to those round them when you get to that section of the Gospel and whisper these words to one another a few times, getting louder each time.

- The words from Ephesians are so beautiful and encouraging. Have verses 16-19 written out, and ask both sides of the congregation to face one another and make Paul's prayer their own for the people facing them. Alternatively, ask everyone to pray in these words looking at the people next to them. Make sure no one is left out.

- Have a flower arrangement incorporating a child's lunch box.

PROPER 13

Sunday between 31 July and 6 August inclusive

2 Samuel 11:26-
  12:13a or Exodus
  16:2-4, 9-15
Psalm 51:1-12 or
  Psalm 78:23-29
Ephesians 4:1-16
John 6:24-35

Jesus is the Bread of Life who satisfies our hunger and sustains us on our journey to heaven.

All-age talk

Ask who had a meal yesterday, and express surprise that they are thinking of having another meal today – some have already eaten today and are still planning to eat lunch! They can explain to you that our bodies need food every day for them to stay strong and healthy, and for the children to grow. We run on food like a car runs on petrol.

Produce a loaf of bread. Remind everyone of how Jesus had fed all those people with enough bread and fish, and they had all enjoyed their meal. Now they are all running after Jesus the next day as well. Some of them want to hear what Jesus says, some want to come and be healed, some want to come because it's exciting going where everyone else is going and they don't want to miss out on anything. And lots are going because they remember those nice tuna sandwiches – the meal they ate with Jesus.

Why does Jesus want them to have come? Collect various ideas, and draw out that Jesus wants them to be there because they know they will meet with God if they're here with Jesus.

But Jesus knows all too well why some of them have really come, and he tells them so – 'You're looking for me because you ate the bread and were satisfied.'

And then he helps them to understand how God feeds us not just with bread for our bodies, while we live on this earth for seventy years or so (keep holding the bread), but in another way as well. He gives us spiritual food which keeps us alive through this life and right on into life beyond physical death. With that feeding we won't be finishing as soon as we die, but going on living for ever.

The people thought that sounded pretty good bread to have, and asked Jesus if he would give them some, so they could be fed spiritually as well as physically. And Jesus told them (lift the loaf of bread up high), 'I am the Bread of Life!' So it's Jesus himself who we feed on.

What does that mean? Obviously we're not like cannibals, eating Jesus up – he didn't mean that. But if we think how satisfied we feel when we have been very hungry and then eat a good meal, that's how our spirits feel when we spend time with Jesus – contented and satisfied, happy and full of energy and health. And just as we need to keep eating ordinary food every day, so we need to keep spending time with Jesus every day, so that, spiritually as well as physically, we will be growing strong and healthy, and we'll stay that way even when our physical bodies get old and weak, and when they stop working so that we die. Even then we'll be spiritually bounding with life and energy, ready to spend eternity alive in God's company.

All-age ideas

- Have wheat and bread as the focus of one of the flower arrangements today.

- Have a home-baked loaf brought up at the offertory for Communion.

- Have the words of the Gospel written out in full, with the people's words in bold, and someone else reading the words of Jesus, so that the Gospel becomes a lively teaching conversation.

PROPER 14

Sunday between 7 and 13 August inclusive

2 Samuel 18:5-9, 15,
  31-33 or
  1 Kings 19:4-8
Psalm 130 or
  Psalm 34:1-8
Ephesians 4:25-5:2
John 6:35, 41-51

Just as bread is the visible form of life-giving nourishment, so Jesus is the visible form of God's life-giving love.

All-age talk

Tell everyone that you are about to show them some vitamin B and some energy, some life-giving essence and some potential penicillin. Have a drum roll or dramatic chords on the organ as you whip out of a supermarket bag a loaf of bread.

But this is just an ordinary loaf of bread – how can something so natural and ordinary be all that clever, invisible, scientific stuff? Well, it is! If we were really hungry we could try it and find out how much better it made our bodies feel. (A hungry person can do this.) We eat our way through loaves and loaves of bread every day because we have found that it does us so much good and comes in a form we can easily take naturally – by eating!

So bread is the visible form of all kinds of goodness and life-giving nourishment. And when Jesus talked of himself being the Bread of Life, he was describing how he is the invisible God in visible form – in the familiar shape of a human being, who we can talk to, watch, touch and listen to.

So why couldn't the religious leaders understand? Why did they find it offensive that Jesus said this?

- Jesus seemed too normal and familiar – they knew him as their carpenter.
- They thought the Son of God should look greater than Moses.
- Their expectations blinded them to seeing the very person they had been waiting generations to meet, when he was standing there right in front of their eyes.

245

We too need to make sure we don't miss God in the ordinary. In fact, God made everything, so nothing is just ordinary, and God can speak to us through his creation, as long as we are ready to notice and listen. Here are some examples.

We often see heavy rain, but usually just moan about it spoiling our hair or stopping a match. Suppose we start actually looking at it and seeing there a picture of how generous and fulsome God is; so many individual droplets of rain – or petals in a tree full of blossom!

Or think of the wide night sky describing God's overarching love; the regular days, nights and seasons showing his faithfulness.

In a dog's dogginess and a young child's openness we can see God showing us the importance of being honestly ourselves; when we see weeds and wild flowers growing over a rubbish dump we see God telling us about redemption, and how everything can be made new and beautiful.

All we need to do is train our spiritual eyes to look, so that we don't miss out on anything God is wanting to say to us, even through the ordinary things.

All-age ideas

- Try this dance/mime of having our eyes and ears opened to notice God. Have a group (of mixed ages and genders) being very bustly and busy – perhaps miming the jobs they themselves do during the week. Walking around between them is someone who keeps tapping people on the arm to show them something, but they are just brushed aside, in a rather irritated way. Finally one person is alerted and shown a flower, so that they really look at it and then in wonder upwards, giving God thanks and praise. They too now wander around trying to alert others, until one by one they are all able to enjoy the world and recognise God's love in it. The mime ends with all raising their hands in worship and moving off back to their places, looking expectantly around them as they go.

- Have the separate sections of Ephesians used in a time of Penitence, like this:

Therefore each of you must put off falsehood and speak truthfully to his neighbour.

Lord, have mercy.
Lord, have mercy.

Do not let the sun go down
while you are still angry,
and do not give the devil a foothold.

Christ, have mercy.
Christ, have mercy.

Do not let any unwholesome talk
come out of your mouths,
but only what is helpful for building others up.

Lord, have mercy.
Lord, have mercy.

PROPER 15

Sunday between 14 and 20 August inclusive

1 Kings 2:10-12; 3:3-14
  or Proverbs 9:1-6
Psalm 111
  or Psalm 34:9-14
Ephesians 5:15-20
John 6:51-58

God's wisdom may appear foolishness without the God-given grace to understand.

All-age talk

Begin with the short quiz given in the All-age Ideas.

Are the people who knew the answers to our quiz necessarily the wisest people here? No. (Though of course they may be!) Real wisdom is different from knowing lots of facts. Remind everyone of the Brownie story about the wise owl. The children are sent to her because they want to find out who will be the little people who do secret good turns all around their house, and wise owl tells them to go to a pond in the woods and recite a poem. (Any Brownies, present and past, can join in the poem!)

Twist me and turn me and show me the elf;
I looked in the water and there saw . . . MYSELF!

The owl had been very wise because she had been able to help the children understand a deep kind of magic – whenever they did their good turns, they would be not just Imogen and Rebecca, but real Brownies! And they'd go on being Brownies whenever they did their good turns, long after they'd become Guides and grown up and had their own children who were learning the wisdom of the wise owl!

Wise people are good to go to when you want to talk things over, but you don't want to be told exactly what to do. Wise people are those who really listen to you – to how you are feeling inside as well as what you are saying. Wise people think carefully before they speak, and like learning from their mistakes.

We could say that WISDOM is all about
Walking In Simplicity Dreaming Of More

or we could say that to become WISE we need to
Wonder and ask questions
Imagine
Seek God
Expect to learn from him

All-age ideas

- Have lady Wisdom and lady Folly both calling out to invite people their way, as a group walks up and down deciding, one by one. Each lady has a big sign on a stick. On the front these say 'Wisdom' and 'Folly', and on the back there are pictures of a rising sun with rays of light, and a skull. As each person decides to go down one way or the other, the lady in the chosen place turns her notice around so that the person can't see it but the rest of the congregation can.

- Consider making some pictures from the newspapers into acetates to project on an OHP. (Office shops will do this for you.) Play some music such as Britten's *War Requiem* or the soundtrack from the film *Schindler's List* as you project the pictures and then verses 15-16 from the Ephesians passage.

- The quiz:
    1. What is H_2O?
    2. How many legs does a spider have?
    3. What animal pretended to be Red Riding Hood's grandma?
    4. What is the current exchange rate for dollars?
    5. What do you call a cake made with eggs, flour and sugar but no fat?
    6. Who scored for Manchester United in their last match?
    7. What are nine sevens?
    8. What comes straight after a red light?
    9. What is another name for Rose of Sharon?
    10. How many balls in one over?
    (Answers: 1. water; 2. 8; 3. wolf; 4. check in newspaper; 5. sponge; 6. check in newspaper; 7. 63; 8. red and amber; 9. St John's Wort/hypericum; 10. 6)

PROPER 16

Sunday between 21 and 27 August inclusive

1 Kings 8:(1, 6, 10-11)
22-30, 41-43 or
    Joshua 24:1-2a, 14-18
Psalm 84 or
    Psalm 34:15-22
Ephesians 6:10-20
John 6:56-69

'To whom else could we go? You alone have the words of eternal life.'

All-age talk

Have a show of hands for a few choices – Who's for football, who's for rugby? Who's a lark and loves the early mornings, who's an owl and loves to stay up late? Who's a 'dog' person, who's a 'cat' person?

All these are a matter of choice, and happily we are all different so we all like to choose different toppings on our pizzas, different music to listen to and different colours to wear. It's wonderful and important that we are all different.

But there are some things we can't choose, because it's been decided that there is a collective good way of going on. So we all drive on the same side of the road whatever part of the country we're in; we all go to school and learn how to read and write and do maths and science; we all pay taxes on what we earn so everyone, both poor and rich, can use schools and hospitals and so on.

In our first reading, from the Old Testament, Joshua wants the people to decide, before they go in to the promised land, whether they really do want to serve the Lord their God or not. He makes it quite clear that they will only be choosing wisely if they do choose to worship God, as he is real and powerful, and the other gods are not. It's a little bit like asking a football team if they are going to choose to play with a football or a matchbox in an international match. There really isn't much point in playing with anything other than the real thing!

In the Gospel we heard of some of the crowds choosing not to walk with Jesus any more because he seemed to be making out that he was the Holy

One of God. Jesus asked his disciples if they were going to turn away as well, and Peter spoke for them all, and for us as well. 'Lord, who else could we go to,' he asked, 'seeing that you are the one with the words of eternal life?' When we know that God is real, and that Jesus really is the Holy One of God, what else can we do but make the sensible, wise choice and commit ourselves to following him? That's the wisest, most important choice we make in the whole of our life.

All-age ideas

- As a follow-up to the all-age talk, it may be helpful to provide the opportunity for making a renewed commitment to serve God and become a follower of Jesus Christ. Depending on the style and tradition of your church this could involve a time of worship to reverence God's presence, with prayer ministry available for those wishing to make a definite and public commitment; or you could have a time of silent reflection in God's company followed by the baptismal declaration of faith.

- If anyone can lend some toy items of Roman armour, these could be used in a display based on the passage from Ephesians, with strings going from the appropriate verses to the appropriate items of armour.

PROPER 17

Sunday between 28 August and 3 September inclusive

Song of Solomon
2:8-13 or
Deuteronomy 4:1-2,
6-9
Psalm 45:1-2, 6-9 or
Psalm 15
James 1:17-27
Mark 7:1-8, 14-15,
21-23

We need to be careful never to replace the timeless commands of God with man-made traditions.

All-age talk

Probably quite a lot of us washed before we came out today. Why do we keep ourselves clean by regular washing? (Collect ideas and reasons.) Conclude that there are good reasons for washing. It's all to do with keeping healthy as well as being pleasant to sit next to! Our Gospel reading today was talking about what makes us unclean. If we are talking about our bodies, what sort of things make us unclean, or dirty? (Collect a few ideas.)

Now it was traditional for Jewish religious people to do lots and lots of washing. Some of this was to keep everything clean and healthy, and, having lived as wandering nomads in hot desert country, all that was very important. But there was another kind of 'being unclean' which wasn't to do with bodies but souls. Sin is your soul, or spiritual nature, being unclean and in need of a good clean-up. They believed that eating certain foods or not following special rituals would make you unclean.

But whereas it's *outside* things that make our bodies unclean and in need of washing, Jesus explained that with our souls it's thoughts and wants from deep *inside* us that often lead us into sin, making us unclean. Like what, for instance?

- Like when we have mean, unkind thoughts;
- when we feel like hating or despising people because they've got what we want;
- whenever we want what we know is wrong and against God's way of living;

252

- when it seems like a clever idea to lie our way out of trouble;
- when doing something unselfish seems too much hard work and we can't be bothered with it.

When we are baptised, we're dunked in water, partly as a sign that we're being washed clean from sin. (And in some churches, the priest washes his hands just after the bread and wine are brought to the altar, as an outward sign that he wants God to wash him clean of sin, ready for this special part of the service.)

So if those wrong and bad thoughts and drives make us sin, so that our souls are unclean, how on earth can we get clean again? Can we scrub our souls with soap and water, or soak all our nastiness away in a hot bath? No, we can't. But there is a way of getting our souls clean without leaving any stain of sin at all. It's a two-stage washing process, rather like putting stuff out for the laundry because we know it's dirty, and then having it washed clean. And it's called *repentance* and *forgiveness*.

Once we realise that our souls are messy and dirty with sin, and that makes us sad, we bring all of it to Jesus, tell him how sorry we are and how we would love our souls to be completely clean again. That's *repentance*.

What Jesus does is to take our souls and soak away all the sin in a wonderful bath of *forgiveness*, that leaves us feeling free and happy and spiritually clean.

All-age ideas

- Have an arrangement of washing products, such as a laundry bag with some clothes in it, washing powder/liquid, a laundry basket and some pegs.

- Give everyone a peg to hold. While a cluster of songs and hymns is sung, focusing on repentance and forgiveness, suggest we all look over our souls to see what needs a good wash, and bring it to Jesus for his cleansing forgiveness.

PROPER 18

Sunday between 4 and 10 September inclusive

Proverbs 22:1-2, 8-9,
    22-23 or
  Isaiah 35:4-7a
Psalm 125 or
  Psalm 146
James 2:1-10 (11-13)
    14-17
Mark 7:24-37

Jesus comes fulfilling the hope of healing to wholeness; he shows that mercy has triumphed over judgement.

All-age talk

Introduce the talk with the short sketch given in the all-age ideas. Bring along a couple of different masks and ask volunteers to come and put them on. Point out how Farouk has now turned into a fierce tiger, and we might be scared of him; Mazin is now a clown and looks even funnier than usual! Thank the volunteers and restore them to their normal identities.

One of the things that all grown-ups do is to put on different masks for different people. We need to learn from the children, especially the very young children, how not to. What sort of masks do grown-ups wear? Not usually animal or clown masks, but masks all the same!

Like the woman answering the phone in the sketch, we put on a special voice for people we want to impress, we wear special clothes and try to give the other person the impression that we are efficient, cool, witty, deep or dependable. Why do we do that? Because we know that most people are influenced by outward appearances, and most people are fairly judgemental. If we can persuade them that we are worth respecting, then we reckon they will be more likely to listen to us and take notice of us.

Is that how we want it to be? Think instead of young children, who simply act as themselves, and haven't yet learnt the game of pretending who they are. You can see in the direct look in a young child's eyes that there is something there which

254

grown-ups call innocence, because they are real; and we all regret losing that in all the clever pretending and wearing of masks.

As Christians, we are called to break that destructive cycle. We are *not* to judge from outward appearances, or just be friendly and respectful to wealthy, important-looking people. For us it's different because we know that every person we set eyes on is made and loved by God. And if we treat every person with the respect and love which they deserve as God-made human beings, they won't feel that they need to put on masks when they are with us. We will be joining Jesus in allowing people to be who they are, so that they are helped to wholeness and integrity.

All-age ideas

- Here is the sketch to introduce the all-age talk.

    Pauline Carter is sitting at her office desk working and answering the telephone. She can have the script in front of her, so she won't have to learn it.

    (Phone rings. Pauline answers it in bored, automatic voice.)

    Good morning, Pauline Carter speaking, how can I help you? . . . *(Suddenly sits up straight and adjusts hair, changes voice to be very efficient and respectful.)* Oh Mr Townsend, good morning. How can I be of assistance? . . . Yes, certainly, I'm sure that would be convenient . . . I'll just check the date . . . Yes, Monday at eleven forty would be fine . . . Certainly, I'll arrange that . . . And you, too, Mr Townsend . . . Thank you so much . . . Goodbye.

    (Carries on working. Phone rings again. Pauline answers it in efficient, friendly mode.)

    Good morning! It's Pauline Carter here. How can I help you? . . . *(Suddenly raises eyebrows and slumps back in seat, getting on with work while the other person talks. She's obviously not really listening.)*

Ah . . . oh, hi . . . mmm . . . ah . . . ah . . . no . . . look, I'm really busy here . . . yeah. OK . . . Bye.

(Carries on working. Phone rings again. Pauline answers it in bored auto voice.)

Good morning. Pauline Carter here. How can I help you?

- Suggest that in the Peace we share a sign of God's peace only with one or two people near us, but look at them as a child made by God while we share the Peace of God with them, and think about what we are saying.

PROPER 19

Sunday between 11 and 17 September inclusive

Proverbs 1:20-33 or
  Isaiah 50:4-9a
Psalm 19 or
  Wisdom of
  Solomon 7:26-8:1 or
  Psalm 116:1-9
James 3:1-12
Mark 8:27-38

Loving obedience to God is shown by Jesus to be a quality rich in courage and wisdom, a quality to be highly respected.

All-age talk

Ask for volunteers and spread them around in the aisle. Explain that all you want is for them to do as they're told. Then give a series of instructions, such as right hand in the air, run on the spot, stretch arms out to the sides, touch your toes, touch your nose, and so on. Hardly give them time to think. Finish by telling them to go back to their seats and everyone can give them a round of applause for giving us such a stunning example of perfect obedience.

Point out that it's quite easy to be obedient when someone's shouting out instructions, and the things aren't too hard. But if you had told them to push everyone off their chairs, or give all their money to the vicar, would they have rushed to be obedient and carry out the instructions? Hopefully not! God forbid that we should be so keen to obey anyone that we fall in with any dangerous or wrong instruction. Teachers often come across children who have done something really stupid, and give the excuse that their friend told them to. Is that a good excuse? No, of course it isn't, because we have to think when we are asked to do anything, and refuse to do it if it seems selfish, dangerous or wrong. (It isn't just children, either – grown-ups will give as an excuse that everybody else does it, which is just as foolish an excuse, since everybody else could well be doing something dangerous or wrong.)

So where have we got to with obedience? That we are not meant to leave our brains and consciences behind. That means we are measuring every

257

instruction up against the one we really trust to know what is right and good – underneath all the other obedient things we do there is a deep solid rock of obedience to God. That is what keeps us obedient wherever the instructions we are given are sensible and good, because measured up against the solid rock of our God we can see clearly that it's right to do what we're told here. In being obedient we are also being obedient to God.

And it's also what stops us obeying foolish, dangerous or wrong instructions which we might get from other people. Because when measured up against the solid rock of our God we can see clearly that to obey in those cases would make us disobedient to God.

Obedience to God is what matters more than anything, and Jesus showed us that.

All-age ideas

- Have different voices reading today's Gospel.

- Use part of the letter of James at the time of confession, to help people bring to mind their own misuse of speech.

'People can tame every kind of wild animal, bird, reptile and fish, and they have tamed them. But no one can tame the tongue. It is a restless evil, full of deadly poison.'

We want to apologise to God and one another
for the unkind things we have said
behind people's backs.

Lord, have mercy.
Lord, have mercy.

We want to apologise to God and one another
for the cruel things we have said in anger.

Christ, have mercy.
Christ, have mercy.

We want to apologise to God and one another
for anything we remember saying
that must have grieved the heart of God.

Lord, have mercy.
Lord, have mercy.

PROPER 20

Sunday between 18 and 24 September inclusive

Proverbs 31:10-31 or
 Wisdom of
 Solomon 1:16-2:1,
 12-22 or
 Jeremiah 11:18-20
Psalm 1 or Psalm 54
James 3:13-4:3, 7-8a
Mark 9:30-37

The truly great in God's eyes are those who are prepared to be last of all and servant of all.

All-age talk

You will need to bring along a Christening gift of some kind (Peter Rabbit bowl, silver spoon or locket), a 5 or 10 metre swimming badge, an item of school uniform, several cups or trophies, a graduation certificate or gown, and a driving licence, a few brown envelopes and a clock.

Ask for a volunteer to help take everyone on a whistlestop tour of a lifetime. Work through a person's life (you can call them the name of the volunteer), presenting them with the trophies which mark each stage of the climb to power and greatness. As a baby they are presented with special presents. As they grow up they start doing clever things like swimming and riding bikes. They wear special clothes to show they're old enough and clever enough to be going to school and learning loads more things every morning. Perhaps they have a hobby – in sport or music – and they do so well that they keep winning cups and trophies for it. As they get older still, they're off to university, and a few years later, here they are at their graduation. It's congratulations time again. And then there are the driving lessons and the practice and the extra insurance, and suddenly it's the test, and a smart new driving licence. All they need now is the car to drive. But the work's going well and the money's coming in, so they can buy all the things they've always wanted, and here are the bills to prove it. And then, after a good many years of work, this highly respected person is old enough to retire.

They have become a powerful and important pillar of society.

The volunteer is now loaded. Help unload them and thank them for their assistance.

We all have ambitions; we all hope our lives will turn out like our dreams. We want to be successful, liked, appreciated, fit and good-looking. And often we secretly want to be best. Jesus sees all of our dreams, even the secret ones. He knew what the disciples had been muttering about on their way as they walked along. They probably hoped he couldn't hear, because, like all of us, they had a strong suspicion that discussing who had most status was not really Jesus talk. Jesus really didn't care if the important people disapproved of him. He wasn't out to impress anybody, or work his way up, or gain status – he was just there to get on with the work of loving people to wholeness.

And that's what he wants for his followers as well. He wants us to have that freedom, so we can get on with what's really important, instead of wasting our time and energy empire-building in our particular area, impressing people, or collecting status symbols to wear or drive in. What do they matter when we compare them with God's values? Let's learn to be happy and content with nothing but being last, being unnoticed and the servant of all.

All-age ideas

- Act out the Gospel while it is narrated, using a young child. Have the child's parent taking Jesus' part.

- Secrets. Give everyone a small piece of paper and invite them to think of some act of loving service they could do without anyone knowing. When they have thought, they fold the pieces of paper up and bring them out to a collection point near the cross. They can enjoy carrying this out during the coming week – a secret between them and God.

260

PROPER 21

Sunday between 25 September and 1 October inclusive

Esther 7:1-6, 9-10;
  9:20-22 or
  Numbers 11:4-6,
  10-16, 24-29
Psalm 124 or
  Psalm 19:7-14
James 5:13-20
Mark 9:38-50

Don't let your body lead you into sin and risk exchanging eternal life for eternal punishment.

All-age talk

Bring along some salt and a slice of ham.

Explain that salt is often used as a preservative, to keep food fresh and good, and stop it going off. We tend to use freezing for this, but if you haven't got a freezer, salt works very well. Ham and bacon are salty because they have always been a way of preserving pork. When it's salted it lasts, and it still tastes good. (Give the ham to some volunteers.)

At the end of today's Gospel, we heard Jesus saying to his disciples that they were to be like salt – not preserving food, but working in the world to preserve people for eternal life. Presumably he was thinking that if people didn't have preservative, they'd go rotten. Sin is what makes people go bad and rotten, not just in this bit of life that we walk about on earth and in time, but for ever. And that's a terrible thought and we wouldn't want it to happen to anyone at all, would we?

That's why God badly needs some volunteers living in this world, and this parish, going to the local school, shopping in the local supermarket, working wherever you work and belonging to the clubs you belong to. God needs us to work as spiritual salt among all the people we meet and work and live with, helping to keep people fresh and alive for ever, and preventing them from going bad and rotten from sin. Who's prepared to volunteer as God's salt? Let's hope we *all* are!

So how can we do it? First, and most important, we've got to make sure we're still salty ourselves.

If we're letting our bodies or minds lead us deep into sin, then we're not going to be much good at preserving other people, are we? We're more likely to infect them with our sin – even our secret sin. So Jesus tells us to sort out our own sin with God. We need to ask him to help us clean our life up and keep it clean, so we're really salty salt, useful as God's preservative in the world. Get that done, however much it hurts and however difficult it seems – even if it feels as painful as chopping off a hand or a foot. Turning from sin hurts, but it won't kill your eternal life, like the sin will.

Once we're really salty, we can spread around us the peace which only God can give. We'll be treating people with God's love, able to talk with them about the freedom of being forgiven, introducing them to our wonderful friend Jesus, by the way we live and obviously enjoy his company. And we'll be fighting for good and against all that we come across which is evil. We'll be active in making our society more responsible and wholesome because of us living in it.

Is all this an idealistic dream? Could we really make a difference? The good news is that in God's power and strength we really can be salt; all of us here can join the work of preserving life, knowing that through our willingness to be salty, people will be saved for the joy of eternal life.

All-age ideas

- Have a flower arrangement expressing a seashore, with a bowl of salt, sea lavender, stones, shells and seaweed. Give it the title: 'Be salt; keep salty; be God's preservative.'

- The reading from James teaches us to pray for one another in faith. Either in silence, or in small groups all over the church, pray for one another. Hymns or songs of reverence and worship may be sung while this is going on, and anointing may be offered.

PROPER 22

Sunday between 2 and 8 October inclusive

Job 1:1; 2:1-10 or
   Genesis 2:18-24
Psalm 26 or
   Psalm 8
Hebrews 1:1-4; 2:5-12
Mark 10:2-16

Human beings are made responsible for the care of creation but are subject to God in all aspects of their lives.

All-age talk

Invite people to share what jobs they are responsible for, including household chores, professional responsibilities and so on. Have people of all ages contributing so that it is clear that we all have responsibilities of some sort, whatever our age. You could also draw attention to those responsible for particular jobs in church, making it an opportunity for everyone to thank the flower arrangers, servers and choir, cleaners and pastoral team.

Point out that right from the beginning, when Adam was naming the animals, God has made us human beings responsible for looking after this world and each other. That is the important job that God has given us to do. If we all did our bit and everyone acted responsibly to the planet and to one another, under God's guiding hand, we would find that our life together here would be greatly blessed. People would have enough to eat, and many disasters and much suffering would be avoided.

So why doesn't that happen, when it seems such good sense for us to live according to the Maker's instructions?

The trouble is that we all let our own wants and selfishness get in the way. If we, as rich nations, started acting more responsibly, then things we've become used to getting cheaply would be more expensive, and we might have to make do with less. Our greed stops us acting responsibly. So does our short-sightedness, when we want 'lots, now!' instead of considering those who haven't yet been born.

It's even the same in our friendships and marriages. If we are responsible in these, we will

263

be caring for the other person and looking after their needs, sensitive to their feelings and wanting to help them. If one or other or both stop doing that, the relationship becomes hurtful and wearing instead of rewarding. The answer may not be to get out of the friendship or marriage, but change our way of behaving with each other, talking things over with each other and with God, learning to be responsible again. It is grown-up and sensible to know that life can't always be happy, and the person we love can't always agree with us. Giving one another space, understanding that we all have bad days, forgiving one another and working at our friendships – all this is part of being the responsible people God created us to be.

He doesn't expect us to do it without help. God is there with us in all the bad patches as well as the easy rides, and as a community we are to look after one another properly, making sure we're all OK and coming to the rescue whenever someone isn't.

All-age ideas

- If the church hasn't already got a system for community caring, today is a good time to start one. This might involve grouping people to keep an eye on one another's needs, looking out for them and being there for them in any rough patches. Spreading the responsibility like this makes for a realistic expectation of care without overload.

- Married couples may like to affirm their marriage vows today, with the whole community affirming their commitment to the support and nurture of families. Couples who have been married at the church during the last year could receive personal invitations to church this week.

PROPER 23

Sunday between 9 and 15 October inclusive

Job 23:1-9, 16-17 or
    Amos 5:6-7, 10-15
Psalm 22:1-15 or
    Psalm 90:12-17
Hebrews 4:12-16
Mark 10:17-31

The word of God is living and active, piercing right to the heart; only with God is it possible to be saved.

All-age talk

Beforehand set up a kind of treasure hunt, like this. Prepare the following envelopes, numbered clearly, and place them all around the church.

1. Contains the reference Amos 5:14 and a Bible with a bookmark in the right place.

2. Contains a charity envelope with a description of the need for fresh water in many villages, or an immediate crisis concern.

3. Contains a flag of our nation.

Ask for a couple of volunteers, old enough to read, and send them off to search for envelope number 1. When they bring it back, ask them to open it and look up the reference in the Bible. This was part of our first Bible reading today, and in order to understand what seeking God involves, we're doing it. The prophet knew that seeking God actually changes us, helping us to find God. Already our search has led us to pick up a Bible and read it. All of us need to do that – it's no good having a Bible at home if we never open it up and read it! As we heard in our second reading today, the word of God is living and active. If we are really seeking God, we'll have to find out what the word of God says, every day.

Ask for another couple of volunteers to search for envelope number 2. They open it and show the contents. Either describe the needs in the present crisis, or explain how (Action Aid) is trying to provide the basic need of fresh water for villages in Africa and India, where the children die because

265

the water is so bad. We have fresh water there in our taps all the time! What can we do to help these people? Produce a labelled bucket and announce a retiring collection as we show our love and concern. God is leading us to see with his eyes of compassion and love.

Another couple of volunteers search for envelope number 3. Inside is the national flag. Invite people to think about their country – the things that make them happy about it and the things which sadden them. As we seek God's goodness, truth and justice, we'll find that we notice things that need to be changed. Our country needs us to stand up for what is right and fight what is evil. Are we doing that, or leaving it to other people?

The young man in the Gospel was seeking God, and Jesus helped him. The next stage of that young man's journey into God would be to change things in his life. If we set out to seek God, we must expect the same.

All-age ideas

- Outside the church have a large sign with an arrow, saying, 'God-seekers this way!'

- Have the Gospel acted out, with people taking parts and either learning the actual words or the gist of them.

Proper 24

Sunday between 16 and 22 October inclusive

Job 38:1-7 (34-41) or
   Isaiah 53:4-12
Psalm 104:1-9, 24, 35c
   or Psalm 91:9-16
Hebrews 5:1-10
Mark 10:35-45

Even the Son of Man himself came not to be served but to serve, and to give his life as a ransom for many.

All-age talk

Have three chairs placed in front of the altar, in the obvious place of honour. Prepare three 'Reserved' signs.

In the Gospel today we watched two of Jesus' disciples – James and John – coming up to him with a question they wanted to ask. They wanted to make sure Jesus would give them what they wanted, so instead of starting with the real question, they first said, 'We want you to do for us whatever we ask.' Perhaps we try that one with parents or spouses, or the boss sometimes. Like this.

Invite a child and adult to come and read the following script:

Child   Dad, you love me, don't you?

Dad   Yes, son.

Child   You'd give me anything I wanted, wouldn't you?

Dad   Mmm . . . maybe I would.

Child   Well, can I have this really good educational computer game?

Dad   No.

Child   Oh, but Dad, you said . . .

Dad   I only said maybe!

Child   Oh well, it was worth a try.

Jesus didn't say yes either. He asked James and John what they wanted, and was pretty gobsmacked by what it was. Invite two children to read out James and John's question – have it printed out in large, clear letters for them: 'Let one of us sit at your right and the other at your left in your glory.'

What on earth was Jesus to say to that? Point out the three chairs, and have someone place a reserved sign on the main, middle one. Who was this place in glory reserved for? Jesus. Had he pushed for it or even asked for it? No! He was given it by Almighty God, his Father. It was being a servant and being willing to give up his life for us all that brought Jesus to reign in glory. If James and John were to be granted their wish (invite them to go and sit either side of the main seat), what would it show about them, and about Jesus? (Collect ideas. It might show that they were the most important of the disciples, that Jesus liked them better than the others, that pushy people get their way in God's kingdom, for instance.)

Jesus pointed out to them that those places are not his to give anyway as they have reserved signs on them. (Invite someone to move James and John off the thrones and place reserved signs on them.) No one, not even Jesus, knew who they are reserved for. It could be for someone here! What we can be sure of is that the people they're reserved for would be the very last people to ask to sit there, or count themselves more worthy than anyone else!

Jesus tells us that we are all here to bother about serving others, not to bother about being served. Even Jesus himself, the Son of the living God, came as a servant, and gave up his life for the good of others. That's the example we're to follow, not resigning ourselves to it, grudgingly, but happy to have the honour of giving up our lives to serve others in love.

All-age ideas

- While the first reading is read, have a cross brought from the back to the front of the church, or project an image of the cross from a painting on an OHP screen.

- The Gospel works well read with different voices, especially if the readers have prepared by studying the text and thinking through the sub-script, rather as actors would, so that they can act it in the expressions and body language, pauses and so on, as well as the words themselves.

PROPER 25

Sunday between 23 and 29 October inclusive

Job 42:1-6, 10-17 or
    Jeremiah 31:7-9
Psalm 34:1-8, 19-22 or
    Psalm 126
Hebrews 7:23-28
Mark 10:46-52

In Jesus, God gathers his scattered people and opens their eyes to see.

All-age talk

Begin by asking people to imagine a child who has gone outside to play. She has been learning to ride her bike, and is quite good at it now, with a few wobbles. She's happy out there, riding up and down, until she takes a corner a bit steeply, brakes sharply, and she and the bike crash down. The child has a nasty graze on her leg, and is upset and a bit frightened by the fall. All she can think of is getting back home, to the person she knows will make it all better, and there she is, limping up the road, with her leg bleeding, crying out for her mum as she goes.

Most of us have been there. Whenever we're badly hurt, even when we've grown up, there's a young child inside us limping back home, crying, to the place we feel safe, and to the person we know will look after us and make it all better.

It's a good picture of our loving parent God, who is always there, waiting for his hurt and limping children to walk back home to the one who can and does make it all better, however old or young we are, and however we got our wounds. What that walk back home shows is that the child trusts. What our walk back to God shows is that we know and love and trust God to help us.

In today's Gospel we met a blind man called Bartimaeus. He knew he was blind. He knew he missed out in life because he couldn't see. When he heard that Jesus was passing by, he shouted and kept on shouting, so he wouldn't miss his chance. Never mind if the disciples told him to be quiet, he knew this was too important an opportunity to miss, and he shouted hard until Jesus himself heard him. That gave him the chance to do his 'limping home' – he made his way to the person he knew could help him. And, sure enough, Jesus did just that.

All-age ideas

- The reading from Jeremiah can be read chorally, with a group of voices such as men, women and children, or a mixed group of high, medium and low voice tones. Work through the passage experimenting with who reads what, bearing in mind that the object is to help bring out the meaning in the best way.

- The Gospel can be acted out, with a narrator and mime, or with the different voices. Involve everyone by turning the centre aisle into the Jericho street, with the people all standing there, crowding round the action as it happens.

ALL SAINTS' DAY

Sunday between 30 October and 5 November inclusive

Wisdom 3:1-9 or
   Isaiah 25:6-9
Psalm 24:1-6
Revelation 21:1-6a
John 11:32-44

Great is the rejoicing in heaven among the saints of God as they worship their Lord in glory.

All-age talk

Give everyone a sweet which is wrapped in coloured cellophane (or just clear cellophane). This is a special present to everyone to celebrate All Saints' Day. Ask everyone to unwrap their sweet, eat it while they listen to the talk, and keep the wrapper carefully.

We are tasting the sweetness of our All Saints' gift. What makes a saint is someone who tastes the sweetness of God's amazing love and savours it, enjoying it and thanking God for it. Living like that is what transforms their lives, so that when people are with them they know they are in the presence of God. They can detect God's peace, God's love and God's joy.

Now invite everyone to straighten out their wrapper and look at it. When we look straight at it we notice all the sticky bits and fingerprints. When we look not at it but through it, we see beyond all those. That's how saints are with their view of life. They are here in the real, ordinary world, some of it bright and breezy, and some of it heavy with sadness, and a bit messy. But they keep looking through all the experiences of this life, using them to help them understand more and more of the love of God which shines through it all.

We are all called to be saints, set apart as friends of Jesus, walking through this life in his company and dying in his company. What about after that? Our readings today tell us about all the rejoicing that goes on in heaven for those who have gone faithfully through earthly life. It's difficult to describe heaven in ordinary language because heaven is so

272

wonderful that it breaks the vocabulary barrier, and no one can find quite wonderful enough words to give us the full picture.

But we do have some idea. Some of the joy of heaven spilt out into the sky above the shepherds' field near Bethlehem the night Jesus was born, and that was full of angels singing and praising with great delight. Whatever it looks like, we can be sure that there will be a glorious sense of welcoming love and homecoming waiting for anyone who has spent their earthly life close to Jesus, loving God and loving those sharing the earth with them.

All-age ideas

- Give out instruments for the children to play during some of the hymns.

- Have a joyful procession with all the banners and flags.

- Play some music as a background to the reading from Revelation – 'In Paradisum' from *Requiem* (Fauré), for example.

FOURTH SUNDAY BEFORE ADVENT

Sunday between 30 October and 5 November inclusive
For use if the Feast of All Saints was celebrated on 1 November and alternative propers are needed

Deuteronomy 6:1-9
Psalm 119:1-8
Hebrews 9:11-14
Mark 12:28-34

To love the living God with heart, soul and strength, and to love our neighbour as ourselves means far more than any sacrificial offerings.

All-age talk

Beforehand ask three people to practise saying the same sentence, each emphasising a different word so that the meaning is slightly changed.

- WE go to church on Sunday – (as opposed to other people)
- We go to CHURCH on Sunday – (that's our destination)
- We go to church on SUNDAY – (rather than another day)

Also they need to practise saying the same sentence meaning something different.

- Yes, I believe so – (but you're not at all sure about it)
- Yes, I believe so – (automatically because it's written for you to say, but absent-mindedly)
- Yes, I believe so – (after much thought and with deep conviction)

Begin by pointing out how jokes can be really funny if you tell them right, but fall completely flat if you don't. How we say things is as important as what we say. Somebody can be saying nice things but you know they really don't like you and are trying to be nasty. Your friend could say the same things and you'd be happy and pleased instead of upset.

Invite the sentence-speakers to the front and invite everyone to spot the difference in what they are saying. (We go to church on Sunday.) Through stressing different words, they changed the meaning, even though the words stayed the same.

274

In the Gospel today we met a well-educated person, who had been quoting the scriptures every day of his life for a good number of years. He was thought of as fairly expert in his field of understanding God's law. He's been sitting listening to Jesus discussing the matters of law and faith with other experts, and he's impressed. He thinks it sounds as if Jesus really knows what he's talking about. He's so impressed that he asks Jesus a question, addressing him very respectfully as Rabbi, or Teacher. And the question he asks is this (have a volunteer, or everyone, read it out clearly and loudly): 'Which is the most important of the Commandments?'

The trouble was there were so many commandments now (as you speak, gradually unroll a very long roll of paper labelled 'Commandments') that it was all rather complicated and confusing. The scribe needed some help to sort it all out.

And what Jesus does is this. He recites the special statement of faith which every Jewish person knew by heart from childhood. It was this (everyone reads it out clearly): 'Hear, O Israel! The Lord our God is the one Lord.'

Just imagine how God's Son, a Jewish young man, would say that! The scribe could hear, in the way he said it, all Jesus' complete trust in God. He could tell it meant everything to Jesus, and he wasn't just rattling it off by heart. He meant it, completely and joyfully. And that got the scribe excited about his own faith – Jesus' love of God was catching!

When we talk about Jesus, does our love for him show?

All-age ideas

- As a time of confession, use the Lord's prayer, taking far more time over it than usual, speaking slowly and with pauses between the phrases so that everyone can really think about what they are saying.

275

- A credal statement today could be this:

  The Lord our God is the one Lord,
  and Jesus is Lord!
  Glory be to the Father and to the Son
  and to the Holy Spirit,
  as God was in the beginning,
  is now and shall be for ever. Amen.

- The summary of the law can be sung to the tune
  of *London's burning*, in a round:

  You shall love the Lord your God with
  all your heart and all your mind and
  all your strength! All your strength!
  And love your neighbour,
  and love your neighbour.

THIRD SUNDAY BEFORE ADVENT

Sunday between 6 and 12 November inclusive

Jonah 3:1-5, 10
Psalm 62:5-12
Hebrews 9:24-28
Mark 1:14-20

When we are called we need to respond with obedience so that many may be brought to repentance.

All-age talk

Begin by giving out a few messages as if they are notices, rather like this. 'Is Ali Holden here? I've got a message from Molly, your neighbour's dog. She says when you next take her for a walk could you go past the swimming pool as there are some good smells around there. And then there's another message . . . this is for John Bendkowski. It's a message from the rope you used to climb the tree, asking for another high level outing as it enjoyed the view.' (Use inside information so that the messages match up with real life.)

What do we reckon – are those messages true or not? Does Ali take a dog called Molly out for walks? Did John use a rope to climb a tree? Yes! Then what makes us think the messages aren't quite right? It's because common sense tells us that dogs and ropes can't send messages like that, even if they wanted to. Today we are looking at the way God calls us, and how we can work out whether it's really God calling us, or not.

What first alerted Ali and John to the messages given out? It was their names. When God calls us, he gets our attention and speaks directly to us. Sometimes what happens is that we hear a reading at church, or read a passage of the Bible at home, and suddenly a particular bit hits home, and we know it's meant specially for us. It's as if it has our name on it. God spoke into Jonah's heart so that Jonah knew God had a message for him, whether he chose to obey it or not. The fishermen heard Jesus calling directly to them as they worked in the fishing boats. So one thing we can learn about God's call is that it feels personal to us.

277

The next thing to look at is this: is this the sort of message that God would give? With our messages from a dog and a rope, we knew they didn't ring true, so we could laugh at the messages and not take them seriously. But what other things might make us suspect that a call is not from God at all? If it's to do with anything unkind, violent, selfish, greedy, lazy, deceitful, or evil, then the call we think we are hearing is not coming from the God of truth and love. But if we feel God is calling us to something loving, selfless, thoughtful, kind, courageous, honest, or good, then it's likely that God is speaking into our hearts, and we should listen carefully.

Then what? The first time Jonah heard God, he chose to run away from what he was asked to do. That ended up with him being tipped overboard and swallowed by an enormous fish! The second time God called, Jonah chose to do what God wanted him to do, even though he really didn't like the idea very much.

When Andrew and Simon Peter, James and John heard Jesus calling them, they got up straightaway, left everything and followed him to do what they were being called to. If we hear God calling us, and we choose not to listen, or not to obey the call, the terrible truth is that people who might have been helped won't be; people who might have been saved might not get the chance God wanted them to have.

So we need to be ready to hear God calling in the quiet of our hearts, check with our experience of God that the call is true, and then be prepared to obey the call, going bravely wherever God is leading us.

All-age ideas

- Have a flower arrangement focusing on the fishermen, using a flat mirror and some sand, stones and shells, driftwood and netting.

- Give everyone a stone as they come in and suggest they hold it during the Psalm and during the intercessions as a tactile reminder that God is our rock and refuge, whom we can always trust.

SECOND SUNDAY BEFORE ADVENT

Sunday between 13 and 19 November inclusive

Daniel 12:1-3
Psalm 16
Hebrews 10:11-14
  (15-18) 19-25
Mark 13:1-8

We are to be on our guard; great anguish will accompany the last days, but all that is good and loving, wise and true will be saved and celebrated for ever.

All-age talk

Bring along a well-loved and very well-worn companion – teddy or pyjama case. Introduce him to everyone and point out how we can all see just how well loved he is! He bears the signs of being well loved. Probably most of us older ones feel a bit like this – loving has worn us to the shape we are, a bit threadbare and squashed maybe, but perhaps a little wiser and softer and less selfish as a result. Although we know from experience that loving hasn't always been easy, we can say with certainty that it's well worth living lovingly.

Our readings today are helping us to look forward to the end of time, when the sky is wrapped up and the moon folded away. It can sound very frightening, to think of everything we know coming to an end. Whenever there are terrible disasters and famines and wars it can feel as if things are spinning out of control – even out of God's control. Is the end going to be some huge ghastly mistake, brought about by our greed and selfishness?

The Bible reassures us that, however it may look as evil grows and temporarily gains the upper hand, God is always ultimately in charge. As we know, God's way is not to crash into our blundering and force us to change so that disasters are prevented. He has given us that great gift of free will, so that we can choose good or evil in the small and large decisions of life. He longs for us to choose the good that will bring us blessing and peace, but is always there weeping with us in the chaos and suffering that evil leads to, ready to redeem it for good.

And it is that buffeted and battered loving which will last and last for ever. The prophet Daniel gives us a lovely picture of that. All those who have guided others in the right path, he says, will shine like the stars of heaven for ever. All the wise leaders will show up brightly for all to see. If we have set ourselves to live lives of faith and love, there is no way we need be frightened by the last days. After the feeding of the five thousand Jesus told his disciples to gather up the fragments so that nothing is lost. That's how it will be at the end; every scrap of goodness and love will be gathered safely in, so that nothing of it is lost.

All-age ideas

• Place the well-loved friend near the altar, with a sign which reads 'Love remains for ever', so that people can see it as they come to receive communion.

• Have the passage from Daniel read by a group of adults and children, reading alternately, like this:

Children: Verse 1 up to 'fellow countrymen . . .'

Adults: '. . . and there will be . . . till that moment.'

Children: 'But at that time . . . entered in the book.'

Adults: 'Many of those who sleep . . . reproach of eternal abhorrence.'

Children: Verse 3

CHRIST THE KING

Sunday between 20 and 26 November inclusive

Daniel 7:9-10, 13-14
Psalm 93
Revelation 1:4b-8
John 18:33-37

Jesus Christ is the everlasting King whose kingdom is not of this world, but grows in the hearts of his people and lasts for ever.

All-age talk

Beforehand prepare a long length of lining paper on which the alphabet is written clearly. Fix it up where everyone can see it, or ask people to hold it. (Please don't make them hold it high or their arms will drop off!)

Claim that on this sheet you have the whole of the Bible, the complete works of Shakespeare, every love letter ever written, every postcard and Christmas letter ever sent. You also have the names of every person and every place.

At this point a pre-arranged person walks out to protest. Preachers are supposed to tell the truth and here you are telling porky pies. You can't possibly have all that on this sheet of paper. You've only got a few letters!

Meet the challenge by inviting them to find their own name from the sheet, which they spell out letter by letter, and have to admit that they are on the sheet after all. Get someone else to find 'To be or not to be' and 'Come, Lord Jesus'. These are also found to be there.

Our God is like A to Z – the beginning and the end of everything, all thoughts and ideas, all creation, all love, all hope, all existence. That's why we worship God – God has always been. God is, at this very moment, now. (Pause for everyone to become aware of that amazing fact.) And God will always be, for ever. God's kingdom is wherever Jesus reigns as our King. And that means wherever people say, 'Yes!' to Jesus, 'I really want to be in your kingdom!'

And we know what being in Jesus' kingdom is like, don't we? It's full of love and joy and peace, full of forgiveness and patience, full of hope and healing. Today it's as if we've brought out our flags to wave as we celebrate Jesus as our wonderful, everlasting King, who sets our lives dancing!

All-age ideas

- If you have bunting stored away for summer fairs, bring it out today and festoon the entrance to the church.

- Make the flower arrangements reflect the royal dignity and power of Jesus, with gold and scarlet colours, and perhaps including a gold crown.

- As a background to the reading from Daniel, play some evocative music with a sense of awe and mystery.

- Use two voices in the Gospel for the conversation between Jesus and Pilate.

YEAR C

FIRST SUNDAY OF ADVENT

Jeremiah 33:14-16
Psalm 25:1-10
1 Thessalonians 3:9-13
Luke 21:25-36

The gathered hopes of generations remind us to get ourselves ready, so that Christ's return will be a day of excitement and great joy.

All-age talk

Have ready a good supply of inflated balloons on strings. These will be needed later.

Bring out three sweets or apples and explain that three people are going to get them. Give them out completely randomly and then ask if that was fair. Agree with them that it wasn't fair, and often life seems unfair to us. (This is something that all ages know about.) Explain how our world is full of injustice and sometimes cruel and terrible things happen which don't make sense.

Now ask anyone who would like a balloon to raise a hand. Invite these people to come and collect a balloon and return to their seats. You will need them to gather with their balloons later on, when you beckon them.

As Christians we don't have to pretend the bad things aren't there, or try to work out easy answers that don't make sense. God knows there are sad and bad things happening in our world as well. They happened just the same when Jesus was walking around in Galilee. A tower fell on some people and killed them. The people asked Jesus to explain it, but he didn't. He felt very, very sorry for anyone who was ill or whose child had died, and, instead of explaining why, he set about comforting them and doing everything he could to make things better. So that's what we need to do as well while we are alive.

But Jesus did tell us that life wouldn't always be unjust. One day, he said, everything as we know it will finish, and on that day everything you, and everyone else, have ever done which is good or kind, or helpful, friendly or honest will be gathered in, like harvest, and kept. (As you say this, gather all those with balloons together in the centre.) It will be an exciting and very beautiful harvest!

Let's make sure that we grow plenty of love and thoughtfulness and honesty and integrity in our lives, however old or young we are, so that whenever that last day comes, we'll be helping to make it a bumper harvest.

All-age ideas

- If you have a set of advent candles, have the candles lit each week by representatives of different age groups, so that by the fourth Sunday in Advent there is a child, a teenager, a working-age adult and a senior citizen.

- During the Thessalonians reading have some quiet, slow music playing in the background from verse 11 onwards.

- Ask a few people to write these words on large posters for the walls or pillars: 'Heaven and earth will pass away but my words will never pass away.'

SECOND SUNDAY OF ADVENT

Malachi 3:1-4
Canticle: Benedictus
Philippians 1:3-11
Luke 3:1-6

It had been prophesied that there would be a messenger to prepare the way for the coming of the Messiah. Now John the Baptist appears with his urgent message of repentance.

All-age talk

Beforehand arrange for a local builder/decorator to be interviewed, preferably in working clothes and carrying his tools.

Introduce the guest, and ask his advice about a structural problem (either real or imagined). When the builder talks about the importance of all the 'making good', suggest that surely he could just smear some more plaster over the top, and wouldn't that be as good? Or put on thick wallpaper to hide the cracks? Let the builder explain what will eventually happen if the real problem isn't sorted out.

Thank the guest builder and have a couple of the children bring him a mug of tea as it's time for his tea break.

While the builder drinks his tea, explain how what is true for walls and windows is true for us as well. If we have been mean or a pain, or lazy, or if we've been telling lies or living lies, or if there is anything at all in the way we behave which is not right, loving and honest, then we are like a building with bad cracks and damp. As the builder told us, the only way to put it right is to have the wrong things cleared away, and then be built up soundly again.

God can do that in us if we want. He will help us put our lives right, however bad a state they are in. Tell him you are sorry you tell lies, and want to be more honest. He will help you become an honest person who others can trust. Tell God your sister/father-in-law/colleague winds you up and you hate all the rows and want to be more able to cope.

286

God will help you improve those relationships. Tell God you find it hard to share your toys or your money, and want to be more generous. He will help you do it.

But we can't put anything right until we see that there is a problem. It was only when the damp and cracks were noticed that the builder was called in.

John the Baptist spoke about 'repentance'. That means he is saying to us: 'Look at your lives; see those cracks and damp patches; and get them sorted out.'

All-age ideas

- Instead of a flower arrangement, have an arrangement of an open DIY manual, and various tools and materials, with a title: 'Get your life sorted out!'

    This can be done by someone doing their own property up at the moment, or a student on a building course.

- Give everyone a small paper house shape (made and distributed by the cubs or brownies, perhaps). Instead of the usual form of confession, play some music and ask everyone to look at their house as their life, and listen to what God is saying needs putting in order or sorting out. Then the houses are collected up and placed in front of the cross (or people can bring them up to the cross). At the end they can be given out for people to take home and remind them of what they and God are going to tackle together.

THIRD SUNDAY OF ADVENT

Zephaniah 3:14-20
Canticle: Isaiah
   12:2-6
Philippians 4:4-7
Luke 3:7-18

Our period of preparation shifts from repentance and forgiveness to the freed exhilaration of hope, as the momentous truth of God's immanence begins to dawn on us.

All-age talk

Bring with you a sealed envelope containing an invitation to a very special party or wedding. The date for the celebration needs to say 'to be arranged'.

Tell everyone how you have received this letter, and it looked so exciting that you thought you'd bring it to church and open it there. Invite someone to come and help you open the envelope, and someone a bit older to read it out. Show your excitement and start planning what to give as a present, and what to wear, getting suggestions from people and scribbling it all down on a list. Such a lot to think about!

Then stop as you ask to check the date of the celebration. Realise that it only says 'Date to be arranged'. *Date to be arranged!* That means you have no idea when to get ready. It might be ages to wait. It might be next week! Suppose it's next week!

Come to the conclusion that the only way you can be sure to be ready is to get ready straight away.

Put the invitation down and pick up a Bible. As you flick through the pages talk about how you are sure there is an invitation to a party somewhere in here as well. Find the Zephaniah reading and discover that it's the one we heard this morning, with all the dancing and singing in it.

It's going to be quite a day, and we'll need to make sure we're ready for it. But what was the date again? Look and find it's another case of 'Date to be arranged'. Only God knows the actual date. That means it could be a long time ahead or it could be very close, so the best thing to do is to get ready straight away.

What kind of presents would be in order for this party?

Collect ideas like loving kindness, peacemaking, compassion, forgiveness, goodness and self-control. If we start now, we can grow those in our lives.

What kind of clothes would be suitable?

Clean clothes and good habits like honesty, faithfulness, humility, just or fair behaviour, and thoughtfulness. If we haven't got any yet, we can go to God's wardrobe and he'll make them to fit us perfectly. And if we have got them, but haven't worn them lately, now is the time to get them out and put them on again. These clothes get more and more beautiful as you wear them.

The second coming will be a wonderful celebration, and whether we are alive here or the other side of death, we will all be able to see it and take part.

All-age ideas

- Continue lighting the Advent candles with representatives from different age groups.

- Straight after the Zephaniah reading go into an exuberant but simple barn dance, using a mixed age and gender group and either recorded or live music.

- Have the Luke passage read by a group of voices as appropriate. The crowd's words can be written on the handout or on an OHP so that the whole congregation can join in at this point.

FOURTH SUNDAY OF ADVENT

Micah 5:2-5a
Canticle: Magnificat
   or Psalm 80:1-7
Hebrews 10:5-10
Luke 1:39-45 (46-55)

When we co-operate with God amazing things happen.

All-age talk

Try a kind of Mexican wave, first with one side of the church and then the other. The side not involved can enjoy the effect. Row by row, starting with the front row, everyone stands together and then sits together. The row behind gets up as soon as the row in front of them has sat down. Point out that for this to work they all needed to co-operate with one another and also with you, in agreeing to try it in the first place. Today we are watching what can happen when people are willing to co-operate with God.

Last week we found John the Baptist challenging people to sort out their lives and giving them some practical advice. Those who went away and did as John suggested found that once they had started to co-operate with God their lives took on a new sparkle and freshness many had lost. Those of us who took last week's teaching to heart and started looking seriously at what needed changing in our lives will also be here this morning with a new lightness in our step and a more positive sparkle in our lives because co-operating with God is very exhilarating and liberating. Working together with God sets us free. (And if we haven't yet got round to that there is still time for us to shake ourselves awake and use Advent profitably.)

Mary was one of those people who had decided to work together with God. And that meant that God could use her. So he did. It was through Mary co-operating with God that Jesus could come into the world.

Mary and Elizabeth are both pregnant. Mary is expecting Jesus, and her cousin Elizabeth is expecting John the Baptist. It's the same John the Baptist we met last week when he was grown up, teaching people by the River Jordan. Today we have a flashback to before he was born. Any mothers here will know that exciting feeling when the baby you are carrying first moves. Luke tells us that the unborn baby John was so excited at sensing the unborn Jesus, brought along in Mary, that he leapt about in his mother's womb!

Never before had God come among his people so closely. And now his birth into the world was less than a year away. No wonder Elizabeth and Mary were so excited. Having agreed to co-operate with God they found themselves being used for such an extraordinary and important job that they could hardly believe it. And they weren't even rich or powerful! They probably weren't even that well educated!

When anyone (and that includes you and me) says to God, 'I want to spend my life working together with you', God takes us up on our offer. If we don't opt out as soon as he asks of us things we may not want to give, he will be able to work with us in our lives to do amazing things. Imagine if everyone here in church decided to work with God. He could get us making waves in our community which would completely transform people's lives.

All-age ideas

- The meeting of Mary and Elizabeth in Luke's Gospel can be mimed while it is being read, using nativity costumes if you have them. It always seems a pity to have these packed away for most of the year when they are such a useful resource.

- If you have a member of the congregation who is pregnant, it would be valuable to have her lead the intercessions, or take part in a short interview about the way the baby moves, as she will be able to add insights which will help our understanding.

CHRISTMAS DAY

Isaiah 9:2-7
Psalm 96
Titus 2:11-14
Luke 2:1-14 (15-20)

Emmanuel – 'God with us' – is born at Bethlehem into the human family. Now we will be able to understand, in human terms, what God is really like.

All-age talk

You will need to borrow a mobile phone (unless you have received one as a Christmas present!) and a helper who is expert at sorting out OHPs.

Begin by telling everyone you want to show them something on the OHP, and then find that you can't work the equipment properly. Before anyone rushes to your aid, produce the mobile phone, delighted that this is an opportunity to use it to get in touch with an expert. Pretend to use the phone to get through to the expert, and have a mock conversation with them about how to work the apparatus, during which the expert suggests coming to help in person.

Welcome the help and pretend to talk through their (speedy) journey, which can be from anywhere in the world. As you get to guiding the expert down the road and into the church your helper arrives in person, mobile phone to his/her ear. (They have been standing hidden somewhere at the back of the building.)

The expert is able to get the apparatus going, and you enthuse about how much more helpful it is to have them there in person. You can now show the OHP acetate, which says: 'EMMANUEL = God with us in person.' The helper can point out that you've just been saying that it's much more helpful having them there in person. Is that what Emmanuel means?

You can then draw out the similarities – that with Jesus being born into the world as one of us, we have God with us in person to help us live good lives, make good decisions and guide us in

292

all the tricky places. It's not that things won't ever go wrong any more, but it does mean we can always be in touch with the one who can help us sort things out. And that is a truth well worth celebrating in style! Suggest that over the Christmas festivities we live out this truth to one another. It will mean being generous-hearted, thankful, available and willing to meet people where they are, whether that is a group of friends at a party, or relatives we find it less easy to relate to. Welcome God in person to your home this Christmas and enjoy yourselves in his company.

All-age ideas

- The Advent candles will all be lit today, together with a white one in the centre. Continue to use representatives from different age groups for this. Perhaps the centre candle can be lit during the singing of the Christmas Day verse of *O come, all ye faithful.*

- Have people dressed in costume to mime the Gospel. Have a narrator who is sensitive to the actors and is able to give them the cues they need if necessary.

- Have a nativity tableau during a carol and child angels (or simply children) standing round the altar with candles during the consecration.

FIRST SUNDAY OF CHRISTMAS

1 Samuel 2:18-20, 26
Psalm 148
Colossians 3:12-17
Luke 2:41-52

Jesus' perception and understanding of his purpose and work begins to take shape throughout his childhood.

All-age talk

Beforehand cut out two simple white cloth tunics like this, one to fit a three- or four-year-old and a larger one for a twelve-year-old.

Invite a couple of toddlers and their parents to the front and interview them about the coats or jackets the children are wearing. Admire them and ask where they were bought, and what size was needed compared with their last coat.

Tell everyone how Samuel was brought to the temple when he was able to feed himself, and every year his mum brought him a new linen coat she had made. Every year he needed a slightly bigger one as he grew older. Produce your linen ephod lookalike and dress the toddler in it. As you do so, explain that it was worn as a sign of coming before God with a clean heart and mind. Priests all wore them, too.

When God came to earth at Christmas as a baby, it was like him putting on the clothing of being human, and it was God's way of showing how much he loves us and is with us. It also helps us to see what God is like, because we cannot see God, but in Jesus we can see how God behaves. We can see that he enjoys people's company, wants to help them and shares their sadness and joy.

And Jesus didn't suddenly arrive on earth as a grown-up. He was born as a baby (draw attention to the size of someone very small in the congregation) and grew to be a toddler and a child (use other people of appropriate ages to demonstrate), so by the time he was a grown-up twelve-year-old he had experienced all the sort of human things that we experience.

Use the larger tunic with the word 'Humanity' written on it to clothe a twelve(ish)-year-old. All twelve-year-olds start asking questions about God and themselves, and so did Jesus. Part of wearing humanity meant that he developed as a human person and now he was grown-up he was fascinated to know who he was and why he was alive, just as we are. Those questions are important, and need to be asked. They are a sign of growing up. The answers for Jesus (and the answers for us) didn't come all at once. But that visit to the temple seems to have been a very important one for him. He began to understand that he was on earth to carry out God's purposes. That was why he was wearing the clothing of humanity. Perhaps for some of us this Christmas is an important one for finding out God's purpose for us in our lives. We need to come into God's presence wearing the clothes of honesty and openness, and ask our questions.

All-age ideas

- The Old Testament reading can be acted out with a couple pretending to bring a little robe and fit it on a young child who is standing with Eli (someone the child knows well and trusts). Eli says his own words and the couple walk back down the aisle hand in hand or with their arms round each other, looking happy.

- The tunic with the word 'Humanity' written on it can be laid down near the altar for people to see and remember as they come to receive communion.

SECOND SUNDAY OF CHRISTMAS

Jeremiah 31:7-14
Psalm 147:12-20
Ephesians 1:3-14
John 1:(1-9) 10-18

Christ is the way God tells people about himself.

All-age talk

You will need a hairdrier or a fan, or a lit candle to blow out.

Start with a riddle. You're thinking of something which is all around us, pressing against our faces and bodies at 15 pounds per square inch. It goes in and out of us all the time we're alive, and there's lots of it right in front of our eyes. What is it? (Air.) But we can't see it, so how do we know it's there?

Put on the hairdrier or fan, or ask someone to blow the candle out. When air moves, we can see what it does. When we try to hold our breath we realise how much our bodies need air to live.

God is here as well, and we can't see him. No one has ever seen God while they are alive on earth. So how can God tell us what he is like, when we can't see him?

There are ways we can see what God is like by what he does and by what he creates. If we look at the world we can see that God must be generous, imaginative, careful, clever, organised, hopeful and happy to let us work with him.

But God had an even better idea. If he could walk among humans as a human, then all the humans who lived at the time or at any time afterwards would be able to see exactly how God behaves. We could see it in our own human language. The language of doing, thinking, feeling and speaking.

In the Gospel today Jesus is talked about as being the Word, or the Message of God. When we look at how Jesus lived and died, we are looking straight at God, even though we can't see God with our eyes.

And what do we see? John describes Jesus as

being 'full of grace and truth'. Have this written up on a sheet. Around it you can add other people's ideas. Head the page 'Jesus is' and display it for the rest of the service.

All-age ideas

- Have on a banner or poster the words from John 1.18: 'No one has ever seen God . . . But the Son has shown us what God is like.'

- Have a group of mixed voices reading the Jeremiah passage. Work through it together first to see which lines would be best read by male, female or children's voices, and which are best read by the whole group. Aim to act out the feeling and the meaning of the passage through the presentation.

- If you have an OHP, try making up some Christmas cards into acetates as a parish resource. These can be placed behind the words of hymns and carols to reflect their meaning.

THE EPIPHANY

Isaiah 60:1-6
Psalm 72:(1-9) 10-15
Ephesians 3:1-12
Matthew 2:1-12

Jesus, the hope of the nations, is shown to the world.

All-age talk

Beforehand arrange for a knitter to bring a completed garment to church, together with a ball of wool and needles. Also prepare a large paper cut-out of a similar garment, which is folded up so that the first bit that would be made is the only piece showing. Alternatively use the actual garment, folded up at that point.

Begin by showing everyone the wonderful garment that the knitter has made and asking how long it took to make and who it is for. What did it look like at first, when they started making it? The knitter can show the ball of wool and needles, and do a couple of stitches. Hold up the needles with these stitches and point out that it doesn't look much like a jumper/scarf yet! But the knitter went on working at it, knowing that one day it would be ready.

God knew that one day everything would be ready for Jesus to come into the world, but he, too, took a long time making things ready. He started by calling one person, Abraham. (Show the folded garment, but don't refer to it – it is there to be visual reinforcement of what you are saying.) Over the years God went on to prepare all Abraham's family. (More of the garment is revealed.) Until over more years that family became one nation. (Reveal some more of the garment.) But God's plan still wasn't finished. He went on to include not one nation but all the nations and everyone in them. (Shake the whole garment out and display it.) Today is called the Epiphany because the word 'epiphany' means 'showing' or 'revealing' or 'manifesting', and when those wise men arrived at Bethlehem with their presents, God was showing or revealing himself

298

not just to Abraham or his family, not just to the whole nation of Israel, but to all the rest of us in the world as well.

Whatever country you come from, whatever you look like and whatever language you speak, God is saying to us today that he is there for you and no one is left out. You don't have to have the right ancestors to know God. You don't have to pass any exams to know God.

We sometimes get so interested in the presents the wise men were bringing to Jesus that we forget what brought them there in the first place. It was God who called these wise men from other nations to be there when Jesus was still a baby, so he could welcome them as well. They were there representing all the nations, so when God welcomed them he was welcoming each of us.

All-age ideas

- Today's Gospel can be acted out, preferably with costumes, as these may well be available from a nativity play. I am not suggesting a full-blown production with hours of rehearsal. All that is needed is a sensitive narrator, and the characters to mime what the narrator says.

- The wise men can take the collection and offer the gifts today. This emphasises their role as representatives of all the nations coming to be welcomed and offer their gifts. A globe can be offered at the same time.

- Have a bowl of burning incense, gold and myrrh arranged among flowers as a display either as people come in or near where they will come to receive communion.

THE BAPTISM OF CHRIST: FIRST SUNDAY OF EPIPHANY

Isaiah 43:1-7
Psalm 29
Acts 8:14-17
Luke 3:15-17, 21-22

Jesus is baptised, and God confirms his identity and his calling.

All-age talk

Using a flipchart, OHP or large sheet of paper and thick pens, collect everyone's suggestions about what water can do. Some of the suggestions can be drawn rather than written, so that the non-readers can also join in.

Read through all the suggestions to celebrate them, and talk about how Baptism picks up on these qualities of water and uses them to teach us spiritual things. When we are baptised we are 'drowned' to the old ways, given new life, washed clean, and refreshed. If it is practical, have water in the font and pour it as you explain each quality and its spiritual meaning.

Remind everyone that today we have heard about Jesus being baptised, and as he was praying the Holy Spirit came upon him, looking rather like a dove flying down to rest on him. And God told Jesus that he was God's Son, and God was well pleased with him.

Point out any dove symbols there are in the church – in carvings, pictures or windows – and have a cut-out dove shape (you can use the picture below) to show everyone. The dove has become a sign or symbol for the Holy Spirit because of what happened at the Baptism of Jesus.

When we are baptised God calls us actually by name to follow him, and sets us apart to love and serve him through the whole of our life. We can only do that with the gift of the Holy Spirit, so that is what we are given. The more we use it, the more it will grow. The sign of the dove will remind us. Whenever we see a dove or a pigeon, or a wild goose, it will remind us that we belong to God, and have chosen to follow him.

All-age ideas

- Give everyone a simple cut-out paper dove as they come in. Ask people to hold their doves in the palm of their hands during the intercessions.

- Have music as a background to the Isaiah reading, and several readers, reading it chorally.

- Decorate the font with flowers to give the sense of a cascade of water.

- Use the Renewal of Baptismal Vows for the statement of faith, with everyone gathered round the font.

SECOND SUNDAY OF EPIPHANY

Isaiah 62:1-5
Psalm 36:5-10
1 Corinthians 12:1-11
John 2:1-11

As a marriage celebrates the beginning of a changed, new life for the bride and groom, so our loving, faithful God has chosen us and is ready to transform our lives for the good of the world.

All-age talk

Beforehand ask someone in the congregation who still has their wedding dress or bridesmaid's dress to bring it along. Several people could do this – they won't have to wear them unless they want to! Ask a happily married couple to be prepared to talk about their wedding day.

Introduce the people and their wedding dresses, bringing out how special they are because of it being such a special day in their lives. Talk to the married couple so that they show how their love for one another brought them to marriage and how the wedding day emphasised the important step they were taking. If there are couples soon to be married, this would be a good time to pray for them as they start their new life together.

Through the prophet Isaiah, God tells his people that his love and faithfulness is a bit like that of a devoted bride and groom. We have been loved and called, and chosen to live a new life together with our God. He will take us just as we are and gradually change us into being more richly ourselves than we could ever be on our own.

Today's Gospel was all about something changing. Water was changed into wine. That happens naturally every year as the rain falls and gets drawn into the vine to make grape juice, and then the grape juice is fermented carefully to make that new drink – wine. But that wedding day in the town of Cana was different because the change happened straight away. Ask the married couple if they had ordered enough wine for their wedding, and then go over the wedding story and the way Jesus transformed the whole situation. John, who wrote this account, tells us that it showed the disciples they could put their trust in Jesus.

That is true for us as well. Whatever has gone wrong in your life, whatever makes you really sad or angry or disappointed, God will take and change so it can be used for good. Nothing you have to suffer will ever be wasted if you stick with Jesus, and do as he tells you.

All-age ideas

• Have the main flower arrangement with a wedding theme, with ribbon and a framed wedding photograph, a bottle of wine and two glasses among the flowers.

• Have the Isaiah passage read chorally with a group of men, women, boys and girls. Work through the passage together, listening for ways to bring out both the meaning and the poetry through the different combinations of voices. The easiest way to record this is with different coloured highlighter pens on copied sheets. Arrange for one of the group to take the lead and that will keep everyone together.

THIRD SUNDAY OF EPIPHANY

Nehemiah 8:1-3, 5-6,
   8-10
Psalm 19
1 Corinthians
   12:12-31a
Luke 4:14-21

The meaning of the scriptures is revealed to the people.

All-age talk

Begin by telling everyone you are going to drop a pin. Ask people to raise their hand if they hear it. (If the building is large, choose something slightly noisier to drop.) Point out how they all listened to be able to hear it. Today we are thinking about careful listening. Tell everyone you are going to drop the pin again, and this time ask them to notice what their bodies are doing to hear such a little sound. When you have dropped the pin, collect some of the things people have noticed. (These might include things like concentrating, waiting, being very still, cutting out our own noises, putting our best ear forward, turning our hearing aid up a bit.)

Today we are told that God is often revealed or shown to us through the scriptures – through the words in the Bible. (Hold a Bible and open it as you talk about it.) In our first reading we heard how all the people gathered in the square in front of the temple and had God's law read out clearly to them so they could really understand it. And when they heard it like this, they couldn't wait to start living the way they knew God wanted them to live. The reason they heard God's voice that day was because they were really trying to listen, like us trying to hear the pin drop.

When Jesus went to preach at his local synagogue he taught the people that the prophecy from Isaiah was coming true that very day. The ones who were listening as carefully as you listened for the pin dropping would have been very excited. Jesus was giving them a very strong clue about who he really was. And it isn't every day you have

304

the promised Messiah turning out to be someone you grew up with!

The trouble is that lots of them weren't listening at all. And in our lives we are often so busy and preoccupied with things that don't really matter that we make too much noise to hear the still, small voice of God telling us really important things about what is right and what is wrong, and how we can live good lives, full of honest, loving behaviour.

God will always whisper what is good and true and loving to help us. We won't hear an actual voice because God can speak straight into our hearts and minds, so we will just know, suddenly, that what we are doing is very good or very bad, very thoughtful or rather selfish and unkind. Once we know, we can stop the wrong behaviour and change it. But we do need to get used to listening so we can hear God clearly.

All-age ideas

- Make a large card jigsaw of a body outline and a church. During the reading from Corinthians, have two groups of children working on these in the aisle so that the shapes are being built up visually in line with our understanding. The puzzles can be left on the floor so that people walk past (or over) them on their way to communion as one body.

- Act out the Gospel by having it fixed on a scroll. The Gospel reader reads the first section from the Bible as s/he walks up to the lectern. A scroll is handed over and verses 17b to 20a are read from this. When it is handed back the reader takes up the Bible again and walks over to sit down for the rest of the passage.

FOURTH SUNDAY OF EPIPHANY

Ezekiel 43:27-44:4
Psalm 48
1 Corinthians 13:1-13
Luke 2:22-40

At eight days old, Jesus is presented in the temple, and at the Purification is revealed to Simeon and Anna as the promised Saviour who is able to reveal to us our true selves.

All-age talk

Today is a good opportunity to celebrate the elderly faithful and build relationships between young and old. Beforehand arrange for an elderly man and woman to sit at the front with a microphone to answer a few questions put to them by the children about what life was like when they were children. Gather the children round their feet and introduce the elderly people. Since they have been alive a long time they have picked up lots of wisdom. They have lived through things the younger ones here have heard about in history. Invite the children to find out what it was like being a child 70 or more years ago – they can ask about clothes, toys, school, church or food, for instance. After a few questions thank the volunteers and have the children escort them back to their seats.

In today's Gospel we heard about Joseph and Mary bringing the baby Jesus into the temple. All Jewish families did this when their first son was born. They came to give a present, or offer a sacrifice to God and dedicate the child. We've had two wise, elderly people answering questions today. And when Mary, Joseph and Jesus came into the temple there were two wise elderly people there. Their names were Simeon and Anna. They had both loved God all their life, and if any of us do that, we will end up wise and lovable in our old age. You can't love God all your life and end up crabby and narrow-minded.

Jesus didn't have a big label tied round his swaddling clothes saying 'I am the Messiah'. Joseph and

Mary didn't wave flags or shout to everyone, 'Look! This is the baby you've all been waiting for!' From the outside he looked just like any other baby, and Mary and Joseph looked just like an ordinary, fairly poor set of parents, rather dusty after the journey.

So how did Simeon and Anna know that this baby was the one they were waiting for?

Simeon had been told that he would see the promised Messiah in person before he died. He had been listening to God all his life, and because he was used to listening to God, he was able to recognise that this particular baby was the Messiah, God's chosen one.

When we spend a lot of time with another person we get to know how they think, and we understand them better and better. If we spend time with God every day, starting from today, and carry on doing that right into our old age, we will get to know him better and better, and it won't be long before we are able to hear what he speaks into our hearts. It is astounding that the powerful creator of this universe is happy to communicate with individuals like this, but that's God for you. He's hoping there will be some wise and faithful elderly Christians in the future – twenty, thirty, forty, fifty, sixty, seventy or eighty years from now. There could be. It could be us.

All-age ideas

- Have a grandparent and grandchild bringing up the offertory gifts.

- Act out the Gospel as it is narrated, using a young family with a real baby if you have one available!

- Read Simeon's song (the Nunc Dimittis) antiphonally across the two sides of the church.

- Have a display of photographs of those who regularly receive communion in their homes, with space for people to sign their pledge to pray for a particular person daily. It is important that these frail and elderly faithful do not become forgotten by the rest of the church.

PROPER 1

Sunday between 3 and 9 February inclusive (if earlier than the Second Sunday before Lent)

Isaiah 6:1-8 (9-13)
Psalm 138
1 Corinthians 15:1-11
Luke 5:1-11

God calls his people and commissions them.

All-age talk

You will need a mirror. First do a spot of face-painting on a volunteer, writing their own name in mirror-writing across their face. Then show them their face in the mirror. They will be surprised at what they look like because it isn't their familiar face looking back at them. Yet it is their own named self they are looking at.

Whenever Jesus met up with people he seems to have been able to show them who they were; what they were really like. By the things he said, the stories he told, and by the signs and miracles he did, people were able to look at him and suddenly see something about themselves they hadn't realised before. Some suddenly realised that they were lovable and important, when they had always thought they were rubbish. Others suddenly saw that they were living very mean, selfish lives, and knew they wanted to change.

In the event we hear about today, Simon Peter has been fishing all night long without any success at all. It's possible that Jesus had watched them, and noticed how they carried on even when they were tired and disappointed. Perhaps Jesus brought that into his teaching, and the fishermen would have sat up on the beach and thought, 'This man really knows what it's like to be a fisherman like me, working all night with nothing to show for it!' So when Jesus suggested they try again, Simon was doubtful, but willing to give it a go. The huge catch of fish, coming suddenly after all that time they had worked in vain, must have given Simon a shock. It was a bit like looking in a mirror and seeing who he really was for the first time.

He saw that this man Jesus, who had been sitting in Simon's own fishing boat talking to the crowds, was different from anyone he had ever met before. His goodness, his wise teaching and his knowledge of where the fish were, all made Simon suddenly ashamed. We don't know what it was in Simon's life that went through his mind. It might have been some particular sin he still felt guilty about, or it might have been remembering all the general meanness and selfishness, or the bad temper he knew he had.

The important thing for us to look at is how Jesus helped him see himself, and then said, 'Don't be afraid, follow me.' That is what Jesus does with us today as well. So be ready for it. If something makes you suddenly see yourself and you don't like everything you see, Jesus will not be standing at your elbow, saying, 'There's no hope for you, then, is there? You might as well give up.' He will be there, speaking into your heart words of love and comfort and hope: 'Don't be afraid of what you really are. Come and follow me.'

All-age ideas

- Have music played as background to the reading from Isaiah which reflects the sense of overwhelming holiness and wonder of God. Begin with the music on its own, then lower the volume as the reading starts. The reader leaves longer spaces between sentences than usual and the music gives people time to reflect on the vision. Fade the music out during verse 7.

- For the Gospel have different voices for Simon and Jesus.

- Have a fishing net, sand and shells incorporated into the main flower arrangement, or make a boaty display with oars, life jackets, oilskins and waders at the entrance, with a prayer for those who work on the sea.

PROPER 2

Sunday between 10 and 16 February inclusive (if earlier than the Second Sunday before Lent)

Jeremiah 17:5-10
Psalm 1
1 Corinthians 15:12-20
Luke 6:17-26

The challenges and rewards of living by faith.

All-age talk

Beforehand gather a selection of brand-name items relevant to each age group in the congregation.

Begin by displaying each item and drawing attention to the brand name to impress people. Talk about how we are sometimes made to feel we have to have a particular thing in order to be thought normal or worth anything. Sometimes we are teased if we haven't got them. Sometimes we go out shopping to cheer ourselves up, thinking that having more will make us happy. Sometimes we spend money we can't afford to keep up with our friends or neighbours.

Put all the items into a carton labelled 'Very Important' and close the lid. Explain that Jesus turns our ideas of what is important upside down. As you say this, turn the carton upside down. Today we have heard Jesus telling the people that trust in what you can buy and possess is not the good thing the advertisements say it is, and these things don't give us long-term happiness at all.

So what does he offer instead?

Jesus says that we will be much happier if we trust in God rather than in things people say about us, and things people make and sell. Getting stuck in the 'wanting something else' mode or the 'everybody else does it' mode just ends up making us dissatisfied and greedy and selfish, which doesn't bring happiness to us or those we live with. But if we put our trust in God, all the riches of the kingdom of God will be ours. We'll enjoy the lovely and surprising ways God provides for our needs. We'll be able to see what is good and right, and want to work enthusiastically again instead of just going through the motions. We won't be frantically running to keep up with the latest fashion. We won't be so anxious about material things.

Jesus doesn't say we'll have lots of comforts or fame or money if we live like this. In fact he says we will run into insults and people will think we're crazy, and they will laugh at us and make life difficult for us. We can't say we haven't been warned!

But the rewards far outweigh the disadvantages. Putting our trust in God will enable us to live as free, contented and generous-hearted people – the kind of people we would, deep down, probably prefer to be.

All-age ideas

- Have a twin flower arrangement of a dry, dead branch set in sand, and a bonsai tree or a cluster of flowering pot plants, standing in a wide, shallow tray filled with water and a few pebbles. Have a quotation from Jeremiah or Psalm 1 beside the arrangement.

- The Jeremiah passage works well read chorally with men's and women's voices. Work through the reading with highlighter pens to decide who will be reading which parts, and experiment a little. Practise the reading in church beforehand, using whatever sound system is in place, so as to try out the full effect.

- Have a collection of actual items needed, rather than money, for a local project to help the homeless, for example.

PROPER 3

Sunday between 17 and 23 February inclusive (if earlier than the Second Sunday before Lent)

Genesis 45:3-11, 15
Psalm 37:1-11, 39-40
1 Corinthians
   15:35-38, 42-50
Luke 6:27-38

Jesus teaches us to love our enemies and forgive those who sin against us.

All-age talk

Beforehand ask the children to make lots of paper chains.

Remind everyone of what Jesus teaches us in today's Gospel: to love our enemies and forgive those who sin against us. How on earth are we supposed to do it? Surely enemies are people you hate? Why does Jesus tell us to love them, then?

Ask a volunteer to run and skip around a bit and talk about how life can feel when we are happy with ourselves, and everything is going well for us. But sooner or later we get into a mood with someone, someone upsets us and annoys us, someone else winds us up, someone makes our life a real misery, someone lets us down and spoils our plans, someone hurts a person we love, or someone steals from us a close friend or a marriage partner, or our dignity in old age. (At each suggestion, drape a chain around the volunteer until s/he is smothered in chains.) And if we haven't forgiven these people who have sinned against us and hurt us, we end up still carrying invisible chains which weigh us down. The volunteer can walk around bowed down with the heavy chains.

So when Jesus says to us, 'Love your enemies and forgive those who wrong you', he knows it is hard, but he also knows it will set us free to live fully again. Every time we say (and really mean it) 'I forgive you for what you did', a chain drops off. (Pull a chain off the volunteer.) Every time we wrestle with our feelings of hate for someone and ask God to help us sort things out, a chain drops off. (Pull off another chain.) Pull off the remaining chains, with everyone saying 'I forgive you!' for each one.

Jesus doesn't like to see us weighed down with heavy invisible chains of hate and resentment and bitterness against people. He wants us to be free to enjoy life, and he will always help us to do the forgiving. Forgiving is not easy; it's very hard work. If you know there is someone you are finding it very hard to forgive, ask God for the grace to forgive and then work at the forgiving. Don't live with the chains any more.

All-age ideas

• Act out the Joseph story with someone taking the part of Joseph.

• A chant. Have the following words written on the weekly handout or on an OHP: 'Love your enemies. Do good to those who hate you. Pray for those who hurt you.'

   Very quietly the congregation recites these words, repeating them six times. Above this hushed chanting of Jesus' teaching, have three people, standing in different parts of the church, to call out their protests. They should leave enough space between each protest for the teaching to be heard through, and the chant should be the last thing left in people's minds.

   Here are the protests:

   1. 'But you can't expect me to forgive them! Not after what they've done!'

   2. 'It was terrible.
      It was unforgivable.
      How can I possibly love them now?'

   3. 'But they've ruined my whole life.
      Why should I forgive them?'

SECOND SUNDAY BEFORE LENT

Genesis 2:4b-9, 15-25
Psalm 65
Revelation 4
Luke 8:22-25

'He commands even the winds and the water and they obey him.'

All-age talk

Borrow a toy farm set, or a playmat with animals, houses and cars to arrange on it. Also borrow any remote control vehicle.

Set the youngest children arranging their landscape in a space where they can be seen. Then have the remote control vehicle demonstrated in the aisle. As it is directed to run in different directions, talk about the kind of control the demonstrator has over the vehicle; the vehicle has no choice in the matter. Look at the kind of control demonstrated in the children arranging the animals and buildings. Here, too, they are deciding for the animals what is the best place for them to be. These decisions may be sensitive and based on what the animals would probably like best, but still they have no choice, and must remain in the pond or looking over a fence where they are placed, unless the children decide they need a change.

What about our behaviour in this service? We mostly all sit/stand/kneel in all the right places very obediently, though no one can make us join in attentively if we choose not to, and we could, of course, choose to be very disruptive and spoil it for others.

The Bible tells us that God cared about the people he made. As soon as Adam was made he was invited to help God and share in his work. God would bring the animals to Adam, and Adam named them. (Take some pictures or animal models to the children and let them name them.) The gardening was not drudgery, but wholesome and rewarding work, with God and people working together.

This is a picture of us all living in harmony with

God, obeying him, and living as he suggests is right and good for us. It isn't remote control, with God making us do what he wants. It isn't God doing what is best for us whether we want the best or not. It is God loving us and inviting us to work with him. He lets us choose whether to live this way or not. He hopes we will choose what he knows will make us really deep-down happy, but if we choose ways that mess things up for us or others, he won't stop us. He will just be there ready to dry our tears and help us try again when we realise how foolish we have been.

All-age ideas

- Have sounds to accompany the readings. For the Genesis passage have glockenspiels and triangles, and the sounds of breathing. For the storm in the Gospel reading use shakers and other percussion instruments building up and dying down.

- Using green and blue streamers (made from lengths of crêpe paper) have a group of dancers starting still on the floor and gradually boiling up to a turbulent storm which settles when a voice calls above the noise, 'Be Still!' The dance can either be accompanied by the percussion music, or by taped music, such as the storm section from Beethoven's *Pastoral Symphony*.

315

Sunday before Lent

Exodus 34:29-35
Psalm 99
2 Corinthians
  3:12-4:2
Luke 9:28-36 (37-43)

God's glory makes Moses' face radiant, and it transfigures Jesus as he prays on the mountain. Our lives, too, can become increasingly radiant as the Spirit transforms us.

All-age talk

You will need a hand mirror.

Begin by asking everyone if they have noticed how people often look like their pets, particularly dogs! Perhaps they choose a pet which reflects their own character. Today we are looking at how spending our lives with God makes us more and more like him.

Use the mirror to catch the light and throw it on to people's faces. Mirrors are excellent at spreading light around, because they are able to reflect light. In the first reading today we saw Moses, who was a close friend of God. He was the person who led the people of Israel out of Egypt, where they had been slaves, and through the desert to the promised land. When Moses had been on a mountain in God's company and was given the Ten Commandments, he came down from the mountain with his face glowing and radiant. Like a mirror, he was reflecting some of the glory of God. Sometimes if people are really happy – a bride and bridegroom getting married to the one they love, students hearing they have passed all their exams really well, or children on their birthday – we talk about them looking radiant, or glowing with happiness. How we are feeling and thinking inside changes the way we look.

When Jesus was on earth, three of his close friends were on a mountain with him when he was praying, and they saw him not just with a radiant face, but completely shining, or transfigured. What they were seeing was the glory of God in Jesus, who

316

was and is completely at one with God, his Father. They heard God's voice explaining who Jesus was and telling them to listen to him. Not like listening to music in the background, but really attentive listening, like you would listen to instructions for flying an aeroplane if you were the only person on board able to bring it safely to land.

When we live our lives close to Jesus like this, listening to his quiet voice guiding us, talking over our problems and happiness with him, and working at living a good life, then gradually our faces will start to show some of God's glory, and our lives will start to shine, reflecting God's loving nature like mirrors (flash the light again) reflecting the light.

All-age ideas

• Have a mirror on the floor with a flower arrangement and lots of small candles on it, so that the picture of reflecting light and beauty is expressed.

• During the reading of the Gospel, have music playing, starting at verse 29. This can be provided by the organ or music group, or you could use recorded music.

• For the penitential rite, give out small pieces of shiny paper (cut from wrapping paper). Explain that the cleaner, smoother and shinier the mirror, the better it works. Ask people to bring to mind anything in their life which needs cleaning, smoothing down or polishing. Give them time to tell God about it, and receive his forgiveness, so that they are all able to reflect God's love better.

FIRST SUNDAY OF LENT

Deuteronomy 26:1-11
Psalm 91:1-2, 9-16
Romans 10:8b-13
Luke 4:1-13

Following his baptism, Jesus is severely tempted out in the desert, and shows us how to overcome temptation.

All-age talk

On matching sets of three graded sizes of card, from A5 to huge, write these two messages, with the print and thickness increasing with the card size.

I want it and I want it now.

Love God and love one another.

Begin by explaining that Jesus went into the desert after he had been baptised, and had a very hard time out there being tempted. We all know what it feels like to be tempted. It's when we want something or want to do something which we know is wrong. (Show the middle-sized 'I want it and I want it now' card.) Ask someone to hold this card, but don't make them stand with their arms in the air for ages.

Jesus was being tempted to turn the stones into bread so he could eat them, but he knew that this would be using his power in a selfish way. He remembered that he loved God and he loved other people (display the largest 'Love God and love one another' sign). Ask someone else to hold this up.

As you can see, the love for God and other people stayed bigger than the temptation, and so Jesus was able to stand firm and not let the temptation get the better of him.

Whenever Jesus was tempted he always remembered that his love for God and other people was much stronger than the 'I want'. Put these signs down.

Now let's see what happens with us. First we get a little temptation inside us. (Give one helper the smallest 'I want' sign.) It isn't very big and we remember the right way to live (give the other helper the middle-sized 'Love God' sign) so we don't give way to the temptation.

But as we think about it more, this happens. (Exchange the small 'I want' for the middle-sized one.) And now there's a battle going on inside us, because the 'I want' is the same size as the 'Love God'. If we're not careful the 'I want' will get even bigger! (Swap it for the largest 'I want' sign.) And when we let the 'I want' get bigger than the 'Love God', even for a minute, we're in danger of falling into temptation, and doing or saying what we really know is wrong.

Jesus shows us how not to do this. As soon as you feel a little 'I want' coming on (show it), remember that you love God and you love other people more than you want what is wrong. (Display the middle-sized 'Love God' sign.) And if the 'I want' gets bigger in you (show the middle-sized 'I want') think hard about how you and God love each other (show the largest 'Love God' sign) so that the 'I want' is less strong and you can fight it; and instead of giving in and doing what you know is wrong, God will be helping you to stand up to temptation and win.

All-age ideas

- On the walls have poster-sized versions of the advertisements below so that people can see how temptations use truth but distort it.

With the posters have a heading: 'Always read the small print!'

During the first reading have a family bringing baskets of fruit and vegetables to lay in front of the altar.

319

SECOND SUNDAY OF LENT

Genesis 15:1-12, 17-18
Psalm 27
Philippians 3:17-4:1
Luke 13:31-35

If only we will agree to put our faith in God, he will fill our lives with meaning and bring us safely to heaven.

All-age talk

Beforehand collect some 'special offers' from your junk mail during the week and from local shops. Also make one sign that says, 'Not today, thanks!' and another that says, 'Yes, I'll go for it!' Ask everyone (or just the children) to shout out the words on the signs whenever you show them.

Start by talking about the special offers in your collection, referring to those which people of different ages in the congregation might find interesting, amusing and completely ridiculous. Ask a volunteer to display the general view of people about various offers by holding up the appropriate sign. Point out that in all these special offers we are free to choose whether to take advantage of the offer or not, and if it's something we really want and like we're likely to say, 'Yes, I'll go for it!' If we don't think we need the item on offer then we don't think it's worth having and we're more likely to say, 'Not today, thanks!'

Jesus' special offer to us is extremely good value. He offers to make himself at home in our lives and set us free from all the things that imprison us, so that we can really live to the full, not just now, but after death as well. For ever, in fact. How much does it cost? Nothing. Or rather, everything, but Jesus has already paid the complete cost for us.

As it's such a good offer you'd think that everyone would rush to take him up on it. (Display the 'Yes, I'll go for it!' sign.) But today's Gospel tells us that there have always been lots of people who have refused the offer and turned it down. (Display the 'Not today, thanks!' sign.) In our Gospel reading we see Jesus really sad. What has made him so sad is that he has been longing to give people the love he knows they need and yet they won't let him give them this free gift which could make their whole lives rich.

Perhaps we don't think we need God's love and help. Perhaps we are afraid to accept because it seems just too good to be true. Perhaps we think it can't be possible because we don't think we're worth something as good as this. Whatever the reasons, lots of us humans end up saying 'Not today, thanks!' to the best special offer ever. That means losing out on all the good things God is hoping to give us during our lives on earth and our lives in heaven. Things like joy and peace of mind, contentment and fulfilment, a sense of really being alive and living life the best way there is.

Abram was a 'Yes, I'll go for it!' person. He took God up on his offer and believed God would put his action where his mouth was. As a result his life was greatly blessed. And God did keep his promise to make Abram's descendants as many as the uncountable stars in the sky.

God will never force us to say 'Yes, I'll go for it!' when we really want to say 'Not today, thanks!' But before anyone says 'Not today, thanks!' to God's special offer of his freely given love, they would be wise to think it over very carefully. It's such a fantastic offer that the only wise thing to say is, 'Yes, I'll go for it!'

All-age ideas

- A mime using people of different age groups. One person stands with arms outstretched and beckoning, and all the others move slowly and wearily around, as if building their own lives with heavy stones. They take no notice of the beckoning person. Then just one person stops building long enough to look up and notice the person reaching out. As soon as they begin to respond by reaching out, the person comes to meet them and give them food and drink. This person now goes to nudge others to notice, until several have relaxed and are enjoying the refreshment and the newfound friendship of one another. At the end they all turn and reach out to those who have refused to lift their eyes from building, and everyone freezes in this position. This can be done with a musical background, perhaps while a hymn is sung, or in silence.

• At the penitential rite have people fold their arms and close their eyes as they think of the times they have failed to reach out to others in love, and chosen not to get involved with what God has asked them to do. As they call these things to mind with sorrow, ask them to unfold their arms and open their hands in a gesture of openness, both to receive God's forgiveness and to commit themselves to reach out in love from now on.

THIRD SUNDAY OF LENT

Isaiah 55:1-9
Psalm 63:1-8
1 Corinthians 10:1-13
Luke 13:1-9

We have God's invitation to come and drink freely of his Spirit, but if we keep refusing his offer it can eventually be withdrawn.

All-age talk

Have some different varieties of bottled water and some cups, and offer drinks to a few people around the church. Ask some to describe what it feels like to be really thirsty – when your mouth feels like sandpaper, and all you can think about is the drink you long for.

God says to us, 'I am like a drink of water to you when you're really thirsty. I can quench your thirst, make you feel better, keep you alive, refresh you and comfort you.'

What we need to do is take what God offers us. We need to say, 'Thanks, Lord God. I'll accept what you are offering and drink deeply from you.'

Sometimes if we're thirsty we're not too fussy about the source of the water. (I was so thirsty once in Spain that I drank from a fountain and spent the rest of the holiday regretting it!) Some water isn't clean and can make you very ill. With water we need to make sure we can trust it. And it's the same with spiritual water, too.

Suppose we are thirsty to understand who we are, why we are alive, why there is so much evil and suffering and why things go wrong. There are lots of people offering us easy answers or giving us things to take our minds off this deep thirst. Some of those things (like drugs and alcohol abuse, and materialism) are bad for us.

The only way to be completely and safely satisfied – physically, mentally and spiritually – as the whole wonderful human being you are, is drinking in God's Spirit. Don't be distracted. God is pure, faithful, true and full of love; the best drink there is.

All-age ideas

- Have an arrangement on a table of a carafe of water and a glass, with the text: 'Is anyone thirsty?'

- In small groups all over the church pray for those who thirst, both physically and spiritually, while passing a drink of water around the group.

- At each section of the intercessions have a glass of water brought and placed on a drinks tray in front of the altar, so that people will see it and call to mind the prayers as they gather at the altar to receive communion.

FOURTH SUNDAY OF LENT: MOTHERING SUNDAY

Exodus 2:1-10 or
  1 Samuel 1:20-28
Psalm 34:11-20 or
  Psalm 127:1-4
2 Corinthians 1:3-7 or
  Colossians 3:12-17
Luke 2:33-35 or
  John 19:25-27

While we are here in this life, given one another to care for, we can learn the lessons of mutual love and support and shared suffering.

All-age talk

Ask for two volunteers of about the same height (or several pairs of volunteers) and tie the ankles of each pair together. They can practise walking three-legged around the church. As they do so, point out how difficult it is until you get the hang of walking in step with one another. This is one of the most important lessons we can learn in life.

We are all given other people to live with. People in our families like brothers and sisters, mums, dads, grandparents, aunts, uncles and cousins. Is it easy, just because we are related? No! Sometimes it's very good fun, like when we're all getting on together and making one another laugh, and listening to what the others are saying, and the others understanding when you come home fed up.

At other times it's very hard living with those close to us. Like when everyone wants something different and no one wants to do the washing-up, and so on. That's a bit like when we get in a tangle of feet in the three-legged race and trip one another up. When we start to think it would be a lot easier to live on our own without other people around.

What Saint Paul suggests is that we need to live in step with one another, learning to do things like forgiving one another, being patient, letting someone else have the best sometimes, co-operating instead of getting at each other's throats all the time. That's the Christian way. That's Jesus' way. It may also

325

mean comforting one another, sharing one another's suffering. It's really learning to love in the way Jesus talked about love.

When we live like this, we and the people we are joined up with, in our families and at school and at work, won't need to keep tripping one another up. We'll be able to live more supportively, enjoying one another as God meant us to.

All-age ideas

- Have families (preferably three generations) welcoming, collecting the offering, and leading the intercessions today.

- If flowers are given out today have enough for the older mums too. There isn't any rule about motherhood finishing when your children are grown.

- Gather the children in the aisle and all turn towards them and pray for them, their growing and their families.

FIFTH SUNDAY OF LENT

Isaiah 43:16-21
Psalm 126
Philippians 3:4b-14
John 12:1-8

When we are privileged to share in Christ's suffering, we also share in his new life.

All-age talk

Have some perfumed oil burning throughout the talk, a shell showing the mother of pearl, and a dish of smoothed beach pebbles. Ask for a volunteer and fasten a string of pearls round their neck. Let them walk up and down to show everyone.

Explain how pearls come about, a bit of grit or sand getting inside the shell and rubbing so it hurts. The way the mollusc deals with this is to coat the grit with layers of mother of pearl and in the end something beautiful results from the pain.

Look at a pebble. The beauty often comes from the violent battering and explosive forces of molten rock, which has been worked on by the waves and sand to smooth those scars to beauty. Today we are shown how God can turn terrible suffering into something very beautiful.

We join Jesus with his friends at a celebration meal, knowing that there is suffering ahead. That's never nice or comfortable to think about. We can get some idea of what that felt like if we think of how we feel when we are dreading something. You may be dreading a visit to the dentist or a maths test, or an operation or moving house. You know it has to be done, but that doesn't take away the unease and dread. Jesus knew the suffering would be terrible, but he knew it would be worth it because through it people would be set free from their sin.

At the meal, Mary, one of Jesus' friends, smoothes some sweet-smelling oil on to Jesus' feet – rather like aromatherapy. It was very expensive stuff, and you're probably wondering why she did it. Judas certainly thought it was a waste of money. She did

327

it because she loved Jesus. And she loved Jesus because through him she knew God accepted her as she was and forgave her and loved her. (We all long to be accepted as we are and forgiven and loved. When we are, we blossom; when we're not, we shrivel up inside.)

In Jesus' country it was usual to anoint the body of your loved ones with fragrant oil when they had died, so when Mary poured that sweet-smelling ointment on Jesus' feet she was looking ahead to when he would have to suffer and die out of love for us. Loving us was going to be very painful and cost his whole life, but it would be turned into something beautiful because through Jesus dying we can all know for certain that we are accepted as we are, forgiven, and loved completely.

All-age ideas

- Give everyone a small pebble as they come in, and at the time of confession ask them to hold their pebble, look at it and feel it, noticing the faults and scars on it. Play the soundtrack of waves on a beach as they call to mind their faults and habits which need smoothing and transforming by the waves of God's love.

- Have a bowl of incense burning, or an oil burner, so that the room is filled with fragrance during the Gospel. After the Gospel sing *May the fragrance of Jesus* (Graham Kendrick) while people reflect on the story they have heard.

PALM SUNDAY

Liturgy of the Palms:
Luke 19:28-40
Psalm 118:1-2, 19-29

Liturgy of the Passion:
Isaiah 50:4-9a
Psalm 31:9-16
Philippians 2:5-11
Luke 22:14-23:56 or
    Luke 23:1-49

As Jesus rides into Jerusalem on a donkey, and the crowds welcome him, we sense both the joy at the Messiah being acclaimed, and the heaviness of his suffering which follows. Jesus' mission is drawing to its fulfilment.

All-age talk

Ask about football matches people have watched which have been really memorable and exciting. If you happen to have any players in the congregation, ask them to talk about a particularly memorable moment of triumph, and how it felt to have the spectators sharing the exhilaration.

When Jesus rode into Jerusalem all the crowds were on his side, cheering, waving and singing, pushing for the best view, and excited not just with Jesus as a hero but at what was a turning point for their side – their country. There would have been some there on that first Palm Sunday who saw it as a political statement, others as religious revival, others as a festive carnival of some kind.

So why did Jesus ride into Jerusalem on a donkey?

He was doing something the scriptures had said would happen to the promised Messiah. This meant he was giving a very strong hint to the people about who he was. He was saying that the Messiah had now come and was entering the holy city of Jerusalem as a king. But instead of all the rich clothes and grandeur of an earthly king, Jesus was riding on a very humble animal that was often piled high with people's luggage and shopping. It was a bit like using a shopper bike rather than a Rolls Royce, stretched limo or BMW.

All the crowds that day cheered Jesus, but a few days later, once he didn't look like a winner any more, many of the same people had turned against him and were yelling for his blood.

What kind of supporters are we? Do we support our team only when it's doing really well, or do we hang in there even after a run of lost games? Do we stick with our friends even when they go through a bad patch? Do we keep trying even when a marriage gets shaky? And, perhaps most important of all, are we happy to sing God's praise in church on Sunday but ignore him or deny him by our behaviour and language and choices during the week?

These are Palm Sunday questions which we need to ask ourselves today.

All-age ideas

- Give the children coloured crêpe-paper streamers to wave in the procession, and choose songs which are joyful and don't need books for at least part of the route. Encourage the children to shout and dance and sing – children were very noticeable on the first Palm Sunday.

- Look at some imaginative ways of presenting the Gospel using different voices, singing it, using slides as a visual focus, changing the lighting during the narrative, or using expressive mime during the narration.

EASTER DAY

Acts 10:34-43 or
  Isaiah 65:17-25
Psalm 118:1-2, 14-24
1 Corinthians
  15:19-26 or
    Acts 10:34-43
John 20:1-18 or
  Luke 24:1-12

It is true. Jesus is alive for all time.
The Lord of life cannot be held by death.
God's victory over sin and death means
that new life for us is a reality.

All-age talk

Take along a few Easter cards you have received, and show them around, describing the pictures on them. There are probably some fluffy new chicks, young lambs skipping about in the spring fields, lots of flowers, and some decorated eggs. And we probably all gave and received a chocolate Easter egg today. So all this says that Easter is a happy, festive occasion, in tune with the new life of springtime, with all the new birds, animals and flowers.

What else? Some cards have a garden with an empty tomb, and three crosses on a hill in the distance. Others have made all the flowers into the shape of a cross. So what do these cards tell us about Easter? They tell us about another kind of new life, which doesn't happen naturally every time winter is over, but only ever happened once. It wasn't an ordinary thing at all. It was so completely amazing and impossible that people are still talking about it two thousand years after it happened! Do you know what it was? (Let them tell you.)

Well, that's impossible, surely. People can't come back to life again. It just doesn't happen. The fact that it actually did happen – that Jesus really did die on the Friday, and he really was alive again on the Sunday – shows us that Jesus must be more than a human being. He must be God as well as human. And he must be still just as much alive now as he was then. No wonder we want to celebrate and give one another flowers and cards and Easter eggs! Spring is nice to celebrate, but this is the most

331

wonderful event ever. It means that nothing, not even death itself, is out of God's reach for saving and transforming.

When you eat your chocolate eggs, and open your Easter cards, remember what we're really celebrating today: Jesus is risen. Alleluia! (Everyone can shout back: 'He is risen indeed. Alleluia!')

All-age ideas

- Have one flower arrangement consisting of three levels. The lowest arrangement has rich dark purples with only a few hints of gold. Gradually the colours blend into the gold, yellow and white of Easter at the top arrangement. This will be a visual reminder of the journey to Easter through the suffering of Good Friday.

- Part of the children's day during Holy Week could be given over to creating a banner proclaiming the message of Easter. This can be made of fabric, with the design stuck (with double-sided sticky tape) or appliquéd on to the background, or of heavyweight wallpaper using either paint or collage work.

- The Easter garden presents a wonderful opportunity for different age groups to work together. Consider having a garden outside the church as well as inside.

- Encourage everyone to bring bells to ring in a burst of praise with the organ or music group just before singing the Gloria.

SECOND SUNDAY OF EASTER

Acts 5:27-32
Psalm 118:14-29 or
    Psalm 150
Revelation 1:4-8
John 20:19-31

Having seen Jesus in person, the disciples are convinced of the Resurrection. We too can meet him personally.

All-age talk

Beforehand place a tape or CD in your pocket. Begin by telling everyone that you have got an orchestra in your pocket and asking them if they believe you. Then show them the tape or CD. Now they have seen with their eyes they know exactly what was in your pocket. And now that they understand what it is, they can see that you were right – you did have an orchestra in your pocket, but not in the way they expected!

Jesus had told his friends that he would have to suffer and die before rising to new life, and they hadn't understood what he meant. Even when Jesus was dying, nailed to the cross, they didn't realise that this had to happen if we were to be saved from sin and death. Instead they felt miserable and let down and lost and confused. They didn't believe because they hadn't seen for themselves. (Put the tape back in your pocket.)

Then, on the first Easter evening, Jesus was suddenly there with them. He was alive, talking with them and they were so excited and overjoyed to have him there again. Now that they had seen him they knew it was true that he was alive. (As you say this bring out the tape from your pocket again, but don't refer to it. It will simply help them make connections.)

But it was also different from what they might have thought. Jesus wasn't exactly the same as before. With this new life he was able to be there without having unlocked the doors. He could appear and disappear. But he was a real person, not a ghost. He didn't make the disciples feel scared; he filled them with peace and happiness.

At last they began to understand what he had meant when he had talked to them about dying and rising again. They began to understand that God's love had to go right through death, loving and forgiving the whole way, so as to win the battle against evil. When Jesus came through death and out into the light of new life, he was like a butterfly coming out of its chrysalis – the same but completely different, free and beautiful.

Thomas and the others needed to see Jesus with their eyes for quite a few times after the Resurrection. They now had to learn that he was always there with them, even if they couldn't see him.

All-age ideas

- While singing the *Caterpillar* song, have a few children with painted net butterfly wings and wrapped in green towels to look like caterpillars. They are squirming around, pretending to eat plants and then curling up during the chrysalis part. Then they throw off their towels and fly about all over the church, ending with arms raised in front of the altar.

- Today's reading works well with different voices and a narrator.

THIRD SUNDAY OF EASTER

Acts 9:1-6 (7-20)
Psalm 30
Revelation 5:11-14
John 21:1-19

Those who know Jesus and recognise that he is the anointed Saviour are commissioned to go out as his witnesses to proclaim the good news.

All-age talk

Beforehand prepare some masks from thin card, and mount them on sticks so that they can be held up in front of people's faces. Here is the pattern.

Begin by asking for two volunteers (of different age groups) and giving them a brief interview: What is your name? What is your favourite colour? What do you enjoy doing? How did you get to church today?

Explain that it's nice for us all to know who these people are, and suggest that we all get to know the name of someone in church today. We may see them there regularly but have never actually discovered their name!

Notice how Jesus made a point of calling Simon Peter by his name in today's Gospel. 'Simon, son of John, do you love me?' And in the reading from Acts about Saul meeting Jesus on the Damascus road, again Jesus calls him by his name: 'Saul, Saul, why are you persecuting me?' And on the first Easter Day when Jesus met Mary in the garden he called her by her name, and that's when she recognised him as Jesus.

Produce the 'happy' mask and ask for a volunteer to 'wear' it. Talk about the way we sometimes pretend we're different from the person we really are, because we think God and other people will like us better. This person is pretending to be happy. But if we are pretending, and God knows that inside we are really feeling very grumpy or sad, then the mask we are wearing makes him sad. This person is pretending to be very holy and good. But if we are pretending, and God knows that inside we are feeling angry and resentful, then the mask we are wearing makes him sad.

Jesus wants us to trust him with our real selves, even the bits where we make mistakes and get our lives in a mess. He speaks to us by our real name and will spend our lifetime teaching us who we really are. (Take the mask away.)

All-age ideas

- Have this written on the handout, or displayed on the OHP so that each person is able to join in with the responses.

  Leader My child, where are you?

  All Here I am, Lord, right beside you.

  Leader That is not the person I know and love. Where is the real you, my child?

  All Here I am, Lord. Surely you recognise me now?

  Leader I recognise the face you wear, but where is the real you that I love?

  All Suppose I showed you and it was unacceptable?

  Leader It is the real you that I love.

  All Then just as I am, O Lamb of God, I come!

- Alternatively, this can be done by a hidden voice and someone wearing a mask, which is put aside at the end.

- The Gospel can be mimed as it is narrated.

FOURTH SUNDAY OF EASTER

Acts 9:36-43
Psalm 23
Revelation 7:9-17
John 10:22-30

Asked if he really is the Christ, Jesus directs his questioners to look at his life in action and see for themselves that he and the Father are one.

All-age talk

Begin by explaining that you are going to pretend you have just arrived from outer space, and you're going to work out what the climate is on planet Earth. Walk around picking up on the kind of clothing people are wearing and using that to give you clues about the weather outside. Point out that as humans we are quite good at working things out from signs and clues. What can you tell about the faith of the people who built this church, for instance? (People can share their ideas aloud, or with one another in pairs.)

Signs and clues help us to learn about life and make up our minds about the truth of things. If you claimed that you had just had a bucket of water thrown over you, you would expect people to be more likely to believe you if you were soaking wet, and less likely to believe you if you were completely dry. Show some muddy football kit belonging to one of the children. What was Sam doing yesterday, do you think? Is it more likely to be ballet or football?

Today we heard about some people who came up to Jesus at the feast of Hanukkah and asked him to tell them plainly whether he was the Christ they had been waiting for. Jesus told them to look at the signs and work it out for themselves. Let's look at those signs and see where they lead us. Ask for suggestions and then draw the ideas together. Jesus healed the sick, opened the eyes of the blind, gave the deaf their hearing back, and showed people in lots of ways that he loved them and enjoyed their company. And that's just what the scriptures had said the Christ would be like! So the signs lead us to recognise that Jesus really is the promised Messiah, or Christ.

All-age ideas

- In order to alert people to signs which lead us to understand Jesus better, fix arrows on the floor and walls and pillars before the service. They should all point to the cross. Reference can be made to these during the penitential section.

- In the penitential section draw people's attention to the arrows which direct us to the cross. Ask people to think about things they have done and said which have not helped direct people to Jesus; dishonest or unloving behaviour that has not helped people know God's love.

- Have someone hidden who is blowing bubbles, and two others who catch sight of a few bubbles and follow the trail back to the origin and the bubble blower. This can either be mimed or involve conversation about following signs. One of the pair can be convinced there is someone blowing bubbles, while the other is sceptical and keeps thinking of different reasons for the existence of the bubbles, such as soap in the organ, or somebody thinking clean thoughts.

- Have the passage from Acts mimed as it is narrated, with some real linen displayed at the beginning.

FIFTH SUNDAY OF EASTER

Acts 11:1-18
Psalm 148
Revelation 21:1-6
John 13:31-35

Christ, breaking through the barrier of sin and death, allows us to break into an entirely new way of living which continues into eternity.

All-age talk

Beforehand ask a family to help you by providing a couple of clothing items which are now too small for their child to wear. Or you could borrow a cub/brownie sweater which once you would have been able to get into. Also find a sprouting acorn, or a similar example of life bursting out of confines.

Begin by talking about the way we grow out of our clothes. Sometimes we like a sweater or jacket so much that we want to go on wearing it even when it's a bit short or tight, but eventually we realise that we just can't get into it any more, and we'll have to hand it down to someone younger or smaller. As you talk about this, use the children and their skimpy clothes to illustrate how silly it looks and how uncomfortable it feels to wear something which is much too small for us, and then try the same garment on someone it fits to see the difference.

Remind everyone that we are spiritual as well as physical, and we can grow out of things spiritually as well. Some of the early Christians thought that it wasn't right for non-Jewish people to be allowed to join the Church. Today we heard how Peter realised that was like wearing a sweater which was too small, and God's ideas were much bigger than they had thought. He wanted everyone to be part of his love, with no one left out. So the early church very sensibly took off that outgrown idea.

When we are very young, we are taught to pray prayers we can understand. That's wonderful. But if we are still praying like a three-year-old when we are thirteen or twenty-three, or fifty-three, we are wearing skimpy spiritual clothes that we have really outgrown. Unless we realise that, and take them off, and find ways of praying that fit, we won't be able to move forward where God wants us to go.

Take a look at the acorn. Acorns are lovely to hold and play with, just as they are. But the oak tree can't become its huge, leafy self unless it breaks out of the acorn, and leaves that behind.

Jesus gives us all a rule, or command. We are to love one another. As soon as we start this kind of responsible, caring love for one another, we are bound to start growing. Sometimes the growing hurts. Sometimes the growing feels exciting. Sometimes the growing is hard work. And always the growing will be breaking out of where we were before. This means that, like children growing taller year by year, we will not be able to keep wearing the same old spiritual clothes. God won't let us get set in our ways because he goes on having exciting plans for us right through our lives, no matter how old we get.

All-age ideas

- Have the Gospel read chorally by a group of voices, using different age groups, against a background of music. Start playing the music before the reading begins, and leave space for the music after verse 32, and again at the end.

- Last week the arrows all over the church pointed to the cross. Use the same arrows this week, but have them pointing to the people. Draw attention to this at the time of confession, when everyone can bring to mind the command to love one another, and direct others to God by loving behaviour. This will then lead on to recall the ways in which we fail to love one another.

- Have everyone holding hands all over the church, either as they sing *A new commandment* or during the Lord's Prayer.

SIXTH SUNDAY OF EASTER

Acts 16:9-15
Psalm 67
Revelation
   21:10, 22-22:5
John 14:23-29 or
   John 5:1-9

The continuing presence of God, as Holy Spirit, leads us, as Jesus promised, into a personally guided outreach to all nations.

All-age talk

First fill the space of the centre aisle with chairs and obstacles. If yours is a fixed pews building, have people to sit down as obstacles in the aisle. Remind everyone of how, in today's Gospel, Jesus was talking to his friends at the last supper they had together before he was crucified. Jesus knew his friends were dreading the future without him being there with them. Perhaps they thought it would be a bit like this.

Ask for a volunteer and blindfold them, twizzle them round and send them off down the aisle. As they walk hesitantly, bumping into the obstacles, you talk about Jesus' friends thinking that living without Jesus around would be like trying to get round the difficulties of life blindfolded, and with no one to help or guide them.

Rescue the volunteer and remove their blindfold. As this person knows, you don't feel very safe all on your own and unable to see where the obstacles are. It is frightening and could be dangerous. Sometimes our life can feel like that, and it isn't a comfortable place to be.

What Jesus wants his friends to know is that God doesn't have that in mind for them at all. Although Jesus knew he wouldn't be there physically with his friends for ever, he promised them that they (and we) would have a personal guide right there with us. Let's see how that changes things for us.

Blindfold the volunteer again, but this time appoint a sensible, caring guide who steers them round the obstacles, talking to them and helping

341

them along. (You may want to have primed this person beforehand.)

Watch them together, and then talk alongside the rest of their journey about God's Holy Spirit being with us to teach and explain things to us, to guide us and help us through the dangerous parts of life, so that we are not left alone, but working in partnership with our loving God.

All-age ideas

- Have labelled paper flags from many different nations displayed around the church. (Perhaps the uniformed organisations could provide these.) Or focus on a few countries and have displays of the needs and problems facing the people there, examples of their bread, and pictures of their people, together with the national flag. During the intercessions people can be encouraged to walk around the church, praying for the needs as music from the countries is played or sung.

- The meaning of the reading from Revelation is brought out well if it is read chorally by a group of people who have prepared it prayerfully, splitting the phrases among different voice tones – high, medium and low. If you have an OHP consider making some acetates from coloured pictures of light and water to show during the reading.

Ascension Day

Acts 1:1-11 or
  Daniel 7:9-14
Psalm 47 or
  Psalm 93
Ephesians 1:15-23 or
  Acts 1:1-11
Luke 24:44-53

Having bought back our freedom with the giving of his life, Jesus enters into the full glory to which he is entitled.

All-age talk

Begin by staging a Mexican wave, which runs through the whole church or assembly. Point out how it only worked so well because all of us as individuals were working together as a unit of energy.

Remind everyone of the events leading up to today, giving them a whistle-stop tour of Jesus' life, death, Resurrection and post-Resurrection appearances. Explain how the disciples needed that time to get used to Jesus being alive and around, though not always visible or physically present.

Now they were ready for the next stage in the plan. Jesus leads them out of the city and he gives them his blessing, telling them to hang around Jerusalem without rushing off to do their own bit of mission work. (Enthusiasm is wonderful but it can sometimes make us race off to start before we've got everything we need.) The disciples have got to wait because God is going to send the Holy Spirit to empower them and equip them for the work they will be doing. It will make it possible for the news of God's love to spread out through the world like our Mexican wave.

When Jesus had finished giving the disciples their instructions and his encouragement, we are told that the disciples watched him being taken into heaven, until a cloud hid him from their sight. Those are the only practical details we have, so we don't know exactly how it happened. But we do know that the disciples were in no doubt about where Jesus had gone, and they were full of joy and excitement as they made their way back to the city to wait for the Holy Spirit, as Jesus had told them to.

A lot of years have gone by since Jesus ascended into heaven – about two thousand years. But that isn't much if you aren't stuck in time as we are, and God isn't stuck in time. He's prepared to wait to give us humans the chance to turn to him in our lives, and we don't know the date when Jesus will return. We do know that in God's good time he will come back, and everyone will see his glory together, both the living and those who have finished the earthly part of their life.

In the meantime, we have been given the Holy Spirit, so that God can be with us in person every moment of our life, helping us and guiding our choices, steering us safely through temptations, and teaching us more and more about our amazing God. All he waits for is to be invited.

All-age ideas

- Any artwork or writing that the children have done on what the Ascension is about can be displayed around the building, and time given in the service to looking at it.

- Have a beautiful helium balloon at the ready. Write on it an Ascension message that the children would like to send. After the service two representative children can let the balloon float away.

- Children can wave white and yellow streamers during some of the hymns.

SEVENTH SUNDAY OF EASTER

Acts 16:16-34
Psalm 97
Revelation 22:12-14,
   16-17, 20-21
John 17:20-26

Jesus lives for all time in glory; we can live the fullness of Resurrection life straight away.

All-age talk

Beforehand ask a few people to bring awards they have been given. These should include things that probably lots of others have as well, such as a five-metre swimming badge and a driving licence. There may also be a darts cup or a music certificate.

Begin by showing the awards and talking briefly to the award-holders about how these have been well earned, and give us an idea of the standard that has been achieved, so they are something to celebrate. Probably lots of us have similar awards that we have been honoured with, which is well worth celebrating. (A round of applause may be in order.)

When Jesus entered heaven, about forty days after he had come back to life on the first Easter Day, the whole of heaven gave him a hero's welcome. They said he was worthy to receive power and wealth and wisdom and strength, honour and glory and praise – everything good they could think of.

They wanted to honour him like this because Jesus had managed to do such an incredible thing. He had lived a human life and gone on loving all the way through it without once giving in to temptation, turning against God's will or putting his own wants first. Through loving people enough to die for them, he had been able to break the hold death has over all of us, so we can live freely and happily in God's company. (Another huge round of applause for Jesus.)

Now go back to the swimming badge. This badge proves that Susie is able to swim. What God is saying to us today is that Jesus has won the victory for us, so we are all able to live this incredible new,

345

free and happy life in his company – the sort of life we saw Paul and Silas living, as they sang their hearts out in the middle of a very nasty situation.

It is as if there's a wonderful pool just waiting for us to enjoy, but perhaps we're only holding our badges at the edge of the pool, instead of getting into the water and using them. Let's plunge into the life Jesus has won for us and enjoy it to the full!

All-age ideas

- Banners celebrating the fullness of God's glory in heaven and earth can fill the church with colour today, and the flowers, too, can express the colour and variety of full life in Christ.

- If you have some banners in church, don't leave them leaning against walls. Have them carried round the church during the entrance hymn, interspersed with others proclaiming the words: 'The Lord reigns!'

- The Acts reading needs to be really imaginatively read so that everyone is caught up in the excitement and drama of it. Have it acted out, or read with different people taking the parts.

PENTECOST

Acts 2:1-21 or
  Genesis 11:1-9
Psalm 104:24-34, 35b
Romans 8:14-17 or
  Acts 2:1-21
John 14:8-17 (25-27)

As Jesus promised, the Holy Spirit is poured out on the apostles and the Church is born.

All-age talk

Beforehand make five red, yellow and orange flame shapes (about 30 centimetres high) and hide them around the church.

Begin by asking for examples of flames, such as on a gas hob, bonfire, forest fire, log fire, candle, acetylene torch, fire-eater, house on fire, match, oil lamp, steel works, steam engine, lighter, Bunsen burner. Draw people's attention to the tremendous power of some of these and the quiet, gentle nature and soft light of others. Fire is something we all have to respect, as it can burn and destroy as well as giving us light and heat.

Send the children off to search for the five flames that are hidden in the church, and tell the adults about our need to seek out the Spirit expecting to find, just as the children are doing now. They trust that what they have been told to search for will be there, and it will. We need to believe that if we seek God we will find him – and we will.

When the children return with the five flames, you can remind everyone of the way the Holy Spirit is described as being like tongues of fire, with the sound of a rushing wind. (You can get everyone to make this sound as the flame-carriers run round the church.)

Like fire, the Spirit can be strong and powerful in our lives. (The first flame is held up.) Sometimes the Spirit is gentle and quiet, whispering deep into our needs and telling us what is right. (The second flame is held up.) Like fire, the Spirit is warming, spreading love and a real desire to put things right,

347

and stand up for goodness and truth. (The third flame is held up.) Like fire the Spirit is purifying, burning away all that is evil and selfish in us, so that we can become like pure refined gold, glowing with the light of God's love. (The fourth flame is held up.) And, like fire, the Spirit is enlightening, shedding light for us on the Bible, our conversations and relationships and the events of our lives, so that we can see God more clearly through them. (The fifth flame is held up.)

All-age ideas

- Make three flags using yellow, orange and red lining material and bean sticks. During one of the hymns have three people standing in a triangle waving the flags gradually upwards and downwards. Or they can be used individually at different parts of the church to express worship as people sing.

- Have each side of the congregation facing each other and praying for each other to receive the Holy Spirit in their lives afresh. They can pray silently or aloud, or in unison with this prayer, said once loudly and then whispered softly.

  Holy Spirit of God,
  come upon these people
  whom you know and love so well,
  and fill them to overflowing!
  Amen; let it be so.

- Have a time of shared expectant quietness after the prayer, with some quiet music being played and sung by the music group or choir.

- Have the church decorated with flame-coloured flowers, ribbons, streamers and balloons.

TRINITY SUNDAY

Proverbs 8:1-4, 22-31
Psalm 8
Romans 5:1-5
John 16:12-15

The unique nature of God is celebrated today, as we reflect on the truth that God is Creator, Redeemer and Life-giver.

All-age talk

Beforehand prepare a cake. Also get together two eggs, a bag of sugar, a bag of flour and some margarine, and a mixing bowl, cake tin and wooden spoon.

Set the cake tin down and tell everyone that today we are going to have a cake again, because it was so nice last week having the children's cakes, and today is another important day, Trinity Sunday. So we are going to have a Trinity cake. Ask various helpers to bring the eggs, sugar and flour and margarine and place them in the cake tin.

Proudly present the cake, inviting everyone to take a slice, and let the children point out to you that you haven't got a cake at all. You've just got the ingredients. But isn't a cake just ingredients, then? Let them help you understand that you'd have to mix them together and cook them before you had a cake.

Now let it suddenly dawn on you that it's a bit like that with the nature of God. God is the Father who created the world, Jesus Christ who saved us, and the Holy Spirit who gives life to the people of God. But they aren't separate from each other, any more than these separate ingredients are a cake. To be a cake all the ingredients need to be co-operating and working together. Then they become something which is not just eggs, flour, sugar and margarine. Produce the real cake and point out that you wouldn't say, 'Have a slice of eggs, flour, margarine and sugar with your cup of tea.' You'd call it by its name: a cake.

In the same kind of way, when we talk about

God we are talking about our Maker, and we're talking about the risen Jesus who has rescued us from sin and death, and we're talking about the Holy Spirit who brings us into new life. We know that the word 'God' means all three persons in a wonderful harmony, a community which is still One.

Give the Trinity cake to whoever is in charge of refreshments after the service, so it can be shared out then.

All-age ideas

• Use three different voices for the Proverbs reading. Work through the text prayerfully and listen to the places where single voices or a group of voices seem to be indicated. Split the single voice sections between the three people, according to the sense of the phrases and linking meaning with voice type.

• Put clover and shamrock among the flower arrangements today to express the 'three in one' nature of God.

• Give the children green streamers to wave during some of the hymns, and have three young people waving green flags during the creed or a hymn.

• Use the baptismal statements of belief for the Creed.

PROPER 4

Sunday between 29 May and 4 June inclusive (if after Trinity Sunday)

1 Kings 18:20-21
  (22-29), 30-39 or
  1 Kings 8:22-23,
  41-43
Psalm 96 or
  Psalm 96:1-9
Galatians 1:1-12
Luke 7:1-10

The good news we have been given is not just for us, but to pass on to the rest of the world.

All-age talk

Bring with you a newspaper, a TV remote control, a mobile phone, an airmail letter and, if possible, a trumpeter (failing a real one, a recorded version will do nicely).

Begin by picking up the newspaper and reading out a few headlines. Talk about this being one of the ways we use to get other people to hear our news. People used to use a town crier. (You could ask a loud-voiced volunteer to demonstrate. The news they bellow is written on a piece of paper: 'There is only one real God. He made us and he loves us!') Pick up the remote control and explain that now we don't have to shout so loud because we invite the town criers into our homes and sit them in the corner to tell us the latest news. We can even switch them off!

Another thing people used was a trumpeter. (Have this demonstrated briefly.) That got people's attention so they would listen to what you were saying. Now we have this to get people's attention, and get them listening to us. (Demonstrate the mobile phone.) People used to send their news by pigeons, and now we send it on a metal bird. (Show the airmail letter.)

What has stayed the same all through the years is that people always want to pass on their news. And today we are being told that the news the town crier shouted to us (they can do it again) is such good news, not just for us but for everyone, that we need to make sure we pass it on. Like honey

351

or peanut butter, we are not to keep the good news to ourselves, but spread it!

We can tell people about God's love by behaving in a kind and loving way, by being generous with our time and money, by praying for our friends and for difficult situations, by living by God's rules, and by bringing our faith into the conversation instead of only mentioning it among our church friends. And who knows, God may also call some of you to tell the good news as newspaper reporters, in government, on television or as a famous sports star. However you do it, do it!

All-age ideas

- Have the items used in the talk arranged in front of the altar with the sign: 'The Lord is God! (Don't keep the faith, spread it.)'

- Have a clapping message passed all around the church: 'The real God loves you, pass it on.' As you say it you do these claps: clap your own hands, right with your partner, your own again, left with your partner, clap your sides, clap your own hands and then both hands with your partner. When someone has clapped it with you, you find someone else to do it with until eventually everyone has caught the message.

- The 1 Kings 18 reading of the prophets and the sacrifice is excellent for reading dramatically, either using the *Dramatised Bible* or arranging it with different voices yourselves.

PROPER 5

Sunday between 5 and 11 June inclusive (if after Trinity Sunday)

1 Kings 17:8-16 (17-24)
  or 1 Kings 17:17-24
Psalm 146
  or Psalm 30
Galatians 1:11-24
Luke 7:11-17

*Our God is full of compassion;
he hears our crying and it is his
nature to rescue us.*

All-age talk

Bring with you a pair of balance scales. These can be either a heavy-duty kitchen type or a children's educational toy. You could even use a small portable seesaw and have two children to demonstrate it. It's the balancing of weights that matters.

Demonstrate the scales/seesaw with the help of some children, reminding everyone of the way the scales are balanced when there is the same weight both sides. Sometimes our lives can feel like a seesaw or a pair of scales. We might be really happy, and everything is going well, and our team is winning, and we passed our driving test on the eighth attempt, and our operation was successful, and someone has just changed our nappy and fed us. However old or young we are, we all know what it feels like to have the 'joy' side of the scales full up.

Other times we may feel that everything is against us. Our best friend is moving away to another town, our team has lost for the third time running, the washing machine floods the kitchen, and you fall over and graze your knees. Sometimes the pain is so deep that we can hardly bear it – like when someone we love dies, or we are suddenly let down by someone we thought we could trust, or we are faced with serious illness. We all know what it feels like to have the 'sadness' side of the scales full up.

We heard today about the way God looked after a widow and her son and Elijah, and made sure there was just enough food for them so they didn't starve to death in a terrible drought. And we heard about another widow, beside herself with grief, whose dead son was brought to life by Jesus and given back to her.

So does it look as if our God is only interested in us when the happy side of our scales is full to bursting? No, it proclaims loud and clear that our God is tenderly interested in us all the time, during those terrible times of sadness we sometimes have to go through, as well as the times of great joy we dance through. And that is because he really loves us.

All-age ideas

- Have a jug of oil, a jar of flour and some bread rolls incorporated into one of the flower arrangements with simple, wild flowers.

- Have different voices to read the story of Elijah.

- Show slides or acetates of faces from all over the world which focus our compassion on the greed, poverty, pain, violence, vulnerability and loneliness of many. This can be done in silence or with music suggested by the young people. They are particularly good at putting together pictures and music with sensitivity. If slides and OHPs are not suitable for your church, have the pictures mounted and carried around the church, or fixed on the walls, and encourage the congregation to move around and pray.

PROPER 6

Sunday between 12 and 18 June inclusive (if after Trinity Sunday)

1 Kings 21:1-10
   (11-14), 15-21a
   or 2 Samuel
      11:26-12:10, 13-15
Psalm 5:1-8
   or Psalm 32
Galatians 2:15-21
Luke 7:36-8:3

God has the authority and the desire to forgive our sins completely and set us free from guilt.

All-age talk

During the week collect a few well-known parish voices on tape, perhaps from choir practice, children's ministry planning, or the scout or brownie meeting. If you can have some photographs taken at such things, these can be displayed as people come into church. You will also need a length of string with a Lego person tied on one end, and a pair of scissors.

Begin by playing the tape and letting people experience the 'Good heavens, that's me!' factor. Remind everyone of how you feel when a raffle ticket is called and you suddenly realise it's the same as the number staring at you from your own hand, or when you catch sight of yourself unexpectedly in a mirror when you're out shopping.

Ahab, David and Simon were all given that shock in our readings today. They had all done wrong, and yet hadn't really recognised it. Now, suddenly, they are shown the truth about themselves, and it isn't a pretty sight.

Like them, we don't always know when we've done wrong or sinned. We might have had a little tug of conscience but quickly stamped it out so we could go on doing what we wanted to be doing! If you're in doubt, think to yourself, 'Am I happy for God to see me saying this, or doing this, or thinking this?' And if you're not happy with God seeing how you behave at school, or with particular people, or at work, or at your club, then the way you are behaving is probably wrong, and you need to change it.

355

Sometimes we will need to point out gently to one another where we are wrong. That's all part of loving one another and helping one another to live God's way.

Show the piece of string with a Lego person tied on the end. Explain that whenever we fall into sin, we cut ourselves off from God (cut the string and let the person drop). God longs to put things right, but he can't, unless we call out to him and say, 'I've fallen down! I'm sorry!' As soon as we turn to God like that, and ask him to forgive us, he ties us on again so we're not cut off any more. And the funny thing is we end up closer, if anything, because being forgiven is so wonderful that it makes us love God more than ever.

All-age ideas

- The story of Naboth's vineyard is an excellent one to act out, with different people speaking their parts, either reading them or studying the text first and saying the words. Jezebel can read her letter in a suitably cunning and evil way.

- Create a sketch of a modern-day equivalent to Naboth – an innocent victim of those in power.

- Have a sheet of paper with the shape of a cross cut out of it, and fix it on to a mirror, so the effect is of a cross made out of a mirror. This can be used at the Confession, to remind people that Jesus' love will reflect back to us the state of our inner selves, just as a mirror shows us our outer appearance. Give them time to be shown things they want to put right before the prayer of confession is said.

PROPER 7

Sunday between 19 and 25 June inclusive (if after Trinity Sunday)

1 Kings 19:1-4 (5-7),
  8-15a or
  Isaiah 65:1-9
Psalms 42, 43 or
  Psalm 22:19-28
Galatians 3:23-29
Luke 8:26-39

God is close through all our troubles, and can bring us safely through them.

All-age talk

Bring with you a small loaf of bread, a pillow, a calendar and a clock, writing paper and envelopes, and a briefcase. Place these prominently around the church.

Begin by reminding everyone of how our God hears us laughing and being happy, and is happy for us. He also hears us when we are crying and feeling sad, and his heart goes out to us, and he feels sad for us and quickly comes close to comfort us with his presence. Even if everyone else has let you down and rejected you, God never has and never will.

All of us will have some sad times in our lives, and today we are going to look at how God looks after his friends when they are going through a rough time. So even if you are in a really happy phase at the moment, it's a good idea to be prepared! And if today you are feeling a bit like Elijah, exhausted or chucked out, vulnerable and unable to see any hope, then God offers his help straight away.

Ask someone to go and find something to eat, and something to sleep on. As they go, explain how God is very practical, and starts by providing our practical needs – in this case, sleep and food. As the body of Christ, we church people can do that for one another.

Ask someone else to collect things to do with time. As they go, tell everyone that God gave Elijah time, and he didn't rush him. So we mustn't rush one another to get over a heartache either. People whose loved ones have died, or whose marriages

357

are broken, for instance, need time, and we, in love, must give it to them, just as God does.

Ask someone to find some things for helping us keep in touch. While they are fetching them, talk about the way God was in contact with Elijah, and we are helped in our troubles if God's people make a point of keeping in contact through the dark days, and don't leave us feeling isolated. That's why sympathy and get-well cards, short visits and short phone calls can be so comforting. People need to know that we are all praying for them, too.

Ask someone to find something you might carry to work. As they collect it, talk about the way God knows when we are ready to move forward, and gives us a job to do. The job he gave the healed wild man in the Gospel today was to tell the people in the area about what God had done for him. Elijah was told to go back and continue his former work of being God's spokesman. The job God gives is one that only we can do, and it may well put to use the experiences we have suffered, so that they are turned into opportunities for good.

Leave all the objects out to remind people.

All-age ideas

• As an accompaniment to the Elijah reading, use sounds and music. If you work through the passage, ideas for sounds will come to you but here are some to start you off. You could have metal clashing for the swords, crunching footsteps and insects buzzing, restful music as Elijah sleeps, shakers behind God's voice, howling wind noises, crashes and bangs, crunching cellophane paper for fire, and sad, quiet music behind Elijah's tale of misery.

• Involve different voices at the Gospel reading.

• Psalm 43 can be expressed in movement, with accusers pointing and jeering at the one who is alone and afraid, till two people, light and truth, come and take her hands and lead her to the altar, where she kneels with arms raised in worship.

PROPER 8

Sunday between 26 June and 2 July inclusive

2 Kings 2:1-2, 6-14 or
   1 Kings 19:15-16,
    19-21
Psalm 77:1-2, 11-20 or
   Psalm 16
Galatians 5:1, 13-25
Luke 9:51-62

*When we are called to follow Jesus,
that means total commitment,
with no half-measures.*

All-age talk

You will need someone who can do gymnastics or dance. Ask them to prepare a sequence of moves which need total commitment in order to work, such as somersaults and cartwheels, pirouettes and arabesques.

Begin by asking the gymnasts or dancers to perform their demonstration. Briefly interview them, thanking them and asking whether they could do these things first time, or whether they had to practise. Draw attention to the commitment that has to be given to anything you want to do really well. You can't 'half do' some of those moves, or you'd probably fall flat on your face.

As Christians we are called to that same kind of commitment. We can't 'half do' it. When we commit ourselves to following Christ, it's going to affect the way we talk, the way we behave with our friends and our enemies, the way we spend our time and our money. It's going to affect all our thinking and the choices we make. So it's a bit like deciding to do a double somersault, or a triple pirouette – it takes a lot of dedication and courage to launch off.

Elisha, in our Old Testament reading today, watched his teacher and master being taken to heaven, and was then chosen to be Elijah's successor. He had been a loyal and hardworking student, and now he was off to carry on his master's work for God. But, of course, he wouldn't be left alone to cope on his own. God was going to be his strength.

Imagine if you were just launching yourself into a triple somersault and all your strength suddenly

359

wasn't there. You'd certainly notice it was missing! In fact, you wouldn't be able to do any of those clever moves without strength.

In our Christian life, God's Holy Spirit is the strength. It enables us to do those triple somer- saults of caring love for those we don't much like, and the double pirouettes of co-operating when all we want is our own way. Real loving is very hard work, and it takes lots of dedication. With God's strength we can do it, and then we will be moving freely and beautifully through life, in the way God called us to, and knows will make us, and others, truly happy.

All-age ideas

- For the Galatians passage consider using Eugene Peterson's version in *The Message*. This is partic- ularly good for the sinful nature and spiritual fruit lists.

- In a time of prayer, ask various groups of people to stand so that the others can pray for them in their ministry – all those, for instance, who are involved with learning, teaching and education, those in industry and commerce, those caring for children, those who have time during the day to pray, and those whose sporting or leisure activities bring them into contact with people who don't know Jesus.

PROPER 9

Sunday between 3 and 9 July inclusive

2 Kings 5:1-14 or
  Isaiah 66:10-14
Psalm 30 or
  Psalm 66:1-9
Galatians 6:(1-6) 7-16
Luke 10:1-11, 16-20

In Christ we become a new creation.

All-age talk

Beforehand write out clearly on different colours of paper, six or twelve (depending on numbers of children expected) healings that may well have taken place when the seventy were sent out. (For example, a blind woman got her sight back; two children were dying of a disease, and now they're playing outside; a young man can now walk again; a boy who stuttered can now speak clearly; a family feud has been sorted out.) Give these to different adults to hold in different places around the church when the talk begins. Also give each adult some food to give the children who come to them. Some will be given a sweet each, some a bun each, and some a piece of dry bread.

Begin by reminding everyone that Jesus sent out seventy of his disciples in pairs, to different towns and villages. Let them suggest some reasons for the disciples being sent in pairs. (Friendly; supportive; safer.) So you are going to send people out around the church in pairs, on a mission to find a notice the same colour as the slip of paper you give each pair.

Before they go, tell them to be careful, travel light, not stop to speak to strangers on the way, eat what they're given, say 'Peace be with you' to the person holding their colour, and tell them the kingdom is very near. Get the pairs to repeat the instructions. As they go off around the church, some people can try to make some of the older ones talk on their way. As they reach their paper, the adult there can remind them of their message, if necessary, and give them their food and the notice. The pairs return to

361

you and you can enthuse with them over all the wonderful things that have happened.

Thank them for all their hard work, and tell everyone about Jesus wanting everyone to be made like Naaman in the Old Testament story today – restored and like a new person. But we're still short of workers in this harvest of people. We need to pray that God will send more workers. And we need to make ourselves available, in case it's us he can use!

All-age ideas

- At the time of confession, ask people to imagine that our selfishness and bad temper and so on showed up on our skin. Wouldn't we want Jesus to forgive it completely, with no scars, so we were no longer covered in sin-bumps? Spend time addressing any particular sin-bumps you are ashamed of and embarrassed about, asking God to sort them out and forgive you. Remind them that when they hear the words of absolution, those sin-bumps will be completely gone.

- Have a flower arrangement like a cornfield, with wheat and grasses, poppies and cornflowers, and have a scythe beside the arrangement with the words from Luke: 'Ask the Lord of the harvest to send out workers into his harvest field.'

PROPER 10

Sunday between 10 and 16 July inclusive

Amos 7:7-17 or
  Deuteronomy
    30:9-14
Psalm 82 or
  Psalm 25:1-10
Colossians 1:1-14
Luke 10:25-37

Straighten your lives out and live by God's standards of love.

All-age talk

Bring with you an egg cup, a whole egg in its shell, and a boiled egg which someone has eaten, so that just the shell is left, with a spoon hole at one end. Put this into the egg cup upside down so that it looks like a complete egg ready to eat. You will also need an egg spoon.

Begin by talking about those times you've desperately needed help, like missing the bus when you're already a bit late, or being caught in a downpour on your way to school, and you're hoping one of your friends will happen to drive past and see you. Perhaps the man who had been mugged in Jesus' story felt a bit like that, if he was still able to think after the beating-up he'd been given. Perhaps in the daze of his injuries he heard each set of footsteps coming nearer, and hoped that now he'd get some help. But no, the footsteps quickened up when they got nearer and then went off into the distance again. And the man still lay there, unable to move.

Perhaps he had almost given up hope when the Samaritan, a foreigner, stopped and came to peer at him to see what was wrong. Perhaps, as he swayed in and out of consciousness, he was half aware of being carefully given first aid, of being comforted and reassured that he was going to be all right. Those are good things to feel and hear, when you're in great need. You have no power at such times to make anyone care for you, so all you can do is rely on other people choosing to treat you well.

And that's what we're being taught today: that as Christians we are people called to treat others well, whether we're told to or not, whether anyone sees us or not, whether we want to or not. Why? Simply because our God says that this is the right and good way to live.

In our first reading Amos the prophet was sent to tell the people in Israel that the way they were living was disgusting by God's standards. He said they needed to sort out their values and behaviour to bring them in line with their calling as God's people. They didn't like being told that at all.

And the man in today's Gospel, to whom Jesus told his 'good neighbour' story, could recite the rules he was supposed to live by off by heart: 'Love the Lord your God with all your heart and with all your soul and with all your strength and with all your mind. And love your neighbour as yourself.' But for him and for lots of others, those words are like this boiled egg. It looks wonderful and full of goodness. But if I start to dig into it (do that) with my spoon, I find that all the inside is missing, and there's nothing of any goodness there at all.

We must be brave and dig into the words we sing and pray together today, and look at what we find inside. Perhaps there will be rich meaning, and you will know that the words your mouth says are backed up with the way you live. Perhaps you will find the words are just a shell, and your life doesn't back them up at all. If so, come to God today and ask him to fill the shell with new meaning. He can do that, and he's waiting for you to ask.

All-age ideas

- As part of a flower arrangement today, have a few bricks built up and a spirit level lying along them. Include the words: 'I am setting a plumb line among my people . . .'

- Have a group acting out the story of the good Samaritan, but make sure the first section – the conversation with the expert in the Law – is included in the acting. It can be done either using the *Dramatised Bible* or dramatising it yourselves, working closely with the text. Or a contemporary version can be worked out.

PROPER 11

Sunday between 17 and 23 July inclusive

Amos 8:1-12 or
   Genesis 18:1-10a
Psalm 52 or Psalm 15
Colossians 1:15-28
Luke 10:38-42

Against impossible odds God has reconciled us to himself, in Christ.

All-age talk

Beforehand make a pair of large card ears, about 30 centimetres high, and a pair of large card hands, about the same size.

Start by asking for two volunteers, one of whom holds the ears to the side of her head, and the other who has the hands fixed to her own hands with large rubber bands. Remind everyone of the two people in the Gospel for today, both very good friends of Jesus. Their names were Martha and Mary and they were sisters. Jesus often went round to the home where they lived with their brother Lazarus, and they all enjoyed one another's company.

(Alice) is like a cartoon picture of Mary, because what she liked to do was sit and listen to Jesus and she could listen to him for hours. She probably liked listening to all sorts of people, and may have been the kind of person people could talk easily to because they could see she was interested in them. Mary's idea of cooking a meal was probably beans on toast, and she probably didn't notice the dust creeping up until she could write in it.

(Laura) is like a cartoon picture of Martha, because what she liked best was doing things for people and making sure they had clean shirts and well-balanced meals. Her idea of cooking a meal would be something like roast chicken with all the trimmings. If you wanted something done, you'd ask Martha.

Now people sometimes get upset by today's Gospel because they think Jesus is saying that everyone ought to spend their time listening like Mary, and that busy, practical people like Martha

365

aren't somehow as good. But, of course, Jesus isn't saying that at all. His own life was full of work and activity, travelling, preaching, teaching and healing, and none of that would have got done if he hadn't been a doer.

But he also spent hours late at night, or early in the morning on his own with God, talking things over and quietly listening. And he knew that this was a really important part of the doing. He knew we need to keep the right balance between input (the ears) and output (the hands). On that particular visit to Martha and Mary's house, the listening was more important than the doing. What we all have to do is notice when we need to listen, and be ready to stop what we're doing and listen.

All of us need to set aside a quiet time to be with God morning and night, every day. It doesn't have to be long, but it has to be there. If we neglect that, our ability to discern right behaviour will start to slip, and we risk sliding into the kind of life that hurts God so much. Spending time quietly with God is not an optional extra for people with time on their hands, it's an absolute necessity, as well as being refreshing, rejuvenating and problem solving! (If there is a parish or diocesan weekend planned this year you can mention that as well.)

All-age ideas

- The force of the Amos prophecy can be emphasised with several voices, or even a choir of voices, divided into the same ranges as for singing – soprano, alto, tenor and bass.

- Ask people to hold first their ears and then their hands as you pray for God's blessing on everyone's listening and activity in the week ahead.

PROPER 12

Sunday between 24 and 30 July inclusive

Hosea 1:2-10 or
  Genesis 18:20-32
Psalm 85 or
  Psalm 138
Colossians 2:6-15
  (16-19)
Luke 11:1-13

Keep asking for God's Spirit and he will keep pouring out his blessing on you.

All-age talk

Bring along some strips of bedding plants, or a packet of seeds and a flourishing plant of the same or similar variety.

Proudly show the results of your horticultural exploits, and talk about what your hopes are for the seed or the tiny bedding plants. You don't really want them to stay as they are because, although the pictures on the labels show wonderful flowers or fruit, at present they are only dry dusty things, or boring leafy things, in spite of your recent planting efforts. What you are hoping is that they will eventually grow and flourish, until they flower and fruit as you know they can if all goes well.

That's how God feels about us. When he plants us into life, he knows we have lots of potential, lots of good possibilities. Since he loves us, he really hopes that we will grow, spiritually as well as in our bodies. He doesn't want us to stay the same as when we first begin in our Christian life, because he knows that if all goes well we shall one day be full of flowers and fruit that will help the world.

If I want my little plants to grow I will have to give them things like water and food, and make sure I give them plenty of light. And, being plants, they will just sit there and let me give them the things they need to grow nicely. I also need to talk to them!

God wants to give us lots of things to make us grow. He wants to drench us in his Spirit, warm us with the light of his love, and feed us with his word and in communion. He also wants to talk to

367

us! But because we are humans, and not plants, we sometimes turn away from his light, and put up huge umbrellas against the rain of his Spirit, and refuse to let him feed us, and block our ears to stop ourselves hearing what he says. And when that happens, we stop growing and we wilt and weaken, and we never get to bear any fruit.

Today God is saying to us, 'Let me give you the gifts you need to grow as Christians; keep asking me for them, keep looking for me, and I promise that you will receive everything you need to grow into strong, healthy plants with beautiful flowers and fruit.'

All-age ideas

• Use the Lord's prayer from Luke today.

• Decorate a door with flowers around it and a notice on it from Luke 11:9.

PROPER 13

Sunday between 31 July and 6 August inclusive

Hosea 11:1-11 or
    Ecclesiastes 1:2,
      12-14; 2:18-23
Psalm 107:1-9, 43 or
    Psalm 49:1-12
Colossians 3:1-11
Luke 12:13-21

True richness is not material wealth; true security is not a financial matter.

All-age talk

You will need the packing boxes for various consumables, such as a computer, electronic game, microwave, brand-name shoes, or luxury biscuits. You will also need such things as a CD, gardening and teenage magazines, and a film carton. Choose the items to suit the interests of the people in your congregation, and have enough for one person to hold all at once with great difficulty. Finally, you need a pocket Bible and a tiny spray of flowers.

Remind everyone of the story Jesus told us in the Gospel today, about the farmer who thought that having a bumper harvest, and therefore a financial windfall, meant total security, so that he could just do as he liked and take no care of his soul. His greed had made him foolish. As it happened, he was going to die and face God that very night, and he wasn't in the least prepared for death.

Ask for a volunteer to help you explain something. Explain how all the advertisements tell us that if we get a particular brand of yoghurt or car or shampoo, everyone will like us and fancy us, and we'll be really happy. Sometimes we get taken in by this lie, and start wanting to have things so we'll be safer or happier or better liked.

Go through the things we like to get, piling the packages into the arms of the volunteer as you talk. When they are completely loaded up, and have no hands left to hold anything else, point out the problem with all this 'having' being important to us. It means that when Jesus offers us his Word and his Love (offer the Bible and flowers), we simply haven't room to take it, and we turn it down, because our minds are too full of what we've got and what we want, and how we're going to hang on to what we've got.

And that is a tragedy that lasts not just for a few years but for ever. We need to put down our wanting and having, so that we can take the really important wealth that God offers us. (The volunteer is helped to unload, so they can hold the Bible and flowers.) These are the things which will make us content and happy and secure, whether we have all the other good things or not.

All-age ideas

- Have a flower arrangement in a cash box. Or have buttercups and daisies in a simple and generous arrangement.

- Have the Hosea passage read by a parent who has their toddler with them as they read, or ask parents to lead their toddlers round the church just before the reading.

- Use this short sketch:

A	I've got a new bike with 36 gears.
B	Well I need a new bike with 36 gears. I'll ask my parents.
C	Why shouldn't I steal a decent bike? I'll never have the money to buy one.
A	I'm going to Florida again this year.
B	We might go to Florida if I can persuade Mum to work more hours.
C	It's not fair. Everybody else goes to Florida. We stay with Nan at Clacton.
A	I am a rich, complacent fool.
B	I am an envious fool.
C	I am a resentful fool.
A, B, C	And we're all trapped by money!

PROPER 14

Sunday between 7 and 13 August inclusive

Isaiah 1:1, 10-20
Psalm 50:1-8, 22-23
Hebrews 11:1-3, 8-16
Luke 12:32-40

Have faith in God, and get yourself ready to meet him.

All-age talk

You will need a pair of swimming flippers. Have ready a couple of large freezer labels with the words 'I believe in God' written on them.

Ask for a volunteer to walk up and down the church, so that everyone can see the way this person normally walks. Now give them the flippers to wear. As they are being put on, explain that today's readings teach us about how our faith in God affects the way we live. Remind them of Abraham and the way he was ready to get up and go when God asked him to, even though he didn't know exactly how the move would work out. He trusted God to want the best for him, and had faith that God would look after him.

Now that the volunteer is wearing flippers, is he going to walk in the same way as before? Well, let's see. As the person walks up and down, point out that we can all see the effect the flippers are having on the walking – it's a very distinctive flipper walk!

Put the freezer labels on the flippers, explaining that when we decide to walk with faith in God, that is going to affect the way we walk through life. It will give us a very distinctive faith walk. The readings today tell us the kind of things to expect. We will be stopping doing what is wrong and learning to do what is right. We will be noticing the needs of those around us and in our world, and making sure we help out with our time and prayers and money. We will be building up treasure in heaven by our loving kindness, patience, honesty, thoughtfulness and self-control.

All-age ideas

- The parables in the Gospel can be mimed while it is being read.

- In a flower arrangement express the idea of treasure by the container chosen, and have treasure items included in the arrangement. Have the text of Luke 12:34 beside it.

PROPER 15

Sunday between 14 and 20 August inclusive

Isaiah 5:1-7 or
  Jeremiah 23:23-29
Psalm 80:1-2, 8-19 or
  Psalm 82
Hebrews 11:29-12:2
Luke 12:49-56

When we fix our eyes on Jesus our lives will reflect his nature.

All-age talk

Beforehand prepare a number of heavy carrier bags and a rucksack, and have a sack or strong dustbin bag. Label the bags 'I want my own way', 'It isn't fair', 'So what?', 'I'll never forgive them' and 'No one will notice'. Also bring the local school's PE kit.

Begin by showing everyone the PE kit and draw from them what it is, who wears it, and why we do PE dressed like this instead of in our best clothes, or in bridesmaids' dresses, or Mickey Mouse suits. Establish that it's more practical and comfortable to wear light clothes like this which don't get in the way of our running and jumping.

Refer to the letter to the Hebrew Christians in which following Jesus through our lives is said to be a bit like running a race: we need to look where we're going. That means keeping our eyes on Jesus and his way of living. This will keep us on the right track in our own lives, reminding us to be honest instead of telling lies, thinking of other people's needs instead of just wanting our own way, and sharing our ideas and fears with God instead of ignoring him most of the time.

But often we run our Christian life in very unsuitable clothes. At this point ask for a volunteer, and load them up with all the bags, explaining what each represents, and how we weigh ourselves down with all this luggage. As you hand over the sack for them to stand in, point out how difficult we make it for ourselves by hanging on to all these attitudes which make Christian living extra hard. The volunteer can try running to prove the point.

373

Today we are being given a useful tip for Christian living: get rid of all these unhelpful habits (name them as you take them from the volunteer), so that we are free to run God's race-track uncluttered and 'light'. Then we can concentrate on Jesus, and learn to live his way – the way of love.

All-age ideas

- Have a display, linked with a flower arrangement, of a PE kit or an athlete's running kit and trophy.

- Collect newspaper pictures and headlines from the week which direct people to pray for the needs of our world. These are held, or fixed on pew ends, the floor, pillars and doors, and people are invited to walk slowly around the church building, being the Church in action as they pray for the concerns they see. The choir or music group will help people's prayer if they sing something like *O Lord, hear my prayer* (Taizé) while people are quietly moving around the church praying either silently or in small groups.

- Put the PE kit, used in the all-stage talk, near the altar so that when people gather round the table for Communion, they are reminded of the need to run uncluttered.

PROPER 16

Sunday between 21 and 27 August inclusive

Jeremiah 1:4-10 or
    Isaiah 58:9b-14
Psalm 71:1-6 or
    Psalm 103:1-8
Hebrews 12:18-29
Luke 13:10-17

God sets his leaders apart to challenge prejudices and assumptions, and alert people to the truth.

All-age talk

Bring along a couple of long scarves tied together.

Ask a volunteer to help you explain today's teaching, and get them to stand on the scarf. Wind the scarf round the back of their neck, and join the two ends so that the volunteer is forced to stand bent forward, looking down in a fixed position. Looking sideways is quite difficult, and looking up and into people's faces is almost impossible. Remind everyone of the crippled woman in today's reading from Luke's Gospel, whose back was set into this position so that she had lived the last eighteen years of her life looking down at her feet, unable to see the world properly, or have a face-to-face conversation.

What Jesus did was to release her from this locked position. When he saw her he felt so sorry for her and longed to set her free. And when he placed his healing hands on her back and told her she could now move again (untie the scarf), she found that she could stand upright, and see all around and look into people's faces again! That felt wonderful, and she praised God for all she was worth.

Now ask for another volunteer, and tie them up in the same way. Explain how people can be just as crippled and stuck in their thinking and living, even though their bodies look and work quite normally. Habits of grumbling about everything, wishing for things we can't have, or being so set in our ways that when God asks us to help someone we see it as impossible because it doesn't fit in with our plans – these things can mean that spiritually

375

we are stuck and unable to look up and around. So can spending all our time thinking of one thing, whether that is a hobby, an addiction, an ambition, our health or fitness, or even a person. If we haven't looked up to God's face for ages, we might find we're stuck in the 'head down' position.

God is offering to release us from such crippling habits. He is the one who can put his healing hands on our lives (untie the scarves) and set us free again. It feels so good, and no one needs to stay trapped any longer.

All-age ideas

- Have the Gospel acted as it is narrated, staging it in the whole church context, so that the crippled woman walks up the aisle from the back of the church, and the leader of the synagogue can walk over to the lectern to tell the congregation when to come and be healed.

- Have a display at the back of church showing a child developing in the womb, a new-born baby, children of different ages, young people and adults, arranged in a continuous line. Along the line are the words from Psalm 71:5-6.

PROPER 17

Sunday between 28 August and 3 September inclusive

Jeremiah 2:4-13 or
  Ecclesiasticus
    10:12-18
Psalm 81:1, 10-16 or
  Psalm 112
Hebrews 13:1-8, 15-16
Luke 14:1, 7-14

When we live God's way, both individually and as a community, we will be greatly blessed.

All-age talk

Bring along a front door mat (if possible with 'Welcome' on it), an oven shelf, a first-aid box and temperature chart, a white flower, a purse or wallet, and a stone or piece of local rock. Also ask a happily married couple of many years if they would mind standing up at one point in the talk to help people focus on faithfulness. Place the objects (but not the married couple!) on a table at the back of the church, so that people pass it as they walk in, and start wondering.

Begin by asking everyone which they think would be better for drinking from – a fresh water spring that even bubbles out during dry weather, or a well which is cracked and leaks so the water doesn't stay in it. When they choose the spring, remind them of how sad God was about his people turning away from his excellent offer of life, and choosing instead a way of life that would be about as useful to them as a leaking well. He got his prophet, Jeremiah, to tell them how he felt, and hoped people would realise their mistake and make a more sensible choice: to live God's way.

The letter to the Hebrews, or Jewish Christians, gives them some good, practical guidelines for living God's way, and we are going to look at these guidelines today. They are all about loving one another.

Ask a volunteer to go and fetch from the back table something which reminds them of people coming to visit your home. When they bring back the welcome mat, explain that we are told to 'practise hospitality', which means making people welcome,

377

making them feel at home, being interested in them, and giving them our full attention when we listen to what they say. This may be at home, or with passengers on public transport, or with visitors to our church or school or workplace. Make every visitor to your home feel valued and loved.

Let someone fetch the 'prison bars' (oven shelf), and hold them up in front of their face. We are told to keep in mind those who are in prison, and pray for them by imagining we are there in prison with them. Imagining it can help us pray. Some people are in a real prison with bars, others are imprisoned by their bodies or their disappointments or their fears. All of these people need us to pray for them and befriend them.

Ask someone to find something which reminds them of being unwell and being made better. As they come back with the first-aid box and temperature chart, explain that we are told to pray for all those who are ill or in pain, and look after them however we can.

Now ask the married couple to stand and celebrate with them the joy of being together. We are told to honour marriage, and help one another keep our marriages healthy and strong. God wants us to be faithful to one another in all our friendships and family relationships, even when it gets difficult. As someone fetches the white flower, explain that it is a sign of purity, and God wants all our relationships to be honest and pure, with nothing we are ashamed of or need to hide from other people.

The next object to be fetched is the wallet or purse, and this reminds us that God wants us to live free from the love of money. Money is very useful, and it's good that we can have enough to live on and be able to give presents to one another and so on. But love of money is not good, and only makes us greedy, mean and resentful. You can have a love of money whether you are very rich or very hard-up, so we need to check that and get into the habit of being satisfied with what we have instead of always wanting what we can't get.

There is only one object left, and that is the rock

or stone. Like solid rock under our feet, God is firm and strong and will never forget us or let us down. 'I will never leave you; I will never forget you.' (Deuteronomy 31:6)

All-age ideas

- As people come in, ask them to write their name on a table place name card. At the time of prayer give these out randomly, so that everyone can pray for someone else, and know they are being prayed for at the same time.

- Place the objects from the all-age talk where everyone can see them as they come to gather round for Communion. The appropriate sections of the reading from Hebrews can be written beside each object.

PROPER 18

Sunday between 4 and 10 September inclusive

Jeremiah 18:1-11 or
  Deuteronomy
    30:15-20
Psalm 139:1-6, 13-18
  or Psalm 1
Philemon 1-21
Luke 14:25-33

Following Jesus is expensive – it costs everything, but it's worth it.

All-age talk

Bring along some catalogues with items which would appeal to the different ages and cultures of those likely to be present. Read out several of the items on offer, and ask people to raise their hands if they think each is a good offer. The more varied and unusual, the better. You might try, for instance, the latest sports car, an electronic game, a lawn mower and a Disneyland holiday. Would the items still be good bargains if you had to give up eating, hobbies or driving in order to pay for them? Establish that if something is important enough, we are prepared to give things up for it. If we're not prepared to change our habits to pay for it, we won't be able to have it.

We are called to follow Jesus. We are offered a fulfilling and rewarding life, inner peace and joy, and life that lasts for ever, even beyond our bodily death. That's quite an offer. But what does it cost? What would we have to give up to pay for it?

Have a long and a short piece of card, or two sticks, and show the long vertical one on its own. This looks like the word 'I'. Place the shorter piece across it. Following Jesus costs us the cross – it means deciding to give up the 'I want' way of living, and putting the sign of God's love (the cross) right at the centre of our lives. (Hold the cross you have made against your own body.)

That means that following Jesus is going to cost us quite a lot. It isn't a cheap, throwaway thing like a paper cup. We need to think very carefully about it before we decide to go for it. Is it worth it?

Yes, it certainly is! God made us, so his way is exactly right for us. No one but God can give us the lasting peace and happiness and complete forgiveness we long for. With God we can become more and more our true selves, selves we can face in the mirror and love. With God we can reach out to other people, and be brave enough to stand up for what is right and loving. Although our life as Christians may lead us into some difficult or dangerous situations, we will always have our friend Jesus with us, and that makes it all possible and all worthwhile.

All-age ideas

- Incorporate in a display or flower arrangement some money and a personal finance planner, or some flyers advertising financial advice. The text reads: 'If you wanted to build a tower, you would first sit down and decide how much it would cost . . . In the same way, you must give up everything you have to follow me.' Luke 14:28, 33.

- During the confession section, give out small pieces of clay for people to mould into something which expresses their life. Whenever it goes wrong it can be squashed and started again. Play some reflective music during this activity, and above the music read Jeremiah 18:4-6. Encourage people to bring to God the false starts and mistakes in their lives, knowing that God can always give them a fresh start.

PROPER 19

Sunday between 11 and 17 September inclusive

Jeremiah 4:11-12,
  22-28 or
  Exodus 32:7-14
Psalm 14 or
  Psalm 51:1-10
1 Timothy 1:12-17
Luke 15:1-10

Jesus does not avoid the company of sinners but befriends them.

All-age talk

Gather a mixed group of 'sheep', and appoint a shepherd who is given a crook. Talk about the way the shepherd looks after sheep, finding fresh water and fresh grass, and protecting them from the dangers of wolves and bears. Sometimes a sheep will wander off on its own. (Send one of the sheep to go off and hide somewhere in the church, ensuring that enthusiastic sheep are prevented from going right outside.)

Jesus thought the way we wander off from living good lives was rather like sheep wandering off and getting lost. He loves all of us, and doesn't want any of us to be lost, so, like a good shepherd, he checks that all the rest of the people in the church are OK. (Are they?) Then he sets off to search for the one who has wandered off.

As the shepherd searches for the lost sheep (tell him/her to wait with the sheep when it is found), give some examples of what makes us wander off from God. Perhaps other things crowd God out and take over our life; perhaps we want to disobey God's rules and please ourselves; perhaps some tragedy in our life shakes our faith, and we think God has caused the pain instead of realising that he is weeping with us. Whatever it is, once we realise we are a long way from God, we feel very lost and alone. Sometimes we have got ourselves trapped in habits we can't break out of on our own.

Thankfully Jesus, our good shepherd, is out looking for us, and he will search and search until

382

he finds us. We can help by bleating – which is praying, calling out to God from where we are.

It is very good to be found. As the shepherd brings the wandering sheep, hand in hand, back to the flock, talk about how wonderful it is to know that we are forgiven, and that God loves us enough to forgive us even when we ran away from him. When the sheep comes back to the flock everyone can clap, as, with all the angels of heaven, we celebrate the truth that our God is such an excellent rescuer, full of understanding and mercy, and willing to give up his life to get us back home again.

All-age ideas

- Prepare some people to be ready to pray with anyone who realises today that they need Jesus to rescue them. Have some music, either recorded or from the choir or music group, after the talk while people pray on their own or in small groups for each other.

- Have an arrangement of model sheep, or a picture or poster of sheep on a hillside.

- Dress some of the children in nativity play angel costumes and let them gather round the altar, the older ones carrying candles, at the eucharistic prayer.

PROPER 20

Sunday between 18 and 24 September inclusive

Jeremiah 8:18-9:1 or
   Amos 8:4-7
Psalm 79:1-9 or
   Psalm 113
1 Timothy 2:1-7
Luke 16:1-13

If you cannot be trusted with worldly riches, or even small amounts of money, then you will not be trusted with spiritual riches either.

All-age talk

You will need to prepare this talk with another adult. The two of you will be bosses, standing at either end of the church.

Begin by asking for a volunteer who doesn't mind doing a few jobs. This person stands halfway down the church, and you introduce them to the two bosses they are to work for this morning. They are to serve both people as well as they can.

First one boss gives an order, such as to put three chairs out in a line in the middle of the church. As soon as this is done, the other boss gets annoyed that the chairs are arranged like this and tells the servant to put only two chairs out, facing different ways. The first boss tells the servant to put a hymn book on each chair. The other boss tells the servant to put the hymn books away and put a kneeler on each chair. Continue the orders so that the poor servant is running about the church pleasing no one.

Thank the volunteer, and explain how Jesus said in today's Gospel that it is impossible to serve two bosses like that. Either you end up loving the first and hating the second, or hating the first and loving the second. It is the same with trying to serve God while we are still bound up with materialism, money and possessions. (Have two signs: 'God' and 'Worldly Riches'. These can include appropriate symbols, such as a cross and some money.) It simply can't be done. While God is whispering to your conscience to live simply and generously, Worldly Riches is insisting that you get the latest fashion in clothes or music. While God is expecting

384

you to commit time to prayer and Bible reading, Worldly Riches is expecting you to commit that time to reading the latest magazines and watching the latest videos.

If we choose to serve God (display the 'God' sign) we have to choose not to serve Worldly Riches. (Tear up the 'Worldly Riches' sign.)

All-age ideas

- The Gospel works well with several different voices.

- Instead of the usual collection plate today, invite people to get out of their seats and bring their offering to a plate which is placed at the font or near a cross.

PROPER 21

Sunday between 25 September and 1 October inclusive

Jeremiah 32:1-3a, 6-15
  or Amos 6:1a, 4-7
Psalm 91:1-6, 14-16
  or Psalm 146
1 Timothy 6:6-19
Luke 16:19-31

Wealth can make us complacent so that we fail to notice the needs of those around us.

All-age talk

Arrange for the following items to be in church today, giving different people responsibility for them, so that they will emerge from various people all over the congregation: a pair of sunglasses, some well-known expensive brand of sun cream (the bottle can be empty), a luxurious, squashy cushion, a bottle of champagne (or a champagne bottle) in an ice bucket, and a tape/CD player with some easy-listening music in it ready to play. At the front of the church you need one of those comfortable sun-loungers. Arrange for another person to walk quietly to the middle of the aisle with a begging bowl and sit down there.

Get the sun-lounger out and invite someone to be cosseted and pampered for a few minutes of the morning. They can lie on the lounger, and various people from all over the church bring them all their comforts. Enthuse about each item as you make the volunteer really comfortable. Leave them snoozing in luxury as you pose the question: 'Is there anything wrong with living in wealth and luxury, and pampering ourselves?'

In itself, no, there isn't. Of course it is good to have times of rest and relaxation, and it is fine to enjoy the good things of life. But if we use wealth to cushion ourselves from the real world, shield our eyes from the harsh glare of suffering, protect ourselves from feeling people's pain, block out the sound of people's crying, and deaden our sense of duty, then we run the danger of rejecting all the needs, and not feeling we have any responsibility to do anything about them anyway. (Hold a 'speech bubble' of card over the volunteer, which says, 'What problems?')

In Jesus' story, the rich man was probably a nice guy, and there is no mention of him doing anything really evil. But he simply hadn't noticed the beggar who sat at his own front gate every day. Point out that all the time we've been enjoying indulging ourselves up here, there has been someone begging down there.

It's all too easy for us to ignore the needs. Jesus reminds us to check that our lack of poverty doesn't prevent us from doing the practical caring love we are called to.

All-age ideas

- Use different voices in the reading of the Luke passage.

- Involve the congregation in this, printing it on the handout or showing it on the OHP.

    A Being wealthy is having a meal every day.

    B Being wealthy is having a bicycle.

    C Being wealthy is owning a house.

    D Being wealthy is having lots of exotic holidays.

    E Being wealthy is not having to work, and collecting Rolls Royces.

    All Being wealthy is all relative.
    Being poor is all relative.
    Having needs is part of being human.

PROPER 22

Sunday between 2 and 8 October inclusive

Lamentations 1:1-6
  or Habakkuk 1:1-4;
    2:1-4
Lamentations 3:19-26
  or Psalm 137,
  or Psalm 37:1-9
2 Timothy 1:1-14
Luke 17:5-10

God hears our distress and our crying, and feels it with us.

All-age talk

Bring along a football, a musical instrument, a cross and a Bible. Choose someone to come out and give them the football, telling them that you are letting them borrow this so that you can watch them on television, this week, playing in the next (Liverpool) game. Give someone else the musical instrument and say you'll be looking forward to hearing them on Classic FM tomorrow morning, then.

Are these things really possible? Why not? Obviously it doesn't really happen like that. Just having a football doesn't mean you can get out there and land the goals against fierce opposition. For that you need lots of training and lots of skills. Just having a musical instrument doesn't mean that you can join a top orchestra and get all the notes and phrasing right. For that you need years of training and practice, and a musical gift.

We know about this in football and music, but we sometimes forget it when it comes to our faith, even though it's still true. Give someone the cross and the Bible. Just because they now have these things doesn't mean that they have arrived as a Christian, and can now make all the right decisions, and be perfect in every way. Living Christ's way will take us a lifetime of training and practice, and we are bound to make mistakes and get into scrapes along the route.

So when the going gets hard work, and we find it's a challenge and a struggle to live by God's rule of love, we mustn't get discouraged. Jesus never promised us it would be easy all the time. All training, whether it's in tackling or goal defence, vibrato on the violin or overcoming the break on the clarinet, forgiving wholeheartedly or conquering self-indulgence – all these things are difficult to learn and require dedication and perseverance.

When you are finding it's hard being a Christian, don't give up or decide it's too difficult; go to God and ask for some more help. Throughout your whole life he will provide all the training, practice and gifts you need for the work he asks you to do, whether that work is preaching to thousands, or helping your next-door neighbour.

All-age ideas

- The mood of sadness in the Old Testament readings can be expressed well in dance. Look into any dance contacts you may have with groups using the church hall, and consider inviting them. Some of the Scottish strathspey dances are very poignant, for instance, or the slow Greek dances. A local dancing school might welcome the challenge. Or, for a home-grown dance, while the choir sing or recorded music is played, a group of people from the congregation can move slowly up the centre aisle, hands at their sides, doing a slow *pas de basque* in formation, in the style of a folk dance. At the front they link hands and circle first left and then right, then move into the centre, raising their arms, and back again. They all turn outwards and sway from one foot to the other, before moving back down the aisle again. Keep the steps simple and controlled.

- Ask the flower-arranging team to create an arrangement expressing grief and sadness, with a centre of bright hope, perhaps using purple and dark red colours and cascading foliage.

PROPER 23

Sunday between 9 and 15 October inclusive

Jeremiah 29:1, 4-7 or
  2 Kings 5:1-3, 7-15
Psalm 66:1-12 or
  Psalm 111
2 Timothy 2:8-15
Luke 17:11-19

God can always use even seemingly hopeless situations for good.

All-age talk

Ask for ten volunteers and dish out 'bandages' for them to wear on arms, legs and head. Explain that they are lepers and, because the disease is thought to be very catching, they can't stay with everyone else here but must go and sit somewhere else. Direct them to a place separate from the rest of the congregation. As they go, tell everyone how the lepers of Jesus' day had to leave their homes and live right away from the villages and towns, and look after themselves. How must they have felt? Lonely? Left out? Guilty? Unacceptable? Frightened?

We may not have the disease of leprosy, but there are lots of people in our world, in our country and in our town – perhaps even in our church – who feel lonely, left out, guilty, unacceptable and frightened, like the lepers. People cry themselves to sleep and wake up feeling sad about the day ahead. People who have lost contact with friends, or whose loved ones have died, try hard to be cheerful when they have a big ache of sadness inside them. Lots of people are hurting, and longing for their life to be different.

That's how these ten lepers felt that morning when they saw Jesus walking along the road on his way to a village. They couldn't come too close to him, but they came as close as they could, and shouted to him, 'Jesus, Master, have pity on us!' (This can be written on a sign so the ten 'lepers' can shout it out.) People still cry out to God in their hearts like this. Does God hear?

He certainly does! Jesus shows us what God is like, and what Jesus did was to tell the lepers to go and show themselves to the priest. Why did he tell them that? Because if you were a leper and were healed, you had to show yourself to a priest, so he could check you over and pronounce you fit and well.

Send your lepers off to the priest, who has ten cards saying, 'I declare this leper is now CLEAN. Signed: Revd John Hayward.' Tell them that when they have their certificate of health they are free to join the other people in the congregation.

If any of the volunteers comes and says 'thank you' you can of course use this and praise it. However, since they haven't actually been healed of anything, they will probably sit down in their places. Tell everyone how one leper (choose one) came back to Jesus to say 'thank you'. All the others had been keen to talk to Jesus when they needed help, but they forgot him once he had sorted them out.

Let's make sure that when God answers our prayers, we don't forget to say thank you – even if his answer is not the answer we expect.

All-age ideas

• Give out small pieces of bandage (cut from old sheeting) to people as they come in. At the time of confession ask them to hold their bandage and wrap it round their hand. Just as the lepers were cut off from their community, so our sin cuts us off from God. Ask them to bring to mind the sins that they need God to heal them of, so that their relationship with him can be restored. At the absolution they can unwind the bandages and throw them away.

• Involve both sides of the congregation in these responses taken from 2 Timothy 2:
  A If we died with him,
  B then we will also live with him.
  A If we accept suffering,
  B then we will also rule with him.
  A If we refuse to accept him,
  B then he will refuse to accept us.
  A If we are not faithful,
  All he will still be faithful,
       because he cannot be false to himself.

PROPER 24

Sunday between 16 and 22 October inclusive

Jeremiah 31:27-34 or
  Genesis 32:22-31
Psalm 119:97-104 or
  Psalm 121
2 Timothy 3:14-4:5
Luke 18:1-8

Don't get side-tracked; always pray and don't give up.

All-age talk

Bring along (or ask someone else in the congregation to bring) something which you have made or are making, which requires lots of persistence and perseverance (such as a garment or model, diary or recipe). Talk about the struggle you have had keeping going with it. Use parts of the church building, particularly if it is an ancient one, and draw everyone's attention to some piece of stained glass or carving, and all the persistence and hard work that went into making it. Emphasise the value of doing these things, even though they are difficult.

Jesus tells us to keep going with our prayer, and never give up. Suggest a pattern of praying when you wake up, before you eat a meal, and before you go to sleep at night, showing large posters of logos for these (as below). Or they can be shown on an OHP. If we get into a prayer habit like this, we will be deepening our friendship with God, and getting to know him better.

There is another good habit we need to have as well as praying, and that is reading the Bible every day. There are lots of books and schemes to help us, and we can choose one which suits our age, interests and experience. Show a few of these and draw attention to the display suggested in the all-age ideas. If we don't know much about the Bible there are people in the parish to talk it over with.

However we read it, it's important to pray and read God's word in Scripture so that we really can have God's law of love remembered in our minds and written on our hearts. That way we will be ready for any jobs God asks us to do, and we will be better able to hear him speaking into our lives.

All-age ideas

- Have a display of Bible study aids for all ages and characters, and also a selection of different Bible translations, with recommendations. Consider making arrangements for these to be on a 'sale or return' basis, and have representatives from the children and young people's ministry as well as adults available to talk over Bible reading with people after the service.

- In a flower arrangement have an open Bible and a picture or model of 'praying hands', with the arrangement titled 'Daily prayer, daily Bible reading'.

- Use this short sketch to reinforce the Gospel reading, or prepare people for it:

Woman   Knock, knock.

Judge   Who's there?

Woman   Winnie.

Judge   Winnie who?

Woman   Winnie you going to do something about that money I was cheated of?

Judge   Oh don't worry, that case will be coming up very soon. Now if you don't mind, it's my day off and I'm going to play golf.

(Sign held up saying 'Next day')

Woman   Knock, knock.

Judge   Who's there?

Woman   Winnie.

Judge   Winnie who?

Woman   Winnie you going to do something about . . .

Judge   OK, you don't have to say all that again. I remember. I'll deal with it, madam. Leave it to me. *(Aside)* But not yet because I'd rather watch telly and have a snooze.

Woman   Knock, knock.

Judge   *(Sounding sleepy)* Who's there?

Woman   Winnie.

Judge   Winnie who? *(Aside)* Oh, hang on, I won't ask! I don't know, there's no rest for the wicked. Wretched woman, I'd better do what she asks or I'll never get any peace! *(Shouts)* All right, Winnie, you win. I'll come with you and sort it out *now*!

PROPER 25

Sunday between 23 and 29 October inclusive

Joel 2:23-32 or
  Ecclesiasticus
    35:12-17 or
  Jeremiah 14:7-10,
    19-22
Psalm 65 or
  Psalm 84:1-7
2 Timothy 4:6-8, 16-18
Luke 18:9-14

When we recognise our dependence on God we will approach him with true humility and accept his gifts with joy.

All-age talk

Involve a couple of children in constructing a tower, using building blocks or large packing case cartons. When it is really high, suggest that now they won't need the big block at the bottom any more. Take it away, and of course the whole lot falls down. Be surprised, and protest that you only took one brick away! Then point out that it was the important brick you took – the foundation stone – and everything else depends on that.

Our whole lives depend on God. It's God who gives us life for a start, and provides our planet with what we need to live on. It is God's rain, sunshine and earth which we use to grow our wheat for bread and pizzas. We might sometimes forget to think about God, but he never ever forgets to think about us. He looks after us through our whole lives as we grow up and get old.

We heard another of Jesus' stories this morning, with some more cartoon-type characters. There's Pharisee Ferdinand and Tax Collector Ted.

Both of them have gone to pray. Let's look again at how Pharisee Ferdinand prays. (Display the picture, while a pompous voice reads the part. He needs to sound really smug.) Comment on how awful he sounds, and let people give their ideas of what's wrong with his prayer.

Let's listen in on Tax Collector Ted. (Show the picture, and have someone saying his prayer. This should sound quite genuine.) Comment on the way this person knows he needs God's mercy. And it was this person, Jesus said, who went away right with God, rather than Pharisee Ferdinand who did lots of good things but didn't have any idea of how much he depended on God, and was really only boasting about how good he was.

We owe our whole life to God. Let's not kid ourselves that we don't need him.

All-age ideas

- Act out today's Gospel, or use different people for the different voices.

- If you are using an OHP, transfer on to an acetate a picture of crops ripening, or a rainbow over fields, and put this down as a background to the other things you are projecting.

- With one of the flower arrangements include fruit and vegetables, and a watering can.

ALL SAINTS' DAY

Sunday between 30 October and 5 November inclusive

Daniel 7:1-3, 15-18
Psalm 149
Ephesians 1:11-23
Luke 6:20-31

In Christ we are chosen to be God's holy people.

All-age talk

Bring with you something to inflate, such as a beach ball, or a travel neck-cushion, or a balloon.

Begin by playing a snippet of *When the saints go marching in*, reminding everyone that today we are celebrating the festival of all the saints marching into heaven, and we also want to be among that number.

But what is a saint? You may have some windows with particular saints on. If so, you can briefly draw people's attention to these, and any saintly connections your parish has. Emphasise that although these may be importantly fixed in stained glass now, in their lives they were ordinary people. We may well have lots of saints sitting here now, because we are *all* called to be saints, or God's holy people.

How can you spot a holy person when you meet one? The way they think and talk and behave makes you realise that they are full of God's loving spirit. Show your inflatable. It was designed to be full of air, so at the moment, without air in it, it isn't really able to be properly itself. Ask someone to breathe into it to inflate it. Can we see the air that has been breathed in? No. Can we see the difference it makes? Yes! It has turned this ball/cushion/balloon into what it was designed to be, so now it is really itself, and also very useful.

We can't see the loving Spirit of God either. But whenever people are filled with it, they are able to be more fully their true selves, and it shows in their love for God and their love for others. Lots of inflatables have a valve which stops the air coming in until it is deliberately opened. With us, too, there has to be a definite decision to open up to God's

397

in-breathing of his Spirit. What the saints have done and are doing is keeping that valve open, so that they can be filled with the Spirit, and topped up whenever they get a bit deflated.

One saint – Paul – whose letter we heard this morning, wrote about the whole church being filled with the Holy Spirit of God. The Church isn't supposed to have loads of deflated Christians and one or two saints here and there who are full of God's loving Spirit. The idea of the church is that *everyone* in it is full of the breath of God!

Let God fill you up with his life, and make you into the person he knows you can be. We'll all look different shapes, and we'll all be useful to the world in different ways, just as a beachball is useful for throwing around but not so good as a pillow or a camping mattress. But as God breathes his loving Spirit into us more and more, we will become more and more our true selves – holy people the world needs, marching into God's kingdom with all the other saints.

All-age ideas

- Give out balloons to the children after the service.

- Have the Gospel read chorally with a group of men, women and children.

- Consider hiring a small inflatable bouncy castle for an All Saints' party, labelled 'Be filled with the loving Spirit of God'. Having an All Saints' party is a good alternative to the Hallowe'en culture, and can involve all ages – the Church at play.

FOURTH SUNDAY BEFORE ADVENT

Sunday between 30 October and 5 November inclusive
For use if the Feast of All Saints was celebrated on 1 November and alternative propers are needed

Isaiah 1:10-18
Psalm 32:1-7
2 Thessalonians 1:1-12
Luke 19:1-10

Jesus came to search out the lost and save them. Through him we come to our senses and make our lives clean.

All-age talk

Bring along some wallpaper, paste and brush, and also some foundation make-up.

Introduce these items, talking about what a difference they can make to the look of a room or a face, and how we carefully choose and apply them. The people of Israel were taking great care over their worship, and what it looked like, and we do as well. Point out the colours and clothing, candles and music that we take care in choosing to make our worship beautiful.

So if all this is in God's honour, why was he disapproving of it? The trouble was not in the actual colours and shape of the worship, any more than there is anything wrong with decorating our walls and faces. The big problem was that the people of Israel were pretending to show they loved God, through their worship, but their lives showed that they couldn't care less about his laws of love. They were saying one thing with their worship and something else with their lives.

That was a bit like using nice wallpaper to cover up a crumbling wall with holes in it and damp stains. Before long the underlying badness is bound to show through, and the nice wallpaper won't put the wall right at all. It's a bit like having a spot and smothering it with foundation cream to cover it up. It certainly won't help the spot get better, and may even make it worse.

Zacchaeus knew something was wrong in his life. When Jesus came to his house, he helped him to sort out the problem properly, instead of just covering it over and hoping it would go away. Sin never goes away unless we deal with it properly. It

399

isn't any good trying to make it look pretty or covering it over with excuses. Like Zacchaeus we need to invite Jesus in and deal with it.

Then our worship will be honest and truly reverent, as we pour out our love for the God who has saved us from sin. And however beautiful we make our worship with colours and music, the most beautiful thing about it, as far as God is concerned, is the state of our hearts, which he can see right into.

All-age ideas

- Act out the Gospel, using a narrator and other people reading the different parts.

- Have a ewer and stand, soap and soap dish incorporated into one of the flower arrangements, with the text: 'Wash and make yourselves clean . . . stop doing wrong, learn to do right!'

THIRD SUNDAY BEFORE ADVENT

Sunday between 6 and 12 November inclusive

Job 19:23-27a
Psalm 17:1-9
2 Thessalonians 2:1-5,
   13-17
Luke 20:27-38

Life after death is not wishful thinking but a definite reality.

All-age talk

Bring along some tasters of a particular cheese, tiny chunks such as those you find in most supermarkets from time to time. Bring also a block of the same cheese, labelled.

Show your tray of tasters for the cheese you have brought to recommend. Suggest that people try a taster of it to see whether they like it. Since these tasters came off the main block of cheese, you can guarantee that they will taste as good as the main block. Discuss their findings briefly.

Although we haven't been to heaven, God gives us lots of little 'tasters' which help us find out what it is like. Whenever we sense Jesus giving us peace of mind or joy, or the lovely knowledge that God really loves and cares for us, we are getting a taster of life after death. Jesus lives in heaven so when he comes into us, he doesn't leave heaven behind but brings it with him. So the more we live in God's company and follow Jesus, the more of heaven we will have in our lives even before we die.

Explain that lots of people think Christians are crazy believing that there is life after death. Since they can't see beyond death, they don't think there can be anything like heaven. If I had never seen the yellow daffodil flowers in spring, I would probably think people were crazy burying dry bulbs in their earth at this time of year. But because I have seen what happens to those bulbs, I trust that they won't just rot in the ground. If I were a caterpillar, I would probably laugh at anyone suggesting that one day I would be flying about with colourful wings. It isn't true that the only real things are those we can see.

It is sometimes difficult to trust that what we can't see is still there, but we make the effort to do it whenever we drive in fog, walk along looking around instead of at the path under our feet, or wash our backs. So it is quite possible. And Jesus has told us that there really is life after death, and lots of people saw him alive after he had died. So we aren't crazy for believing there is life after death; we happen to know it's true, and we've already tasted little bits of how lovely it is.

All-age ideas

- Play a recording, or suggest the choir sing *I know that my Redeemer liveth.*

- Decorate the church with brightly coloured flowers and dried flowers, to make it all look bright and beautiful, even in November.

- Make a colourful 'Welcome!' for everyone to walk through as they come into church.

SECOND SUNDAY BEFORE ADVENT

Sunday between 13 and 19 November inclusive

Malachi 4:1-2a
Psalm 98
2 Thessalonians 3:6-13
Luke 21:5-19

There will be dark and dangerous times as the end approaches, but by standing firm through it all we will gain life.

All-age talk

Prepare some large card road signs, and a cereal packet which is labelled 'The last age' on the front and has 'Warnings and advice' with a copy of today's Gospel stuck on the back. Bring these along, together with a packet of cigarettes, and something packed in a plastic bag with the warning of suffocation printed on it.

Begin by asking volunteers to hold the road signs at intervals down the aisle, and ask a couple of people to 'drive their car' among the signs. Talk them through, getting people to say what the signs mean as they come to them, and encouraging them to react appropriately. (If a roundabout sign is used, for instance, they can drive round an imaginary roundabout.) Point out how useful the signs are in warning us so that we are better prepared as we drive.

Show the cigarette packet and read out the warning on that, and on the plastic bag. Lots of things have warnings and good advice printed on them – hair colouring, pain-killers, frozen pies and skateboards – the manufacturer wants customers to be warned of any dangers and know how to avoid them.

Now pick up the prepared cereal packet, and show the 'product name'. Today's Gospel is doing the same thing. It's offering us some warnings and advice for living through this: the last age. We are in the middle of this at the moment. It's the time between Jesus dying on the cross and coming to life again and going to heaven (which has already happened) and the Day of Judgement, or the Second

Coming, which will mark the end of things as we know them. (That hasn't happened yet.)

Jesus knew this would be a very difficult and dangerous age to live in, and he told his disciples to watch for the signs and be prepared. (Turn the packet of cereal round and show the warnings and advice.) Compulsive cereal packet readers will find it may put them off their breakfast. It's the section of Luke's Gospel that we've all just heard this morning.

Pick up on some of the phrases to remind people, and help them see that these things are indeed happening in places all over the world. The signs are there. So what are we to do about them?

Our job as Christians is to stand firm and not get fazed when these terrible things happen, but be in there helping, comforting and doing our best to show and proclaim God's love by our words and actions, even when we get laughed at, despised or persecuted in the process.

Perhaps you are thinking that sounds very hard. Well, you're right, it is very hard and we may feel like giving up. But God promises to be there with us through it all, and will make sure we have all the courage we need to do it. We are warned and prepared specially, because God wants us to be able to stay firm to the end and be saved.

All-age ideas

- As a reflection on the Gospel, try this mime. Play some music from Delirious? ('Sanctify' from *King of Fools* works really well) as a background, or if your parish has more traditional tastes, try some Taizé music, such as *O Lord, hear my prayer*; if tastes are classical try some Shostakovich. Have groups of people all over the church ready to jeer and buffet two or three people who are starting at the back of the church and trying to make their way through the persecution and terror of the last days. One of them gives up and stomps off to the back, but the others make it all the way to the front, reaching out to others along the way in love and comfort, in spite of their treatment. One or two of the jeerers are persuaded to join them. As they reach the front they raise their arms in praise and joy, and everyone in the congregation can applaud. Make the actions slow and deliberate.

* Read part of Psalm 98 in parts using the whole congregation, like this:

Men   Let the sea resound and everything in it

Children the world and all who live in it.

Women   Let the rivers clap their hands *(all clap)*

Men   let the mountains sing together for joy;

Children let them sing before the Lord

Women   for he comes to judge the earth.

All   *(to one another)*
             He will judge the world in righteousness and the peoples with equity.

CHRIST THE KING

Sunday between 20 and 26 November inclusive

Jeremiah 23:1-6
Psalm 46
Colossians 1:11-20
Luke 23:33-43

This Jesus, dying by crucifixion between criminals, is the anointed King of all creation in whom all things are reconciled.

All-age talk

Beforehand prepare a flock of large card sheep. Numbers will depend on your congregation; there need to be at least six.

Begin by talking about the way sheep get easily scared, and will scuttle away a few metres and then stop and eat, and then scuttle away again and eat again. That's why they can easily get lost, because they don't realise how far they have scuttled! Children with little experience of sheep may have noticed a similar 'scuttle, eat, scuttle' pattern in rabbits, who also get scared very easily.

Introduce your flock of sheep, with a volunteer holding each one. Those who are holding them can give them names, or they can be given the names of the children. All through the Bible we read that people are rather like sheep. We get scared (though we usually try to hide that and pretend we aren't scared at all) and we tend to wander off and get lost, and we follow one another into all sorts of rather silly and dangerous places and ideas.

Like sheep, we need a shepherd, and our first reading today told how God was angry with the leaders of his people because they had been bad shepherds, and made the sheep scared, so that they had all scuttled off and got lost. (Send the sheep to do that now.)

God promised that he would be sending his people a king – a good king, whose kingdom would last for ever. Ask for a volunteer and place a crown on their head. But he also knew that his people were like sheep, so this king would not be the kind of king who bosses everybody around and makes them give him all their money so he can be the richest person in the world. God decided that this king would be a shepherd. (Give the king a crook.) And he would go and search for all the lost sheep and bring them safely back to their pasture again. (Send the shepherd king off to do that.)

When the shepherd king has brought all the sheep back, explain that Jesus, the Christ, is our King, and he is the sort of king who knows us each by name, and searches for us when we are lost, and looks after us when he has found us.

In the Gospel today we heard that even when Jesus was dying on the cross he was still searching for lost sheep, right up to the moment he died. Two criminals were being executed with him that day, and one of them, only hours before he died, turned to him and asked for help. Straight away Jesus assured him of forgiveness; he had just brought another sheep back home to its pasture.

Ask the shepherd king to stretch out his arms. Point out that when Jesus, our King, was on the cross, his arms were stretched out like this, so he was in the shape of a cross, and this is the shape of welcoming love.

All-age ideas

- Lay the card sheep from the all-age talk on the floor around the altar so everyone sees them as they gather round to share communion.

- Focus attention on the cross today, surrounding it with flowers, and hanging a crown around it. Or have an arrangement of flowers which expresses the idea of a Shepherd King, with a crown and a crook.

- Gather the children around the altar during the eucharistic prayer, holding the sheep.

407

APPENDIX

Take up your cross, he says

(Proper 7, Year A)

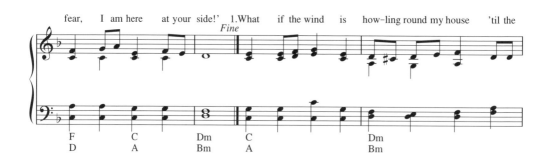

2. What if the rocks are blistering my feet,
   and the sun's heat beats upon my head?
   Near me a grass path beckons with its flowers,
   I'm tempted to go that way instead.

3. What if the tiredness aches behind my eyes
   and my boat is impossible to steer?
   Out on an ocean, drifting and alone,
   am I still, even then, to persevere?

4. Strangest of wonders, wonderfully strange,
   that the cross can set me free.
   Nothing is stronger than the love of God:
   I know very well that he loves me.

Text: Susan Sayers based on Mark 8 and John 14
Music: Susan Sayers, arr. John Rombaut

Script for First Sunday of Christmas
(Year B)

The Trinity is discussing the Incarnation. Father, Son and Spirit are seated as in the icon of the Holy Trinity. (Sounds of arguments and war.)

The Father What they need is the Spirit of God actually alive in them.

The Spirit That's a very personal thing. How can it be done?

The Son Well, as it's personal, it'll have to be done in person.

The Father That's true.

The Spirit It will mean them meeting the Spirit of God in a human person.

(The Father and the Spirit both look at the Son.)

All three speak together:
That's where you/I come in.

The Son How long for?

The Father It'll happen in stages. First, a year or two in ministry, tied to one time zone and in one area, till they get the hang of it.

The Spirit They won't be able to cope for long with God among them in person.

The Father Exactly. It's bound to end in them expelling you.

The Son You mean killing me?

The Father Sadly, yes. But that opens up a new possibility – stage two.

The Spirit How do you mean?

The Father Our love is stronger than death and cannot be destroyed. Through your risen life the Spirit of God will be available for every person in every place and every time zone.

The Spirit So no one needs to lose out!

The Son They'll be able to live the heaven life while they're alive on earth as well as after death!

The Father That's right!

The Son If I'm going to do a couple of years of Godly ministry as a human, I'll have to do all the growing-up bit as well, won't I?

The Father Oh yes – right from conception; you'll need to be part of the whole human experience.

The Spirit But babies are very vulnerable. Suppose they kill him too early?

The Father It's a risk. It's all a risk.

All But if we don't take it, they'll be thrashing about in the dark for ever. They can't save themselves. They need a Saviour.

Human voices, praying earnestly for help:
O come, O come, Emmanuel, save us and set us free!

The Son It's those faithful watchmen calling again.

All And the time is right. Everything's ready.

The Father Gabriel! Come here a moment, will you. We've got some important messages which need delivering personally . . .

Father God, you love me

(Second Sunday of Epiphany, Year B)

2.   Father God, from your love there is nowhere I can hide.
     If I go down into the depths or cross the ocean wide,
     there your love would find me, you'd take me in your hand.
     Your love for me is more than I can ever understand.